CITY
for
EMPIRE

CITY
for
EMPIRE

An Anchorage History,
1914–1941

PRESTON JONES

University of Alaska Press
Fairbanks

University of Alaska Press
P.O. Box 756240
Fairbanks, AK 99775-6240
ISBN 978-1-60223-093-4

Library of Congress Cataloging-in-Publication Data

Jones, Preston, 1966–
  City for empire : an Anchorage history, 1914–1941 / Preston Jones.
    p. cm.
  Includes bibliographical references and index.
  ISBN 978-1-60223-084-2 (paper : alk. paper)
  1. Anchorage (Alaska)—History—20th century. 2. City and town
life—Alaska—Anchorage—History—20th century. 3. Anchorage
(Alaska)—Social conditions—20th century. 4. Anchorage (Alaska)—
Ethnic relations—History—20th century. 5. Pacific Area—History—20th
century. 6. Pacific Area—Social conditions—20th century. I. Title.
F914.A5J66 2010
979.8'35–dc22

                                                2010013803

Cover design by Mark Bergeron

For Maria and Gerry Keffer,
who have made this, and
so much more, possible

CONTENTS

Contents

PREFACE

A NUMBER OF GENERAL BOOKS that trace the early history of Anchorage have been published. Among them are Claus-M. Naske and L.J. Rowinski, *Anchorage: A Pictorial History* (1981); Elizabeth Tower, *Anchorage: From Its Humble Origins as a Railroad Construction Camp* (1999); and John Stromeyer, *Historic Anchorage: An Illustrated History* (2001). The most comprehensive history that covers the city into the mid-1950s is Evangeline Atwood, *Anchorage: All-American City* (1957). Each of these books succeeds in what it sets out to do—provide a broad and engaging overview of Anchorage's past.

A scholarly article by William H. Wilson on Anchorage's first few years is detailed, and Terrance Cole and Stephen Haycox have published good articles on Anchorage and the Second World War. These works are useful and do not propose to place Anchorage in a broad context. Given the city's importance to Alaska, and Alaska's military and economic importance to the United States, it seems that a scholarly treatment of Anchorage's first decades is warranted. Such a work on the city's history since the Second World War awaits another author.

I am grateful to the administrators of the Summer Fellowship Program and to the Faculty Development Committee at John Brown University, where I teach, for providing me with funding that made research for this book possible—especially Vice President Ed Ericson, faculty development directors Galen Johnson and Cary Balzer, and President Chip Pollard. The assistance of Simone Schroder, interlibrary loan librarian at JBU, was, as usual, indispensable. Thanks to Ben Benton and Marilyn Holliday for allowing me to use a laptop through their office at JBU. Rick Froman, chairman of the Division of Humanities and Social Sciences at JBU, graciously made available funding for the photographs included in this book. Mary Habermas, director of the library at JBU, very kindly allowed me to have a large workroom to myself over a crucial two-week period. The librarians at JBU, and at the public libraries in Eagle River and Anchorage, were always gracious and helpful. Over several summers, my parents-in-law, Maria and Gerry, gave my family a place to stay in Eagle River, Alaska, and that made work on this project possible. I have dedicated this book to them.

Once again, I owe many thanks to the following professionals for their help with research: Bruce Merrell, formerly the Alaskana bibliographer at the Z. J. Loussac Library in Anchorage; Bruce Parham, archivist at the National Archives and Records Administration (Alaska Pacific Region) in Anchorage; and Carole Atuk, Wendy Lyons, and Rose Speranza, archivists at the University of Alaska Fairbanks. The editor of my first book with the University of Alaska Press, Erica Hill, took a teaching position at the University of Alaska Juneau when work on this book was beginning. I am grateful for her encouragement in the early stages. As far as my labors were concerned, Elisabeth B. Dabney picked up where Erica left off, and I am grateful for her attention and care. Jim Ducker, editor of *Alaska History*, has been a highly professional scholarly mentor. Chapter three is a revised version of an article published in *Alaska History*.

I thank Mary C. Mangusso, of the University of Alaska Fairbanks, and Katherine Johnson Ringsmuth, of the National Park Service in Alaska, for their helpful comments on a draft of the manuscript. Katherine's collegial conversation and correspondence with me were sources of encouragement. Dan Sparkman, a teacher of Alaska history, has encouraged me for many years. I'm grateful for his goodwill.

I thank Stephen Haycox and the Forty-Ninth State Fellows program at the University of Alaska Anchorage for inviting me to give a public lecture on early Anchorage at the city's main museum. I tested some of the ideas expressed in this book in the lecture and appreciated the feedback I received from members of the audience.

Thanks to my JBU colleagues Trisha Posey and Jake Stratman for reading and critiquing parts of the manuscript that led to this book. Kelly Neighbors and Brittany Jurica transcribed the newspaper articles in the appendix. Kelly also helped me with the bibliography.

I'm grateful to Jack Snodgrass of Palmer, Alaska, who was so helpful in so many ways, and who introduced me to his ninety-three-year-old mother, Alice Snodgrass, neé Mikami. Young Alice Mikami and her impressive family appear in these pages. What a treat it was to talk with Alice and to study old photographs of her family. I am sorry that Alice passed away at the age of ninety-four before this book became available.

Whatever merits this book possesses are due to the help of the people I have mentioned, and others. Whatever faults the book possesses are my responsibility.

À ma famille—Anne, Eleri, et Elliott: je vous aime tant.

INTRODUCTION

A NCHORAGE IS ALASKA'S LARGEST CITY and chief commercial center. At the end of the twenty-first century's first decade, Anchorage's population stood at nearly 300,000, with more than an additional 60,000 living in its metropolitan area.

Most of the offices of Alaska's oil industry are based in Anchorage, and the city is the center of retail and wholesale trading for a large majority of the state's residents. The host of Alaska's largest airport, Anchorage is vital to travel within the state. Anchorage is also a hub for passenger and freight routes to Asia from the United States and Europe. About one-half million tourists pass through Anchorage each year. Some take advantage of the city's museums, symphony, and opera.

Anchorage is the only city in Alaska to host two universities: the University of Alaska (the largest campus in the state system) and Alaska Pacific University, a small private school of Methodist heritage. Anchorage is Alaska's chief port and the headquarters of the Alaska Railroad. With Fort Richardson and Elmendorf Air Force Base on its borders, the city is an important site for the U.S. military.[1]

Anchorage grew slowly from its founding in 1915 to America's entry into the Second World War, when the federal government recognized its strategic value. Between 1940 and 1945, the population of Anchorage grew from about 2,500 to 70,000.[2]

This book traces Anchorage's development from its beginnings to the period immediately following Japan's attack on Pearl Harbor on December 7, 1941. Alaskans, more than many Americans, had long sensed that war with Japan was coming. News about the bombing of Pearl Harbor and other

U.S. possessions in the Pacific came as a surprise in Anchorage as it did everywhere in the United States and its territories, but among Alaskans the surprise was, perhaps, a little less sharp. What the residents of Anchorage could not have known was the extent to which the war that followed would fundamentally alter their community. This book brings Anchorage's story to the point of its transformation.

This book's chief purpose is to describe the development of Anchorage and the ways its public life was similar to and different from the general experience in the American states. As for what to call the residents of Alaska's largest city, the admittedly infelicitous term *Anchorageite* seems unavoidable. The city's inhabitants have used that term from the beginning.[3]

The development of Anchorage is a basic concern of this book. Another is the city's place within the international context that would lead to the world's most devastating war. Thus, at times we focus on the developing trouble in the Pacific. What did Alaskans say and write about Japan and its foreign policy? Or about what American responses to Japan should be? How did Japanese immigrants in Anchorage, and their children, get along in town? To what extent was anti-Japanese sentiment experienced in Anchorage? We will find that the personal experience of Japanese in Anchorage differed markedly from experiences in other places on the west coast, although federal government policy led to the internment of Alaska's Japanese as it did to Japanese living elsewhere in the west.

Early twentieth-century U.S. history textbooks tended to discuss Alaska within an imperial context. One work, published in 1906, viewed the purchase of Alaska in 1867 from Russia for $7.2 million as the "beginning of a general but premature expansion movement" following the Civil War. The text informs us that Secretary of State William Seward, who forged the purchase, had declared that "he wished to see the [American] Union extended from the Pole to the Tropics."[4] Another schoolbook, *The United States as a World Power* (1908), discussed the acquisition of Alaska as a key step on the road to the annexation of Canada.[5] Meantime, in his *History of the American People* (1934), Nathaniel Stephenson considered Russia's sale of Alaska to the United States in 1867 in the context of tensions between Russia and Japan and, a few sentences on, he quoted Secretary of State William Seward: "The nation must command the empire of the seas, which alone is real empire."[6] Arthur Schlesinger's *Political and Social Growth of the American People* (1941) connected the Alaska Purchase to anti-British feeling. The United States, Schlesinger wrote, had relieved Russia of Alaska to prevent the territory from falling into the hands of the English, whose dominion, Canada, separated the territory from the contiguous American states. In a chapter titled "Forging a Colonial Empire," Schlesinger observed that Alaska had been one of America's most profitable acquisitions, a "reservoir of potential riches" that needed safeguarding.[7] Other historians linked the Alaska Purchase to the American annexation of Midway Island, the acquisition of transit rights across Nicaragua (the prelude to the building of the Panama Canal), and to an unsuccessful scheme to acquire the Dutch West Indies. The purchase of Alaska, such authors said, was a major element in William Seward's scheme to draw Asia into the American orbit.[8] Clearly, then, in the first decades of the twentieth century, Alaska was broadly seen an important part of the American Empire, which for our purposes we can see as existing between the Spanish-American War of 1898 and the independence of the Philippines in 1946.[9]

In recent decades historians have had little to say about Alaska's place within the American Empire—perhaps because the territory was always geographically peripheral. But to detach Alaska's past from the American Empire is to lose a basic understanding of the territory's place in the American story. It may have been that Americans never possessed an "imperial temper" like that seen in Britain and France; few Americans were sad to see the Philippines gain their independence after the Second World War. And it may have been that the essence of American imperialism was not militarism but "the extension of the empire of man over brute nature"—a statement that made particular sense in Alaska.[10] But between 1898 and 1942 it was almost true that the sun never set on the U.S. empire, even if American holdings were much more limited than those of the leading European powers.

Early twentieth-century commentary makes it clear that Americans saw Alaska not primarily as a tourist destination or hunter's paradise but as an important imperial holding. In addition to concentrating on the social history of Anchorage, then, this book returns to an older theme, seeking to place the history of Anchorage where the people who built it saw it—in the context of a vigorous American Empire.

Since the civil rights era, there has been an interest in critiquing males of European extraction and Western culture generally. In many ways, this trend has been helpful. Voice has been given to the historically voiceless. In the pages that follow, a Japanese family, the Mikamis, are given substantial attention, not as a result of some sort of literary affirmative action but because the Mikamis really deserve notice. The point is that, fifty years ago, the Mikamis might not have been noticed at all.

Yet the West's peculiar emphasis on self-critique has had at least two unfortunate consequences: one, a romanticization of non-Western, supposedly more simple and more enlightened people, and, two, a kind of self-loathing that has become fashionable and is now deeply entrenched in Western institutions of learning. Hence, for example, the politically pious but irresponsible claim that the internment of American Japanese during the Second World War was the "logical outgrowth of over three centuries of American [racist] experience."[11]

A recent theme in published Alaskan history has been that, in terms of racial and ethnic relations, the Alaskan case has not been substantially different from the experience in the American states. "Prejudice flourished throughout white, middle class America during the 1920s," one text reads. This prejudice was characterized by "anti-labor, anti-radical, and anti-immigrant sentiments. Anyone outside the mainstream was suspect. Alaska proved no exception to this trend ..."[12] There is much to this generalization, and yet it is problematic because there is rarely uniformity in regions or different states or in different areas within states. This book suggests that, at least insofar as Anchorage is concerned, this kind of broad generalization needs some revision.

The writer readily acknowledges his sense that early Anchorage was, on the whole, a place of public civility and cordiality between residents of different backgrounds. Inevitably exceptions must be noted, and the First World War (whose aftermath on the home front is alluded to in the quote above) was an exceptional period. But even here the theme of civility held. Immigrants in Anchorage did not come under pressure unless they sympathized with the enemy or otherwise made themselves seem disloyal to the American war effort.

To summarize, this book strives to accomplish four things. First, it aims to describe the social development of Anchorage from its beginning to the period just after the United States' entry into the Second World War. Second, it wants to place Anchorage within a broader national context. Third, it seeks to situate the city within the context of the problems brewing in the Pacific in the early twentieth century. Finally, it hopes to show that relations in the city between different ethnic and racial groups were mostly civil. This last point is significant, for in recent decades the historical profession generally has focused on conflict, sometimes at the expense of seeing complicated reality.

CHAPTER ONE

Context

W HEN PRESIDENT WILSON signed a bill in March of 1914 authorizing the construction of one thousand miles of railroad in Alaska, he said that the project and the commercial advantages it promised would link Alaskans and the Outside "by many bonds that [would] be useful to both sides."[1] Alaskans agreed. Three weeks before, in the face of spring cold, they had celebrated the passage in the House of Representatives of the Alaska Railroad Bill by a vote of 230 to 87. In celebration, the Tanana Valley Railroad carried happy passengers into Fairbanks for no charge and in observation of the occasion, shop owners in Seward all but suspended business. In Cordova, whistles were whistled and American flags were hoisted. A band in Valdez walked in parade.[2] The vernal equinox assisted the festivities, for it meant "the approach of long days of sunshine and the unlocking of frozen rivers."[3]

Seattle celebrated, too. A parade there was said to have been "the most picturesque ever seen" in the city.[4] What one writer in the *North American Review* described as Alaska's dismal era of scanty population, vacant houses, and cultural despondency seemed past.[5] *The Fort Worth Star-Telegram* made the point this way:

> Before long the United States will build its first national railroad through Alaska and the Patriot with frost-bitten ears will be allowed to stake claims wherever the staking is good . . . . Then Alaska will become the Scandinavia of America and cities as large as Seattle will adorn its seacoast.[6]

There could have been no broad misunderstanding that, the president's words aside, the development of Alaska had less to do with concern about

Alaskans and their well-being than it did with the development of American wealth generally and the U.S. empire more broadly. When the rail legislation was being debated, the *Miami Herald* reminded Congressmen of the territory's minerals, timber, and agricultural land. More importantly, the Navy needed coal and "would need it far more if any war closed the neutral markets of British Columbia," a source of coal that lay within the not entirely friendly British Empire.[7] A South Dakota newspaper expected the imminent availability of Alaska's resources, especially coal, to lessen the cost of commerce in the nation generally,[8] while a U.S. senator observed that the American Navy in the Pacific needed about 300,000 tons of coal annually. The *Star-Telegram* suggested that if the government could oversee the construction of a canal in the malarial heat and mud of Panama, surely it could do the same in "that great country of ice and cold."[9]

In some people's minds, especially as rumors of war in Europe became more ominous, it seemed almost criminal to not break into Alaska's coal fields.[10] Meantime, Franklin Lane, Secretary of the Interior, looked forward to Alaska providing a home for millions of Americans; he envisioned the territory as a host to factories, numerous towns, farms and mills. Lane focused on Alaska because he wanted to bring its "wealth of coal, iron, copper and other minerals within reach of the outside world" and, in the process, enhance American power and prestige.[11]

Some wondered if the Alaska project really had less to do with resources and more to do with government expansion. Critics said that the government's ownership of the railroad in Alaska was the first step in a general scheme to nationalize public transportation—something for which Progressives had been long calling. As the *San Jose Mercury News* observed, "the progressive element in all parties will put the bill through as a simple government ownership proposition."[12]

The counterclaim was that in the absence of private initiative capable of exploiting Alaska for the public good, the government should do the work. Some pointed to the Uncle Sam's heavy involvement in the building of the Union and Central Pacific railroads as a kind of precedent, and Alaska's delegate to Congress, James Wickersham, urged Congress not to leave Alaska's wealth to a "bunch of pirates," that is, the Morgan-Guggenheim Syndicate, whose presence in Alaska was already ponderous. Alaska's riches belonged to the nation and should not be controlled by private interests.[13] Given the

AEC Collection, Anchorage Museum, AMRC-aec-g553

immense difficulties and risks involved in developing Alaska, many observers who were opposed to "socialism" saw nevertheless that only the government could do the job.[14] This was the stuff of the former president Theodore Roosevelt's "new nationalism," which put the "national need before sectional or personal advantage."[15]

While the government exercised substantial control over the Panama Canal, Alaska's railroad was the first major mode of transportation in peacetime to be owned and operated by federal agencies.[16] Thus the railroad symbolized the growth of federal power and influence, as did other legislation passed around the same time. The Merchant Marine Act (1916), for example, provided for a government board to purchase and operate commercial ships. The Smith-Hughes Act (1917) made federal funds available for agricultural and vocational training.[17] Government was extending its reach generally, and Anchorage, as one memoirist said, "was strictly a government project."[18]

What was the country into which Anchorage was born like? What ideas did the Americans who would become Alaskans bring to their country's young territory?

Since the mid-nineteenth century the United States had experienced stunning material growth. By the time work began on the Alaska Railroad, the United States possessed more operating rail lines than Austria-Hungary, Canada, France, Germany, Italy, Russia, Britain, Brazil, and Australia combined.[19] The nation was wealthier, healthier, more urban, and better educated than ever before.

A lengthy stream of facts and figures can be numbing, but they help to make the point. In 1840 the United States possessed 44 cities with populations of 8,000 or more, and the nation comprised about 1.8 million square miles with a population of over 17 million. Seventy-four years later, the nation possessed 786 cities with 8,000 or more residents, and its population of 97 million labored in a country of over of three million square miles (including Alaska and the island possessions). The United States and its empire had become greater in territorial scope than Britain, Germany, Austria-Hungary, France, Spain, Italy, Scandinavia, Greece, the Balkans, Egypt, Japan, and Mexico taken together. Since 1865, the United States had acquired about 24 million immigrants. In 1840, the country produced no oil, moreover, and exported $111 million in goods. By 1912, the United States had produced more than nine billion gallons of oil and exported goods worth nearly $2.2 billion.[20]

Leisure time, improved working conditions, and access to education were more the norm than ever. In 1899, about 3.4 percent of manufacturing jobs were held by children younger than 16 years; ten years later that figure had declined to 2.4 percent. Laws soon passed prohibiting night labor in factories for women and children and capping their workdays at 10 hours. In 1880, 17% of Americans were illiterate; in 1910, the figure stood at 7.7%.[21] "Nowhere in the entire world," said statistician Frederick Hoffman,

> is there an equal amount of widely diffused material prosperity combined with an equal amount of personal freedom, adequate compensation for services rendered, and leisure time for the enjoyment of the pleasures of life. No equal area in the world affords such a range of opportunity for material advancement of every kind and degree as the United States, from the Arctic shores of Alaska to the semi-tropical island of Porto Rico in the West Indies and the tropical possession of the [Philippines] in the Far East.[22]

4

To be sure, not all the news was good. The number of people deemed insane rose from 188 per 100,000 in 1890 to 204 twenty years later. Murder and suicide rates also rose.[23] Labor unions protested against low pay, long hours, unnecessarily dangerous working conditions, and growing corporate power. It is true that industrialization and urbanization caused living standards to rise on the whole, but the pressures they created also led to the creation of slums and heightened alcohol and drug abuse. Large immigrant populations lacked a command of English; the country seemed to be at risk of breaking into subsections of "hyphenated Americans." This caused some to romanticize less racially mixed societies like Australia, New Zealand, and Norway.[24]

On a broader scale, the author of *Protestantism and Progress* (1912) observed that there existed in Western societies a tendency toward oppression that seemed to be vying for eminence with the expansion of freedom[25]—a struggle manifested between colonizers and the colonized, in the First World War, in the postwar American clampdown on politically radical dissent, and in the political cultures that, in the 1920s and 1930s, gave rise to numerous fascistic governments in Europe.

Challenges like these presented Americans with an opportunity to triumph in the name of progress. President Wilson's vision of progress included the government's protection of economic freedom by regulation of monopolies and its work against urban squalor, unsanitary overcrowding, impure food production, and foul working conditions. In an earlier day, Wilson noted, freedom meant that government kept out of the way. Now, in the early twentieth century, government needed to act as a counterweight to self-serving corporations—to take the "heartlessness" out of politics and business.[26] This was an idea at the heart of the Progressive movement of the early twentieth century. Before long, the term *progressive* became trendy and was put to mundane uses. In the 1930s, days were set aside in Anchorage for residents to tidy the town, to help it maintain its "leadership in appearance as well as in progressiveness."[27]

The Progressive Party battled some of the era's troubles; its 1912 campaign song was "Onward Christian Soldiers." In the same spirit, the Christian Endeavor Society's 3.5 million members launched social welfare and educational crusades. Between 1870 and 1920 religious organizations founded more than

100 institutions of higher education. In 1870, less than sixty percent of the American population had spent time in school each year; by 1918 the figure had grown to more than seventy-five percent. This period also saw the establishment of about 225,000 kindergartens, and as of 1918 every state required some formal education. By 1915, the illiteracy rate had fallen to about six percent, and a high school diploma was increasingly seen as necessary for entry-level positions as bookkeepers, cashiers, and managers. As we will see, Anchorageites were as committed to education as other Americans.

Where less than one percent of Americans went to college in 1870, about eight percent did by 1925. Perhaps because of a greater sense of ambition among Anchorage's settlers, students from Anchorage went to university in significantly higher numbers. Students, in Alaska and elsewhere, could study the new disciplines of anthropology, sociology, and economics. Meanwhile, Protestant Americans, fired by the idealism of a social gospel, established Sunday schools and settlement houses; they offered job training, home economics classes, literacy courses, and exhortations to abandon vice for the common good and for the sake of "race progress."[28] These trends expressed themselves in early Anchorage.

Not everyone was impressed by American accomplishment. One European cynic noted that if by progress one meant addiction to cars, distraction, speed, and hype—or if one was comfortable emphasizing scientific knowledge for the sake of usefulness rather than for the simple joy of learning— then, yes, America really was the most progressive of all nations.[29] But another Englishman praised the architecture, egalitarianism, freedom of expression, personal initiative, enterprise, law and order, thirst for education, leisure time, and the wide access to automobiles and radios that he found in America.[30]

Waves of immigration presented challenges, but some American writers were sure these could be parried. In 1914 a Texas newspaper surmised that record-breaking immigration to the U.S.—"the safest and sanest place in the world"—would follow the First World War. A developing Alaska, the writer said, could absorb some of the anticipated newcomers. This would be one of Alaska's several contributions to the cause of American progress.[31] And, indeed, Anchorage was a magnet for immigrants who helped to build up the town, although a few also brought ideas with them that were outside the American mainstream. In 1916, the socialist candidate for Alaska's Congressional delegate had the support of about a quarter of the voters in Anchorage, "where the foreign vote, in opposition to the American vote, was strong."[32] The tensions these words pointed to were offset by other assessments (published in the same newspaper) that expressed delight at the Anchorage region's ethnic variety. To travel along the Alaska railway was to take "a trip around the world."[33]

In the early twentieth century the country wondered if it wanted more immigrants and, if so, what kind. As the Great Depression unfolded in late 1930, the *Anchorage Daily Times* editorialized for wiser immigration policies—policies that brought in truly needed workers rather than laborers who competed with citizens.[34]

The ways different ethnic and racial groups were stereotyped in the early twentieth century now seem crass, sometimes appalling. Northwestern Europeans, chiefly the English, Scottish, Welsh, and Dutch, were said to comprise a restless "race of nation builders"—"a pioneer race"—"a race of heroes"—driven by a constant and mysterious impulse to conquer and subdue and possess. Black slaves and their non-slave descendents, on the other hand, were sometimes depicted as genial, accommodating, happy-go-lucky, and blessed with a penchant for quaint mythology and banjos. The Irish were described as buoyant, vibrant, and possessed of a genius for organization. The Germans were plodding and phlegmatic. Poles were more independent than other Slavs; Italians were restless and roving; Hungarians were of "a Mongoloid blend" and had mingled with the children of Abraham and produced "a type of coffee-house Jew." Of all immigrant groups, the Jews were the most intellectual: "[t]hey cannot forget that Karl Marx was a Jew."[35]

And so it went. Koreans were indolent, a "weaker race" than the gritty and persevering Japanese, although Koreans did seem to be better than Japanese at learning languages.[36] Native Americans were deemed "stubborn and hard to overcome." According to some, Natives were destined for extinction, even if some of their traits would live on in American culture: "the trapper smiled. The Indian sensed his doom."[37] Some regretted the inevitable demise of America's Natives. Others—some in Alaska—called for the establishment of academic programs devoted to Native "race development."[38]

Related to racial views on Natives was the concept of *terra nullius*, whose simple thesis was that organized and settled societies had a moral imperative to acquire and improve unsettled and uncultivated land, even if inhabited.

The consequences of this idea can still be discerned,[39] but it was almost uncritically accepted among Westerners (and adopted by the Japanese) in the nineteenth and early twentieth centuries. "The lands settled [by Americans] were not already occupied by a population with a developed culture and life of their own," one theorist wrote in 1921. "The Indians...were not entitled, by any sort of social ethic which can be seriously considered, to be respected in their occupation of the land as if they had been a civilized people." Alaska, like the Pacific territory the United States had acquired, seemed "empty or inhabited only by uncivilized tribes."[40]

Scholars could appreciate Alaska Eskimo society on its own terms, and they saw the harm caused by Western disease, alcohol, firearms, and cultural dislocation. Diamond Jenness, author of a study on Western civilization's effects on Eskimos, even detected elements of superiority among the Natives, surmising that "[i]njustice and theft, spite and malice" were less common among them because life in the far north was difficult enough without the complications conflict created. Jenness claimed that, even if the Eskimo was "savage" in his customs, "in intelligence he ranks far above the average." Yet for Jenness, as for almost every early-twentieth-century observer, there was no question that on the whole Alaska's Natives would be better off for their interaction with Americans.[41]

The idea that Americans should not occupy Alaska because it was already occupied (albeit sparsely) could not have been taken seriously by very many in the early twentieth century, partly because it stood against the norms of human history (an unbroken record of conquest and domination of some groups by others), partly because human beings are driven by self-interest, and partly because the idea simply had little currency before the Second World War.

Underpinning reflections on race was social Darwinism, the application of a survival-of-the-fittest ideology to human affairs. "The great racial divisions of mankind are very old and well-established," wrote Lothrop Stoddard of Harvard:

> Each race, despite wide internal variation, forms a generalized type possessing a complex pattern of closely linked physical, mental, and temperamental characteristics, which have evolved through long ages of natural

selection that have eliminated disharmonic variations and produced a relatively smooth-working psycho-physical whole.[42]

The theory was applied starkly in discussions of African Americans. One
historian writing for the Yale University Press observed that the

> negro belongs to a period of biological and racial evolution far removed from
> that of the white man. His habitat is the continent of the elephant and lion,
> the mango and palm, while that of the [white] race into whose state he has
> been thrust is the continent of the horse and the cow, of wheat and oak.[43]

Winning in a social Darwinian contest meant conquest in war, or the colonization of militarily weak peoples, or simply moving as far as possible away
from the supposed ignorant barbarism of prehistoric peoples.

Not all agreed that technological superiority implied biological superiority. Some saw that Alaska Eskimos were just as likely to assume their superiority to outsiders as Americans were to assume their own superiority to the
Chinese. Some saw that environmental factors had more to do with cultural
development than mental capacity.[44] Americans who denied that Japanese
could assimilate into North American society, one scholar wrote in 1914,
"based their belief on a theory of race nature which is no longer tenable." But,
even here, a species of social Darwinian thought appeared. While the author
asserted that the "social assimilability of the Japanese is beyond question," he
noted that "[a]dequate specific data are lacking in regard to the desirability of
biological assimilation of the Japanese and white races."[45]Another academic,
Lothrop Stoddard, was convinced by ideologically-driven "scientific evidence
which clearly tends to show that crosses between white and non-white races
are biologically undesirable."

Social Darwinian thinking was also mixed with ideas about the ways
of providence, such as when one author wrote that "in the evolution of the
race and the development of the plan of God, the time had come when it was
for the best interests of the world...that Korea should come under Japanese
tutelage."[46]

Evolution—natural, social and economic—was equated with progress.[47] Thus, in 1915 the *Knik News* noted that with the government's railroad work underway in Alaska, "the process of evolution" in the Anchorage

region would keep step with the railway building; and this would lead to a "race for business."[48]

The intellectual environment Anchorage was born into honored pluck, dash, and determination. Some spoke enthusiastically of a railroad that would connect Anchorage to Fairbanks, Fairbanks to Canada's railroads, and thence to the railroad network of the United States. "With an international railway from Hudson's Bay to Anchorage," one Anchorage newspaper surmised, "the Atlantic seaports would be as close to the Orient as the seaports of the Pacific."[49] That railroad dream, like many others, never came into being, but it points to an early-twentieth-century faith in the capacity of technology to overcome nature's challenges.

Related to this faith was a Christianized conception of heroism that was expressed, in different ways, in the lives of men and women. Thus one late-nineteenth-century feminist text recalled how women had passed through the eras of savagery, mythology, and Judaism, "to the present era of Christianity"—and finally to America, where they were being loosed from the chains of selfishness, redeemed from "the thralldom in which too often the soul is held by the animal propensities," and finally to a "loftier position and...happier sphere."[50] Among the women praised in the book were Lydia Darrah, "an amiable and heroic Quakeress" of the revolutionary period; Mary A. Livermore, an advocate of freedom and loyalty during the Civil War; and Maria Mitchell, "the astronomer who was a librarian of the Nantucket Athenæum for twenty years."[51] A similar book depended on adjectives like enlightened, progressive, accomplished, painstaking, industrious, commanding, dignified, and affable; it praised the Methodist minister Stephen Olin for "continually struggling with great bodily infirmity while engaged in arduous toils," and Isabella Graham, whose good works "were as manifold as the hours of the day."[52] Readers of *Modern Great Americans* (1926) learned that success hinged primarily on a desire to learn—a willingness to risk even health for the sake of knowledge—and, secondly, on persistence. Men succeeded, the author wrote, "because they had iron determination, persistent and utterly resistless will power."[53]

Such were some of the ideas with which the Americans who went to Anchorage were familiar. As we will see, ideas like these manifested themselves in Anchorage's public life. In the person of Mary Mikami, who grew up in Anchorage, we will peer a little into the American drive to succeed.

Other ideas, such as a fierce social Darwinism, had little pull in Anchorage, or perhaps they just seemed irrelevant in the Alaska context. Anchorage was no Eden, but the added pressures of living in early-twentieth-century Alaska forged a certain social equanimity among groups that might have experienced friction Outside. Personal capital was spent on keeping one's financial head above water and on getting through the long, dark winters. There was not energy and personal capital available among Anchorage's residents to expend on unnecessary animosity. Notice, for instance, that the *Anchorage Daily Times* rejected opportunities to worry about eventual extinction of the "white race," which some experts who had examined birthrates among different people groups predicted. Such racial fixations, the *Times* observed, "have a way of making alarmists of otherwise rational people."[54] And in July 1930, when the outlook for the American economy seemed bleak, the *Times* called for a renewal of the citizens' commitment to liberty, to the protection of the weak, and to equal opportunity.[55]

Perhaps most surprising is that Anchorage's small Japanese population seems to have gotten along as well as any other ethnic group. When it came to distant Japan, though, Americans in Anchorage, like their compatriots elsewhere, held more complicated and shifting views. Given all that led to the Second World War and its prosecution and aftermath, it is understandable that general histories focus on tensions between the United States and Japan.[56] But American perceptions of Japanese people were not usually simple and, if they ever were uniform, that was only after war with Japan had begun.

During the Second World War, Japanese would be depicted in publications as apelike creatures. (The Japanese also dehumanized their adversaries.) However, fear and loathing of the Japanese often coexisted with respect—sometimes even the view that, in some ways, the Japanese were superior kinds of people. As one expert wrote, Japan was "in the front rank of progress."[57] The historian and social critic Henry Adams wrote that the Japanese seemed far superior to the Americans in their foreign diplomacy,[58] and one social Darwinian ranking of 12 human groups, published in 1904, placed the Japanese third, behind Russians and the "Americo-Europeans" (placed first), but ahead of "Hindoos," Turks, Chinese, and Arabs, with "prehistoric man" coming in last place.[59] An emblem displayed at the Alaska–Yukon–Pacific Exposition (1909) made Alaska eminent as it presided over representations of the United States and Japan, which were depicted as equals.[60]

Everyone saw that Japan had become a powerful force in the world, and its stunning rise from near isolation in the early 1850s to its status as a world power by 1920 evoked fascination. The "rare charm of Japanese life" could not be found among westernized Japanese, one observer wrote, but

> among the great common people, who represent in Japan, as in all countries, the national virtues, and who still cling to their delightful old customs, their picturesque dresses, their Buddhist images, their household shrines, [and] their beautiful and touching worship of ancestors.... [Japan] has its darker side; yet even this is brightness compared to the darker side of Western existence.[61]

Americans read books with titles like *Japan: Its History, Arts, and Literature* (1902), *Japanese Girls and Women* (1902), *Mysterious Japan* (1921), *The Woman and the Leaven in Japan* (1923), *Unfathomed Japan* (1928), *Awakening Japan* (1932), *A Daughter of the Samurai* (1932), *Beauty in Japan* (1935), and *Living in Tokyo* (1937). Interest in things Japanese found its way to Alaska. In 1917, a writer likened Alaska's natural beauty to "a Japanese painting."[62]

Envisioning an East Asian future inevitably involving Japan, some missionaries hoped the Japanese would adopt Christianity as they had adopted Western technology. "If Japan should speedily become Christian," a minister wrote, "Korea, Siam, and the vast empire of China would be profoundly influenced by the event...while the Japanese Christians...would join the Churches of the West in hastening forward to bring about the redemption of Asia."[63]

Some, then, did not see the growth of Japanese military strength as a threat. And when the Japanese displayed a keen interest in acquiring more influence in Siberia—so close to Alaska—these rather irrelevantly concluded that that would be better than having Siberia taken by the Germans, who had pushed the Russians out of the First World War.[64]

But most commentary on Japan focused on its rise as a military and economic power. If war came in Asia, Basil Chamberlain wrote in *Things Japanese* (1902), Japan "would be as the drum-major marching at the head of the line."[65] Another writer familiar with Japan suggested that the Western nations' day had passed and that Japan was poised to become as potent in international affairs as England had been decades before.[66] The *San Jose*

Mercury News noted that Japan aspired not only to commercial supremacy in Asia but to global rule.[67] When Congressman E. A. Hayes told a crowd in 1906 that the United States should go to war with Japan, it was not because he thought Japan would be easy to beat but because, at that time, Japan was unprepared.[68] The implication that a contest with a militarily ready Japan would lead to American defeat seemed clear.

As the first decades of the twentieth century passed, the Japanese came to be perceived in some quarters as something altogether Other. "The Japanese possess all the deep and subtle contrasts of mentality and ideality which differentiate the Orient from the Occident," a scholar wrote. "The persistent aggressiveness of the Japanese, their cunning, [and] their aptitude in taking advantage of critical circumstances in making bargains" had turned the American people against them.[69]

When some Americans applied social Darwinian theory to the Japanese, they found their own culture wanting. "The real fact," noted the prominent medical doctor William Sturgis Bigelow, "is that the Japanese, from the point of view of evolution and survival of the fittest, are the superior race."[70] Japan's arrival on the world scene was rewarded in 1909 with a seat on the International Olympic Committee, and Anchorage's newspaper readers learned about the skill of Japanese athletes like Shuhei Nishida, winner of the silver medal for the pole vault in the 1932 and 1936 Olympics.[71] Years before, President Theodore Roosevelt, an unprejudiced admirer of military prowess and the recipient of judo training from a "Japanese wrestler," had summarized Japan as "pluck personified."[72]

Well into the 1930s, commentators focused on Japan's stunning national and military rise. The Japanese had learned a lot since the Americans had forced their country open to trade in the 1850s, an American general reported to the *Anchorage Weekly Times*. Japan "had mastered western science, eclipsed western industry in low-cost production, made herself the military equal of the west on land, at sea, and in the air."[73] The general worried that Japan was acquiring the ability to capture Alaska and, from there, launch bombing raids on the American east coast.

Tensions between the United States and Japan grew as both countries extended their power and influence in the Pacific. Japanese observers noticed that the American Monroe policy warned Japan to keep clear of the western hemisphere while, at the same time, the United States was moving deeply into East Asia.[74] American commercial interests, meantime, were increasingly wary of the expansion of Japanese influence in Manchuria.[75]

In 1897, the U.S. military prepared its first contingency plan for war with Japan as whites in Hawaii protested the one thousand illegal Japanese immigrants coming to the islands annually—something encouraged by the Japanese government for practical reasons (a rapidly growing population) and for geopolitical advantage—that is, cultural infiltration. The following year the United States took control of the Philippines and Hawaii, partly to prevent the Japanese from doing so.

Japan's frustration in the face of other national counterweights grew. Japan had beaten China in war in 1895 but the Germans, French, and Russians, eager to preserve their own status and influence, prevented Japan from getting the spoils of war it wanted. Japan showed its strength in China during the Boxer Rebellion (1900), when it sent 8,000 troops to put down the uprising, where the Russians sent 4,800 and the United States, 2,100. Japan agreed to a military alliance with Britain in 1902, and it defeated Russia in 1904—a victory that President Roosevelt greeted with the exclamation "banzai!" But the United States stopped Japan from acquiring all of Sakhalin Island, among other desired spoils. This spurred anti-Western mobs in Japan to torch churches and to attack Americans and Japanese Christians. Japan's victory over Russia revealed how technologically savvy Japan had become.[76]

And there were tensions closer to home. In 1890, the Japanese in the United States numbered just over two thousand. By 1914, that population had grown to more than 91,000.[77] The same year, the U.S. military devised War Plan Orange, which, in the event of a Japanese attack on American holdings in the Pacific, envisioned a counteroffensive from bases in Hawaii, Midway, Guam, and Alaska.[78] Eight years before, San Francisco had attempted to segregate Japanese students from others. The city's mayor was concerned that Asian workers would undermine American civilization; he worried that America, overrun by Asian hordes, was reexperiencing the decline of ancient Rome.[79] And union members in California worried about jobs going to lesser-paid foreigners. The American Federation of Labor called for a law excluding Japanese and Koreans from the country similar to the legislation that had already been passed against the Chinese.[80]

By the early 1920s, American hostility was directed more against the Japanese than any other single group, especially on the west coast, where the large majority of Japanese immigrants lived. Japanese residents not born in the United States, including those in Anchorage, were excluded from citizenship. Some could understand that this caused resentment among Japanese; more were mystified when, in protest against restrictions placed on Japanese immigration, a Japanese patriot committed hara-kiri in front of the American embassy.[81] What kind of people were the Japanese?

On and off again through the early twentieth century, an American war with Japan seemed possible, at times probable, and at moments imminent. At one point, President Theodore Roosevelt sent sixteen battleships on a training mission to the Pacific, although highly placed American officials doubted the United States' ability to prevent Japan from taking Hawaii and the Philippines and attacking the American west coast.[82] The Japanese-American Kiyoshi Kawakami surmised obliquely that American big business was beating the war drum for the sake of the wealth to be gained from selling warships and guns.[83] In a "gentlemen's agreement," the Japanese promised to discourage immigration to California in exchange for an end to San Francisco's school segregation. War talk subsided. But then in 1924 the U.S. Congress passed, and the Japanese government severely criticized, legislation requiring the complete exclusion of Japanese immigrants from the United States, excepting professionals.[84]

All along there was a sense among Americans that the Japanese were particularly capable of ruthlessness. This view was fostered by news of atrocities in Korea, which the Japanese came to rule after their war with Russia. Kiyoshi Kawakami acknowledged that it was difficult for the Japanese to teach inferior Koreans to accept a higher civilization; he recognized that Japan's occupation of the country had not been free of "blemishes and blunders" perpetrated by some Japanese officers high on victory, along with Japanese riffraff who had gone to Korea as laborers. But whatever problems there were, Kawakami continued, they were caused more by "the folly and lawlessness" of the Koreans than by Japanese severity.[85] Some American accounts regretted Japan's heavy-handedness in Korea but acknowledged the Koreans' obstinate inferiority and Japan's record of progress and need for farmland and living space.[86] Arthur Judson Brown, author of *Mastery of the Far East* (1919), somewhat mysteriously argued that the Japanese in Korea were no worse than "the law-less Americans who did their ruthless pleasure in Alaska."[87]

Other observers declined to make excuses. One writer described Korea as living through a "hideous nightmare" and as a henhouse sacked by ravaging foxes; he wrote about "vindictively savage" Japanese sailors machine-gunning helpless Chinese whose ship had been sunk.[88] Another writer contemplated Japan's "reign of terror" on the Korean Peninsula.[89] The astounding brutali-ties the Japanese military would perpetrate against children and unarmed women, let alone vanquished enemies during the Second World War, give credence to accounts of Japanese atrocities earlier in the century.[90] And these claims, recounted in materials read by Americans, helped to promote anti-Japanese sentiment.

Of course, Americans would have done well to pay attention to outrages within their own republic. Through the 1890s, when many of those who went to the new settlement of Anchorage came of age, there were on average 187 lynchings annually. Between 1892 and the early 1950s, there were at least 4,700 lynchings, two-thirds of the victims being black.[91] Some journalists denounced thuggish lynch mobs and, at the end of 1913, they found comfort in a decline in the number of lynchings from the year before.[92]

Like Americans generally, Anchorageites read newspaper articles about interracial murder, one of them titled "Negro is burned to death by mob."[93] And they saw newspaper cartoons in their newspapers that belittled African Americans.[94] In 1936 the *Anchorage Weekly Times* published reports about a U.S. senator from South Carolina who walked out of the Democratic Party's national convention when a black minister rose to give an invocation, and about white men near Detroit wanting to "'see what it feels like' to shoot a negro."[95] There's no way of knowing what reactions to events like these were in Anchorage. The number of African Americans in Anchorage through the first half of the twentieth century was very small and the territory's distance from the American South probably prevented lynching and race-based bru-tality from pressing on residents' consciences.[96] U.S. Army General Simon Bolivar Buckner, in charge of getting Anchorage ready for war with Japan, would bring an explicitly racial outlook and accompanying racial epithets with him to Anchorage, but he was an outsider, he never adopted an iden-tity as an Alaskan, he died in combat at Okinawa in 1944, and he does not represent Anchorage.[97] A recurring theme in the pages that follow is that the culture of Anchorage promoted equanimity and a live-and-let live approach to public life.

The war that would come near the end of 1941 pitted Japan against the empires of Britain, France, the Netherlands, and the United States. It was fitting, then, that the war contributed so monumentally to the growth of Anchorage, which became and remains an important site for the projection of American military power. The purchase of Alaska from Russia in 1867 had taken place within the context of an expanding American empire; it was itself a response to an international context in which leading nations were establishing or expanding empires. Massachusetts representative Nathaniel Banks alluded to this context in 1868. The Pacific, Banks said, would be the "theater of the triumphs of civilization in the future," and Alaska was "the key of this ocean."[98]

The Alaska gold rush of 1900 contributed to American economic strength and to expansion of American influence in the far northwest, as well as in eastern Siberia.[99] By 1914, Alaska had come to be seen as ever more tightly linked to empire—to its preservation, defense, and supply. The word itself soon applied to the resource-rich territory. "Alaska is an empire within its own confines," an Anchorage newspaper claimed in 1917.[100] "Anchorage should in time become a great industrial city," another paper declared. "A great and mighty northern empire is just in the opening."[101] The book *Alaskaland* linked the settlement of Alaska to a stubborn contest for national supremacy:

> God, give us men to tame the wilderness,
> To make Alaskaland a sovereign State;
> Men with God-souls to bide the desert test,
> And build the empire of the *new Northwest!*[102]

The Alaska railroad was built, first of all, because Alaska promised to provide the United States with vast natural resources. The resource discussed most in 1914 was coal—because the Navy needed it after the United States had acquired a Pacific empire to protect. Relative to Britain's, the American Empire was small, but territory gained was territory to be protected because it contributed to American prestige and influence.

Of course, prestige and influence were costly. "If we had a coast line only to protect we would be doing fairly well," the *Philadelphia Inquirer* observed.

> But we have expanded. There are the Philippines to protect; there are the Hawaiian Islands; there is Porto Rico and there is the vastly important Panama Canal. . . . They are as much ours legally as is Alaska."[103]

No one needed to say that Japan was the United States' only serious potential adversary in the Pacific. When in 1914 Rear Admiral Charles Vreeland told a Congressional naval affairs committee that Alaska was weak in defense, Japan was the potential aggressor everyone had in mind.[104]

From the earliest years of the twentieth century, Alaskans and other Americans had been concerned about a Japanese invasion.[105] In 1906 the *Bellingham Herald* warned of Japan's capacity to "strike a fatal blow" against U.S. commerce in the Pacific; the paper's editors observed that "Alaska and Hawaii would be almost helpless in the face of an invading Japanese fleet and army."[106] Others envisioned Japan swarming the American garrisons in the Philippines and then, after a brief conquest, putting coolies to work in Alaska's goldmines.[107] A third scenario envisioned Russia and Japan cooperatively seizing Alaska and Canadian territory.[108]

So the international context of Anchorage's founding was one of wars and rumors of war. In the first decade of the twentieth century, Britain faced crises in Burma (Myanmar), Siam (Thailand), Afghanistan, Sudan, Egypt, Tibet, Venezuela, Samoa, and South Africa.[109] In roughly the same period, the United States faced potentially violent crises with Spain, Chile, Italy, Britain, and Germany. The imperial powers together faced down anti-imperial rebellion in China. Such was the wide world Anchorage was born into.

When the Alaska railroad bill passed Congress in 1914, the U.S. Navy looked to Alaska for coal because it needed fuel to defend America's Pacific empire. And Alaska's natural resources made the territory itself all the more important to defend. Alaska's future and the projection of American military power were bound.

The Americans who went to Anchorage came from a society that seemed contemptible to some among the genteel classes of Europe, but it offered real opportunity to thousands of immigrants and citizens. Few who went to

Anchorage in its first years were committed social Darwinists (many would not have recognized the term), but, inevitably, some did absorb the American emphasis on striving, contending, struggling, and endeavoring.[110] Not many nursed cutting, personal racial hatreds, but some probably did. Many Anchorageites knew Japanese residents personally and got along with them, but they were also concerned about the possibility of war with Japan.

Few who went to Anchorage were intellectuals who closely followed global trends; many, perhaps, shared the customary American impatience with academic complication. Yet Anchorageites, like Americans everywhere, were committed to the cause of general education. Many had not been born in the United States, but most held to or adopted the identity "American." This was better felt than defined.

And, in time, some who went to Anchorage put on an additional identity: Alaskan. Alaskans were independent and long-suffering, modern pioneers. An editorial written in 1916 said that the Alaskan's traits were shaped by the characteristics of the territory itself:

the pure, free air, not tainted with the city's breath, which sweeps over wide distances of mountains and plain[;] the nearness to nature where wonderful sermons are preached, the close association of dangers which teach confidence and self-reliance[;] and a wide charity for the poor devil who gets up against it.[111]

INTERLUDE

Nature

Words like "stunning" may be linked to Alaska more than to any other American state. To consider Alaska is to think of numberless caribou, otherworldly snow-capped peaks, and salmon which, while heaving upstream, make something wondrous of the arduousness of nature. "We saw bald eagles lock talons in midair, tumbling toward the ground like comic-book foes before they soared free," wrote a twenty-first-century travel writer, who also mentioned plentiful whales, a "mammoth mama bear," a congenial porcupine, and a glacier. "Up close, the blue color of the glacier looks more like a Disney World prop than something that actually exists in nature."[1]

The words were nothing new. *McClure's Magazine* chronicled President Warren Harding's visit to Alaska in 1923, recording for readers what he did and said, but also devoting much space to descriptions of America's "great national storehouse."[2] Former Alaska governor Ernest Gruening, too, wrote of Alaska's "sensational splendor," "cosmic dimensions," and its "eternal and undepletable" scenery. "The flora," he wrote, "is riotous, profuse."[3]

Alaska makes the work of tourism marketers easy for the obvious reason that so much of Alaska *really is* breathtakingly beautiful. The point was made in 1917, when the *Overland Monthly and Out West Magazine* published the memoirs of a tourist named Grace Hill. She wrote about a "sedate puffin" and whales coming near as if to offer a greeting. Seward was a modern and attractive town, she wrote, but Resurrection Bay was "like a fairy land." Even severely isolated Nome looked beautiful from a distance. Alaska's wonders made the territory seem like an amazing "land of mystery."[4] And yet, at the end of her essay, Hill wrote that, after a while in Alaska, she was glad to leave "the wastes of the Far North" and return to civilization—namely, Seattle.

This points us to another side of things. Alaska is beautiful, often stunning, but life there is difficult. People speak of Alaska's glories, but also of its thick winter darkness and, for the sleepless, the seemingly incessant light of high summer. People speak of the agonizing cold of January in Fairbanks and of Ketchikan's relentless rain. Depending on one's disposition, having to keep an eye out for bears on nature walks either puts fun into, or takes fun out of, the process. Alaska's mosquitoes form vampire gangs, conducting drive-by hits on whomever.

Whether one focuses on Alaska's particular blessings or challenges depends on the moment's agenda. When the territory's railroad workers wanted higher pay during the Great Depression, they appealed (in part) to the difficult winter weather they labored in. Prospective investors and businessmen, on the other hand, were told that Anchorage's weather cycle was "moderate."[5]

Anchorageites saw that their town could be a key staging area for big game hunters from Outside, or for journalists and travel guide writers. One visitor from Oregon confided in a letter to the *Daily Times* that he would not be content in life until he returned to Alaska to take down big game.[6] Denali, especially, was a tourist magnet: the "mountains of Switzerland are pygmies beside the snowy crests of the Alaska ranges."[7] Alaska Guides Incorporated, based in Anchorage, declared itself ready to organize expeditions for all wallet capacities.[8] And marketers appealed to romantic lore, calling to mind the old-timers who had "tramped the tundras, climbed the mountains, and swarmed through the valleys of the then unknown northland."[9] Certainly there was pay dirt in the perception of Alaska as exotic and awaiting the exploits of the vigorous.

But few Anchorageites were genuinely interested in frontier living. They wanted to settle down. They knew that Alaska's appeal lay partly in the things that made it unusual, but they also knew that Anchorage's long-term well-being depended on the gathering of a steady, well-grounded population. And this, in turn, meant that they needed to create a normal American town.

Anchorageites did not always want to be presented to outsiders as wild and unusual inhabitants of a wild and unusual land. They got tired of Alaska's image as a land of icebergs and frolicsome malamutes.[10] But they also knew that Alaska's extraordinary natural resources attracted tourists and dollars.

Anchorageites advertised Alaska, seeking to bring the right kind of residents to the territory. For Anchorage to realize its potential as an important American city—as a place of influence—it had to be more than a town situated in a winter wonderland. It needed to be seen as a place where winters weren't so bad, and where life was pretty much as it was Outside. So in the late fall of 1923 the *Anchorage Weekly Alaskan* joked that Anchorage's ice cream makers were having a hard time of it since, given the lateness of winter, ice was in short supply.[11] The *Daily Times* promoted the city as a good place to reside year-round because rents were low, food and clothing prices were reasonable, and entertainment was abundant.[12] "If one were to travel the world over," the *Daily Times* said,

> it is doubtful if a locality could be found which possesses a climate as nearly perfect, in winter and summer, as that of the Anchorage district. Climate is not everything but moderate temperatures help a lot when one reads of the heat and storms which so frequently take a heavy toll of life in less favored parts of the world.[13]

A certain Mr. and Mrs. George Roll agreed, opting to stay in Anchorage through the dark months on account of the town's "splendid winter climate."[14]

But however mild Anchorage's winter—and relative to Fairbanks' deep freezing, "mild" was the right word—spring was always welcome. Stores in Anchorage announced spring cleaning sales, advertising scarves, dresses, and lingerie for "her majesty the American woman." Gordon's clothing store in Anchorage advertised its paisleys, plaids, and striped wares as "the most exciting thing fashion has done for many a spring."[15]

What were the Americans who lived in Alaska like? "The people of Alaska are just like the people outside," one U.S. senator said while passing through Anchorage, failing to mention what else they *could* be like.[16] Then again, a writer for the *Los Angeles Times* noted that Alaska produced a "special type of citizen, the like of which is found only in frontier countries." The Alaskan is "wholesome, generous, friendly and hospitable but has the old western spirit of indomitable courage that makes him picturesque and formidable." Another writer, this one a resident of Fairbanks, said that Alaska was a land of "strange enchantments" that "created a strong and subtle spell"; Alaska was a "famed prodigal in lavish generosity" and its "people are warm of heart and supergenerous of gift."[17]

What was true? Were Alaskans—were the Alaskans in Anchorage—just like Americans everywhere, or were they Americans of a special kind because they lived in so special a place?

Into the twenty-first century, they were both. Alaskans were like Americans everywhere. They ate at the same restaurants, wore the same style of clothing, watched the same TV shows.

Yet life in Alaska has always set people apart. When Alaskans go Outside and tell people where they are from, they expect a reaction of pleasant surprise, and they like explaining how they face Alaska's rigors. They like the fact that Alaska is more than twice the size of Texas. They like saying that they can drive to glaciers, and that moose walk past city hall. They take pride in their cold spell endurance, and they recount childhood stories of playing outdoors in summer till midnight.

CHAPTER TWO

Beginnings

IN THE EARLY TWENTIETH CENTURY the Americans who thought about Alaska usually did so in terms of resources—gold, fur, fish, timber—rather than in terms of long-term human settlement. By 1914, another Alaska resource—coal—was gaining attention. Alaska's coal needed to be secured, extracted, and shipped. This made for hard work and contributed to the Alaskans' image as unusually hardy humans. Almost by a process of natural selection, it seemed, settlers who had gone to Alaska and stayed there were exceptional and independent—the fittest. This, some said, set Alaskans apart from dwellers in another parts of the Empire such as the Philippines, where dependence on government direction was the norm. But the Alaskans in Anchorage also depended very much on Uncle Sam.

The use of Darwinian language to express a desire for imperial growth was common. So, too, were rhetorical linkages of Alaska to other parts of the empire.[1] The *Nation* suggested that a government commission be set up to manage Alaska affairs, "much as is done...[in] the Philippines,"[2] and *Current Opinion* compared the paltry development in Alaska to the greater work done in Puerto Rico and Hawaii.[3] The *North American Review* worried about the defensive challenge presented by American possession of the Panama Canal, Hawaii, the Philippines, and Alaska,[4] while Senator George Chamberlain of Oregon said that the building of a railroad in Alaska was second in importance only to the Panama Canal.[5]

Others saw the scheme to build a railroad in Alaska in a global context. The British were growing cotton in Sudan, Europeans had largely financed and built railroads in South America, and some Canadians were talking about building a seaport on Hudson's Bay. Along with schools, hospitals, churches, sanitation, and city planning, exploits like these would bring the world to the plane of high civilization.[6] In *Forum* magazine the American secretary of commerce wrote of Alaska as itself being an empire that (like the Philippines and Puerto Rico) added to the wealth of the greater American Empire. Thus, Alaska had helped to put the United States in a position to fulfill its mission as a "saviour nation"—a nation that made sacrifices for the good of the world.[7]

As war crept toward Europe through the spring and early summer of 1914, American military strategists emphasized the need to shift substantial naval power from the Atlantic Ocean to the Pacific. The completion of the Panama Canal in that year made such a transfer relatively easy. Lieutenant Frederick Mears, who had served in the Philippines during the Spanish-American War and who, from 1909, had been impressive as the superintendent of the American-built railroad in Panama, would now take his skills, along with some of the equipment he had used in Central America, to Alaska.[8] Mears' personal connection to the Panama Canal and the Alaska Railroad symbolized the imperial link between American possessions in the south and far north.

American warships could now pass through the Panama Canal into the Pacific. How would they be fueled? Some coal—not enough—came from British Columbia, a small but important part of the Dominion of Canadian within the British Empire. In May of 1911, some residents of the Alaska town of Cordova showed their distaste for this by reenacting the Boston Tea Party and dumping British Columbian coal into the sea.[9]

In reality, Alaska's development owed much to Canadians—the Sovereign Bank of Canada invested heavily in Alaska rail lines and Canadian engineers helped to build them—but in this competitive imperial context, a resource so essential to the projection of American power needed to be placed firmly in American hands.[10] In 1913, not even Alaska's own coal needs were met by the territory's resources.[11] Unfortunately, by the following year, the Navy knew that the coal from Alaska's Bering field was inferior in steaming efficiency to coal from West Virginia. Reports on the coal in the Matanuska field, however, were more promising. Strategists were worried about the possibility of war with Japan.[12] The Pacific fleet needed 300,000 tons of coal per year. One expert predicted that Alaska contained enough coal to meet the nation's needs for 200 years.[13]

In the spring of 1915, the *Knik News* reported hopefully on testing of Alaska coal done by the *U.S.S. Maryland*. The matter was pressing. "The contrast between the preparedness for war on the part of Japan and of the United States needs no comment."[14] The Philippines especially, but also Hawaii and Alaska, seemed vulnerable. In the words of the Alaska railroad bill that gave Anchorage its start, Alaska needed to be developed to "provide adequate and suitable transportation for coal for the army, navy, and other Government services, of troops, arms, and munitions of war."[15] The Secretary of the Navy, Josephus Daniels, had said that a new railroad in Alaska was "imperative"; President Theodore Roosevelt had made the same point nine years before.[16] Now, in light of growing tensions with Japan, President Wilson called the need for an Alaska railroad to the coal fields "very pressing."[17]

Some viewed the territory as an important site for the projection of American power. Partly because of Alaska's perceived military value, the *Philadelphia Inquirer* praised the American triumph over Canada in a turn-of-the-century border dispute along the Alaska panhandle. How fortunate that the United States was not presented with the possibility of British Navy cruisers and battleships stationed at the Lynn Canal, surrounded by impregnable fortifications.[18] Now, in the context of discussions on the Alaska railroad, Washington representative William E. Humphrey made the case for Alaska's naval significance. "Alaska is the place where, above others to-day, we need a new naval station," he said.

> A battleship fleet in Alaska is in a far better position to strike an enemy in the Orient than one at Hawaii. It is in a far better position to intercept a fleet from the Orient. For naval purposes alone construction of a railroad in Alaska is fully justified.[19]

Another Washington congressman, Albert Johnson, saw the development of Alaska as the next logical step in a process that began with Pilgrim settlement and, in time, led to the acquisition and development of Louisiana, Texas, the West, Puerto Rico, the Philippines, and the Panama Canal. He argued, somewhat improbably, that American interest in Alaska had spurred the Monroe Doctrine of the 1820s, and he wondered if the United States had been guided all along by divine providence. "Open Alaska," he said in Congress:

> This is the opportunity, and it is almost providential. Alaska is to-day...the greatest asset the United States possesses. Guard it well. Do not let it lie dormant at a time when the opening of the Panama Canal is about to divert a great immigration to our Pacific ports.... This railroad means that Alaska, unlocked, shall be opened, peopled, and made prosperous, to take its place as our sentinel and our key to the new Pacific.[20]

A Navy lieutenant commander would have agreed, for he saw that, since the Spanish-American War of 1898, the United States had met its "naval frontier of destiny" in the Pacific—and this new frontier would be supported and strengthened by the old "coast-line naval frontier" of which Alaska formed a part.[21]

Alaska also beckoned missionaries. The *Herald of Gospel Liberty* reported that the story of Christian missions there was as thrilling as from any Asian country. American work in Alaska could advance two empires, the *Herald* suggested—one republican, the other monarchical: "As Alaska is called the coming country of the United States, may she be speedily claimed for the King of kings and her wonderful resources turned toward the advancement of His kingdom."[22]

From afar, the *Miami Herald* linked the Alaska scheme to the symbols of American power. The railroad in the far north, the *Herald* told its readers, was the most extensive such project envisioned since the first transcontinental railroad. Alaska promised to play an important part in the growth of American trade in the Pacific; it had already delivered over thirty times its purchasing cost of $7.2 million in gold; and the territory was vital to Navy interests.[23]

The first surviving copy of the *Knik News* (1915), forerunner to Anchorage's newspapers, alludes to imperial concerns: it considered the U.S. Navy's need for coal and Japan's military strength, and it wondered whether the Japanese would send troops to the war in Europe. The Japanese did not do so, but their capacity to do so seemed beyond question.[24] Anchorage's founding and the interests of American Empire were inextricable.

On the ground, amidst the snow and mud on which Anchorage was built, daily concerns were inevitably mundane. Well before the town was established, and even as observers hoped that Alaska would play an important imperial role, it was fashionable among some to construe the territory as an

Anchorage Museum general photo file, AMRC-b70-19-212

American colony. Early in the century, a few had called for Alaska's independence or for annexation to Canada. Alaskans sometimes felt forgotten and more poorly served than Filipinos and Puerto Ricans.[25] Occasionally this feeling was expressed in ways that could not be taken seriously. An article in the *Weekly Alaskan* suggested that Alaskans might as well migrate to Siberia for all Uncle Sam cared.[26] Another paper complained that the flashy and somewhat shady Anchorage resident Joe Spenard had created more road for automobiles in ten days than the Alaska Road Commission had built in three months.[27]

For all the Alaska hype about rugged individualism, there is no question that early Anchorage was in a state of dependence on government. Where some Alaskans would grow bitter over a supposedly forgetful federal government's neglect, Anchorageites could not miss Uncle Sam's presence among them. Even before the new city had taken rudimentary shape, the *Knik News* provided news about the "government railway scheme," the "government mess house," a "government agricultural experiment station," a "government school teacher," and a government hospital.[28] By the summer of 1915, long and tedious articles with titles like "Regulations Governing the Disposal of the Lots in the New Government Townsite" were published in the *Cook Inlet Pioneer*.[29] Government officials decided where the new city would be founded, how many lots would be available for sale, and at what minimum price ($25).[30] Anchorage's early settlers looked to government to provide livable wages.[31] Government agents received high praise for their energy and capable direction.[32]

The government told settlers when they could purchase lots, and it determined the names of the settlement's streets. Without any sense of irony, land sales that led to the development of Anchorage were called "big government realty transactions"; the rudimentary town itself was called a "government domain."[33] The *Philadelphia Inquirer* informed its readers that the government intended to make Anchorage "a model village" where rules concerning building and sanitation would be strictly enforced.[34]

A shortage of drinking water in the winter of 1915 was the government's problem to solve, as was the problem of eliminating annoying mosquitoes.[35] The government installed a sewer system and sought to provide model housing to railroad employees—living quarters that would serve as "object lessons of possibilities of what the best practical methods of housing, feeding and sanitary conditions should be."[36] Residents could criticize the government sewerage system, but final decisions were not the people's to make.[37]

Government decided how coal would be extracted from the Matanuska fields.[38] Sometimes the new railway in the far north was called the "Alaska railroad"; more often it was the "government railroad."[39] Sometimes the titles were combined, as in the "government Alaska Railroad."[40]

The government's man on the scene, Frederick Mears, ordered automobile and dogsled drivers to stay off sidewalks.[41] The local government determined that no automobile could be parked within 25 feet of a fire hydrant and that "[a]rticles may be hung on the fronts of buildings provided they do not extend more than 12 [inches] from the walls of such buildings."[42] Even after a small majority of Anchorageites voted for incorporation in the fall of 1920, the government continued to provide medical care.[43]

Government seemed to touch everything. An article about Anchorage published in *Outlook* magazine made the point succinctly. When the Alaska railway was up and running and Alaska prospering, it said, "Uncle Sam will stand out before the world as the biggest and best builder that this or any other continent has known."[44]

In a place so isolated, entertainment for families was vital and this, too, partly became a government responsibility. "Your Uncle Sam is teaching employers a few fine tricks on that new government railroad he is building up in Alaska," the *Miami Herald Record* reported.

[O]ne of the first buildings he wanted to put up at the new town of Anchorage (which is the construction camp base for the railroads) was an amusement hall.... So now the men at Anchorage have a government-owned recreation plant, where they can get healthy amusement free as part of their contract with Uncle Sam—model employer.[45]

No one saw a problem of church–state mixing when a wandering preacher roamed into Anchorage and held services in the government amusement hall.[46] Perhaps appeals to the beauty of the region made his work easier. "Who can say that Alaska is not God's country," a high school student wondered. "No tinsel ornaments could have made the spruce trees look so beautiful, nothing but God's own hands could have worked such miracles."[47]

What the traveling preacher thought about the government-sanctioned red-light district on the southeast fringe of town, we do not know. The government did not allow prostitution or gambling in the town proper, but these vices were contained rather than resisted. In the spring of 1915, one "woman alleged to be of the underworld" was asked to move her lodgings to a "less prominent part of town." The next days willing hands pitched in to help move her cabin.[48]

Then there was booze—or, in Anchorage, the attempted control of it. The government reserved the power to seize property on which alcohol was sold.[49] Perhaps this was why Alafar Dunlap's husband had a fatal heart attack following news of her conviction as an alcohol dealer.[50] Almost as grim as coronary failure was the lawyerly prose of the government's case against Mrs. Dunlap:

It appears from the records that the [land] purchaser, Mrs. Dunlap, was arrested and charged with violation of Section 2581 of the Compiled Laws of Alaska relative to selling liquor without a license; that a trial was held on July 14, 1916 and resulted in her conviction and she was sentenced to a term of one year in jail and to pay a fine of $1500. The records also show that this is the third offense of this character committed on said premises by the purchaser. This being the third offense committed by the lot purchaser, it is recommended that a forfeiture of the lot and all money paid thereon be declared in accordance with the regulations as published in Circular No. 491, copy of which is herewith enclosed.[51]

On another occasion U.S. Marshal F.R. Brenneman seized, among other contraband, "ten cases of whiskey, six barrels of whiskey, fourteen bottles of whiskey, twenty eight kegs of whisky, ten boxes of whiskey, one five-gallon tin of whiskey, six gallons of whiskey and three demijohns of whiskey." The importers from San Francisco were not found; the Marshal destroyed the whiskey.[52] The struggle for an alcohol-free town continued.

Different government agents with different concerns squabbled over jurisdiction. "The first thing you know," one official wrote, "the public will begin to think that it is not possible for any two bureaus of the Government to work together."[53] And indifferent bureaucratic rules wrecked good feelings. In July 1917 the Anchorage school's janitor, Charles Brown, was denied one day of sick leave "as the regulations do not permit giving sick leave to janitors."[54]

Red tape got in the way. Locals complained about government bungling and lack of foresight. The government "didn't start to lay the water mains till the freezing weather started," one memoirist recalled.[55] In the pages of the *North American Review*, Secretary of the Interior Franklin Lane criticized the "interlocked, overlapped, cumbersome, and confusing" government activity in Alaska. He listed more than twenty federal agencies with some kind of oversight in the territory. All of Alaska's key problems were related, Lane wrote, and all government direction there "should be in the same hands."[56] Officials in early Anchorage understood that they sometimes needed to forego bureaucratic channels to get things done.[57]

A worker with the U.S. post office decided on the new settlement's name, despite a popular referendum in which Alaska City gained the most votes.[58] In July of 1915 Alaska's governor suggested changing the name of the city from Anchorage to Matanuska, but the idea went nowhere.[59]

If the government controlled Anchorage, Washington state, and especially Seattle, benefited economically from Alaska's development. San Franciscan business interests sought to capitalize on Alaska wealth as part of a grander project to tap into Pacific trade and make their city the second largest in the country. "Nature has decreed that San Francisco is to be a large city"—and, of course, San Francisco did become important.[60] But for obvious geographical reasons, Seattle gained the most from Alaska development.

Like some in San Francisco, a few in Anchorage thought, or hoped, that the young city would someday rival Seattle as the key American settlement on the Pacific: "if the Orient be considered we [in Anchorage] stand without competitor on the entire pacific coast, if distance [to Asia] be counted."[61] If seen in terms of American airpower projected in the Pacific, this aspiration would eventually be borne out.

From the beginning, observers could see that Seattle's business community had a great personal interest in Alaska's development. Washington capitalists invested in the territory,[62] and even before Anchorage was settled, Seattle businessmen became friendly with appointed Alaska railroad officials. In April 1915, some 500 flag-waving residents of Seattle saw Lieutenant Mears off to Alaska.[63]

By 1916 the Alaska Bureau at Seattle's Chamber of Commerce was well established; its letterhead carried the slogan "develop Alaska."[64] The bureau launched letter-writing campaigns to encourage Congress to appropriate funds for Alaska's development. One such letter observed that, with a value of nearly $64 million to the United States, Alaska commerce amounted to over $5 million more than the country's trade with China.[65] It was Seattle, *Banker's Magazine* noted in 1915, which first demanded that the government unlock the great storehouse of Alaska.[66]

Given the economic and shipping infrastructure in Seattle, and the city's relative proximity to Alaska, Alaska almost seemed to be a satellite of Seattle.[67] In 1915 the Seattle Commercial Club had members working in ten departments of interest—among them agriculture, entertainment, and Alaska. Businesspeople knew that Seattle's development as a "world port" depended in part on Alaska's economic growth.[68]

Anchorage's ties to Washington State were clear from the beginning. The government shipped lumber and steel to Anchorage from there.[69] Con artists based in Seattle looked to make money from Alaska land schemes.[70] Washingtonians established businesses in the new town, and the Seattle public library donated books to the Anchorage public school.[71] In turn, the school purchased necessities from Seattle's Lowman and Hanford Booksellers.[72] In November 1923, ice cream producers short on ice because of a late winter wired to Seattle, ordering a shipment of frozen water.[73]

In Anchorage's first years, Washington politicians came under criticism. In 1916, the *Forty-Ninth Star* made the point this way:

> All over Alaska a sentiment is growing against candidates for Alaska offices who make their homes in Seattle and who do not spend an average of three months a year in the country they expect to honor them by voting them into prominent positions. In a business way it is very nice and proper for Seattle to manifest a lively interest in Alaska. It helps all around. But in politics—well, carpetbaggers are just as unpopular in Alaska as they were in Dixieland forty years ago. There was cause for their unpopularity in the land of cotton and there is cause for their unpopularity in the land of gold and one-streak bacon.[74]

In the same year the *Forty-Ninth Star* editorialized in favor of a dubious plan to cede Juneau and its environs to Canada.[75] Alaska, the paper said, would be better off without a city that hosted so many "Seattle buccaneers."[76]

Some said that Anchorage's new residents could be counted as the kind of pioneers—the kind of new pilgrims—who would wrench a stable city from the wilderness. At first, unlike among the Pilgrims of yore, there were few families. According to reports, 500 people lived in Anchorage by the summer of 1915, most of them single men.[77] The wife of an army officer at Fort Liscum in Seward decried the fact that so many of the territory's good men were living in bachelorhood.[78]

Women arrived and the town's composition changed. Among those who applied to teach in Anchorage were Cecilia Burroughs from California, Edna Bond from Iowa, Anna Simonson from North Dakota, Elva Arbuckle from Indiana, Florence Poucher from Washington, and Maude Clifford from Oregon. One official claimed that the school board had received between 400 and 500 applications to teach in the new settlement—the vast majority of them coming from women. Competition for teaching positions was so stiff that not even the president of the Tanana Valley Railroad Company could ensure teaching positions for his cousins Mattie and Effie.[79]

By 1917, Anchorage's population stood at more than 5,500 and Anchorage could be a called a "town of families" populated mostly by settlers from the western states, although the halls of Harvard, Yale, and Princeton were also represented.[80] It could not have been true, as one journalist put it, that "all nationalities" worked in Anchorage.[81] Yet the city's early telephone books and other sources point to Alaska's broad appeal and to the way the town acted as a melting pot. Early on, some worried that the large number of immigrants in the new town were "foreignizing the American" and felt that, thanks to government immigration policies, the livelihoods of American laborers were threatened. It was irritating sometimes to feel as if one could not get along in Anchorage in English.[82] But these kinds of feelings were never dominant.

There was no question that the Alaska Engineering Commission drew an international workforce. One writer noted that, except perhaps in the Foreign Legion, a greater variety of people could be found "nowhere else in the world."[83] William McKenzie from Seattle worked a steam shovel, William Mellish from Alberta was a clerk, and Charles Strum from Nova Scotia was a watchman. Chas Seamen from Finland was a carpenter, and Phil Miller (England), Sam Radish (Serbia), and Mike Papiduk (Romania) were foremen. James Williams from Wales was a fireman and James Van Zanter from the Netherlands was a cook. James Xounas from Greece, Walter Trenach from Austria, Carl Olsson from Sweden, Michael Martin from Germany, and Floyd Reno from Oregon were laborers. Adam Simmons, born in Seldovia, Alaska, was a crane engineer. The job of Simon Samis, from Turkey, was not listed.[84] In the city's first years, local banks published advertisements, and the socialist *Alaska Labor News* published articles, in Greek, Italian, and Serbian.[85]

Among the twenty Andersons listed in Anchorage's 1917 directory were a railroad contractor, three miners, a watchmaker, a "steam shovel man," and the vice president of the Bank of Anchorage. Milo Jonovich owned the Eureka House, Anton Kavacevich owned Tony's Café, and George Pappadopulos ran the Royal Café. Also listed were McIntoshes, McLanes, McMillans, and thirty-seven Johnsons.[86]

Over one hundred immigrants petitioned in Anchorage for citizenship between 1916 and 1920. Twenty-two of these were Swedes, nine were from Norway, five came from Denmark, and a single Icelander added to the Scandinavian mix. Immigrants from the British Empire—Canada, South Africa, Ireland, Scotland, New Zealand, and Wales—renounced their loyalty to England's king in exchange for American papers. Immigrant workers from Italy, Greece, Bulgaria, Switzerland, Germany, Russia, and the Netherlands vowed, as required, that they were neither anarchists nor polygamists. These immigrants had come to the United States via ports at New York, Detroit, Boston, Seattle, Baltimore, Juneau, and Ketchikan. Most of these new Americans were in their thirties. The oldest petitioner to be naturalized in Anchorage between February and December of 1919 was 61 years old; the youngest was 26.[87]

The process of gaining citizenship was helped along by longtime American citizens who vouched for applicants' characters. The Anchorageites George Abraham (a contractor) and Frank Walsh (a carpenter) spoke for the moral character of Hamma Haddad, who had been born in Syria and had come to the United States via France.[88] Michael Durback, originally from South Africa, had made his way to Alaska from Argentina, then New York, and then Washington State. His citizenship application had the support of Camille McGown (a merchant) and Joseph Flower (a barber).[89]

There is no way to know how many Japanese lived in Anchorage between 1917 and 1921, although a dozen is the minimum. No Japanese petitioned for citizenship; as a result of federal law, they were ineligible. Yet some of Anchorage's Japanese residents emphasized American identities: K. Kamada owned the Union Bath House and Laundry, where O. Tanaka was employed. Y. Kimura ran the U.S. Restaurant where S. Tanaka worked. Harry Yokota lived in the Nevada House. How K. Tanaka, Kemoda Sabe, and S. Yamamoto were employed we do not know.[90]

What is clear is that Japanese immigrants in early Anchorage enjoyed freedom of movement and access to the local economy. In 1915, the *Cook Inlet Pioneer* matter-of-factly announced the visit to Anchorage of G. Shinowasa, editor of the Seattle Japanese newspaper *Asahi News*.[91] An Anchorage newspaper cited the names of Japanese en route to Anchorage from Seattle—Mrs. A Shimeko and Harry Fukuhara—among European names without comment.[92]

As we have seen, Japanese residents gave their Anchorage restaurants American names. The U.S. Restaurant, located near the center of town, and the Union Cafe advertised in the city's newspapers. The former offered "chop suey and noodles"; the latter claimed, "We serve the best."[93] More striking is the name of S. Abe's restaurant, the Tokio Café.[94] If Japanese in Anchorage faced the kind of open resentment they might have encountered in San Francisco or Vancouver, they would have been reluctant to announce the Asian origins of their products and to name a business after Japan's capital city.

Writing many years after the fact, one laborer in early Anchorage wrote of Japanese miners in the Anchorage area in derogatory terms, but without vitriol.[95] The memoirist also recalled a "race problem" between Eastern Europeans and others, noting that the "Slovaks" lived and recreated in a segregated area ("they were discouraged from visiting any other"). But then he placed a group of drunken Swedes in an even lesser light, and one gets the impression that the race problem amounted to little.[96] And by 1967, when he published his memoirs, he may have forgotten that, decades before, ethnic segregation was normal. Some of the nicknames one heard in early Anchorage—"Dago Jim," "Pale Faced Kid," "Nigger Jim" (a white southerner)—are unfortunate, but if they appealed to feelings of racial and ethnic animosity, those feelings did not translate into hostile action.[97]

Some tense feelings were probably inevitable. These were expressed in articles in the *Forty-Ninth Star*, though, here too, the tone is more sarcastic than angry. The *Star* derided territorial politicians who proffered the slogan "Alaska for Alaskans," noting that the government men should come to the Anchorage area and make their point, through interpreters, to "Jesus Patagaschsky and his friends."[98] The *Star* claimed that it bore no feelings of ill will toward immigrants. "We admire [their] pluck and energy in striving for employment."[99] Its anger was directed rather at the government, which seemed to give place to outsiders at the expense of the native-born. More interesting are points of ethnic integration. The *Alaska Labor News* reported that a Christmas celebration at the Greek Orthodox congregation in town had drawn a large and contented crowd.[100]

Celts, Greeks, Eastern Europeans, Canadians, Scandinavians, Japanese, and old school Yankees lived and worked together in young Anchorage's public spaces with little of the acrimony that infected some towns and urban centers Outside. Alaska presented settlers with challenges enough—isolation, cold, nowhere to go. There was little use for ethnic animus. A few paragraphs after commenting on Anchorage's ethnic diversity, the writer William Stephenson wrote that there was a spirit of "*bon comaraderie* in Alaska that I have found nowhere else in the world. Perhaps it is a brand not to be found except in the far spaces of the universe!"[101] The overstatement is a little ridiculous but makes a worthwhile statement.

It was also true that, however many foreign-born residents there were in Anchorage, they all knew that loyalty to any power other than the United States could not be affirmed publicly. Indeed, if photographs of public spaces were all one had to go by, the researcher might conclude that the population of Anchorage included few foreign-born. From Anchorage's earliest days, Americans flags were hoisted high. Flags festooned the town on the July Fourth and Labor Day Celebrations. Early on, the Alaska Transfer Company and a watchmaker posted flags on their storefronts. Finkelstein and Shapiro's clothing and furniture store flew an especially large flag.[102]

Early in the century, Americans in Canadian Dawson had put up myriad American flags to the chagrin of Canadian officials. But Americans would not abide by such an act on their own soil. Peace was maintained in Anchorage, in part, because the foreign-born accepted American identities or kept other allegiances to themselves. And while the socialist leadership of 1915–1917 sought to include non-English speakers in their work, they also they recognized that the "Alaskanizing" of immigrants was necessary and supported the idea of night schools where immigrants could learn English.[103]

Anchorage was human. In the old tradition of journalistic battle, J. W. Frame, editor of Anchorage's *Forty-Ninth Star*, called John Troy, the publisher of Juneau's *Empire*, a "sissy boy," "nincompoop," and "an effeminate dude who curls his mustache like the Kaiser."[104] But early residents of the town remembered it as peaceful, safe, and free of crime. Local boosters presented the settlement as family-friendly place of well-paying jobs, free of saloons and almost free of drunkenness. As one lengthy advertisement in the *Forty-Ninth Star* somewhat awkwardly put it: "Bring along a woman, a cow, a dozen chickens and a couple of pigs and quit hunting for a 'job.' Build yourself a HOME."[105]

An article in *National Geographic*, published in December 1915, described Anchorage as almost dull—as a carefully planned, nearly sterile place where treasure-hunters and scoundrels were not to be found, where men fought mosquitoes not one another, and where "the jail has been empty most of the time and the marshal has had practically nothing to do."[106] The city's strong vote in 1916 favoring the elimination of intoxicating liquors in Alaska—640 to 274—pointed to a community interested in law, order, and civility.[107] On the other hand, the vote against prohibition had been substantial, and the city's court records are full of cases brought against bootleggers.

On the whole, Anchorage was a peaceful and safe community. Yet it took less than two years for the small settlement to see its first murder—Sam Kashoff shot Alex Tachoff multiple times[108]—and between 1915 and 1940, the courts in Anchorage heard some 2,400 civil cases and hundreds more criminal cases, many of them involving multiple plaintiffs and defendants.

Anchorage proved the old lesson that wherever human beings gather there will be problems and, sometimes, depravity. In 1918 A. D. Sweet was sentenced by the court in Anchorage to two years in prison for molesting a young girl.[109] And while most parents understood their role in the moral education of children, others seemed indifferent. In 1917 the principal of Anchorage's school reported on a young teenager who had already acquired a reputation as a slovenly and sulky thief and whose parents seemed to have little interest in doing anything about it.[110]

The first civil case came to the federal court in Anchorage in June of 1915. H. W. Nagley alleged that two boat operators owed him $1147. The records do not say whether Nagley got his money.[111] On another day, Peter Boudreau sued the Alaska Labor Union for staging an automobile race in Anchorage on Labor Day. Boudreau alleged that the union allowed an unskilled driver, William Petersen, to get behind the wheel and that, as a result, he suffered a "broken leg and severe bodily bruises" when Petersen drove his car into a crowd. Boudreau wanted to recoup the expense he incurred while recovering in the Alaska Engineering Commission's hospital. The union countered that the race had been sanctioned by city officials, and that Boudreau should not have been standing in the street. Again, the surviving records do not say how the case turned out.[112] In June 1917, Mitchell Weisenberg sued H. Seidenverg (a clothing salesman) for publicly calling him a thief and, thereby, costing him business. Weisenberg wanted $6,000. Whether he got that sum, we do not know.[113]

Given the scarcity of women in early Anchorage's marriage market, the number of divorces in the young city is striking. Perhaps they also point to the stresses life in Alaska brought to a marriage, particularly if only one spouse was committed to living there. Of the first 100 civil cases brought to court between 1915 and 1917, 30 involved divorce. In August 1916 Margaret

Bell sought to dissolve her marriage to Fred, who "willfully and without cause deserted and abandoned" her. Fred helped to make Margaret's point when the court could not track him down. The judge ordered the divorce, and Margaret reassumed her maiden name of Weise.[114]

Anna Gleason wanted to divorce George, who had abandoned her.[115] The same was true for Estella Sherman, who wished to take her leave of William.[116] Hulda Lathrop looked to divorce Robert because he was cruel, lazy, and murderous. "[I]n the later part of January 1915," the court documents say, Robert "beat, threatened to kill, and accused her if [sic] infidelity and a few days later shot at plaintiff, the shot barely missing her head."[117]

The unhappy record continues. Olga McCullough sought to divorce Fred because "during their married life [he] used the plaintiff cruelly and inhumanely by addressing her in violent, offensive, profane and obscene language, privately and in the presence of strangers."[118] Anna Ashton wanted to be rid of Wright who had abandoned her and was living in Seattle.[119] Margaret Agnew had had enough of Benjamin's cruelty, as had Clara Foreman of Virgil's.[120]

In most cases, as these examples suggest, women petitioned for divorces from absent and cruel husbands. But sometimes men were the offended, or claimed to be. Collin Murray wanted to split with Mercy because she had abandoned him in 1908. Mercy said that, in truth, Collin had done the abandoning; she called his divorce suit "cruel and inhuman treatment" and demanded financial compensation. Collin conceded that he had gone to Anchorage from Seattle for employment. He said he had supported his wife and two children all along, but as the case went on he looked the worse and dropped it.[121] George Bray accused his wife of being "the inmate of a bawdy house engaged in the practice of prostitution" but also later dropped the case.[122] John Steen, whose wife Sadie had left him rather than return to Alaska from Seattle, was granted a divorce.[123]

Courts are unhappy places and give one a skewed sense of reality. Most marriages in early Anchorage did not end in divorce and violence was uncommon. If it were obviously untrue that the people of Anchorage "[lived] at peace with one another," as the *Anchorage Daily Times* declared in 1916, it is unlikely the paper would have made such a claim.

INTERLUDE

Socialism

The stresses of life in a new far-northwestern town, along with the pressures of a rapidly changing world, occasionally made for trouble in the workplace. One Alaska Engineering Commission worker, James Wilkinson, struck a colleague and broke his arm. Wilkinson, a "blacksmith orator" known for the hotness of his political views and abrupt personality, was fired for "being quarrelsome and fighting in the shop while on duty."[1] In a letter of self-defense Wilkinson suggested that the poor quality of the helpers he had been obliged to work with during the First World War had driven him to frustration: "[I]f the management had secured competent men to help me when I made complaint there would never have been escuse [sic] for me finding fault with my helpers or the job." He did not ask to have his job back, but he did ask the AEC to pay his fare to Seattle. A handwritten note at the bottom of Wilkinson's letter suggests that the commission agreed to do this.[2]

Whether Wilkinson was a socialist is not clear but, as elsewhere in the United States in the years before the Great War, radical left politics appeared to offer Americans an alternative to the major parties. The reason for the failure of socialism in the United States generally is not a concern here, but it is fairly clear why political radicalism, although briefly fervent, did not take hold in early Anchorage. For where Alaskans were interested in promoting a sense of Alaska identity, leading socialists laughed at slogans like "Alaska for Alaskans," arguing that clear-eyed visionaries from Outside could represent Alaska's interests as well as any resident of the territory.[3] And where Alaskans sometimes felt vulnerable in a hostile world and, therefore, had a strong psychological attachment to the United States and its promise of military power, the socialists called for a vague, theoretical "upward progress of the human race."[4] The rhetoric that appeared in Anchorage's socialist *Alaska Labor News* was often shrill, conspiratorial, pompous, and contemptuous. The ideological world its contributors lived in was far removed from the everyday concerns of Anchorage's residents.

In most respects, the Alaska socialists' platform of 1916, published in Anchorage's *Forty-Ninth Star*, was a nonstarter. A continuous theme in the history of Anchorage to 1941 (and indeed, into the twenty-first century) was a desire for government projects and fiscal appropriations. However, Anchorageites could also see the problems that came with bureaucracy and did not want government ownership of all forms of public transportation and communication. Most Anchorageites did not want government to come into possession of Alaska's fisheries and canning facilities. They did not see that a takeover of government by the working class would somehow magically "make for security and justice for all." Anchorageites might have wanted capitalism to be tamed, its uglier aspects softened, but few wanted to see it overthrown. And socialist initiatives that many Anchorageites favored could be gained via more mainstream political activity.[5] While the town's voters cast ballots 3 to 1 against the socialists in 1916, for example, they also voted about 3 to 1 in favor of prohibiting intoxicating drinks in Alaska and 10 to 1 in favor of an eight-hour work day (reforms the socialists supported).[6] The socialist candidate for Alaska's Delegate to Congress as well as for Alaska governor, Lena Morrow Lewis, frankly acknowledged that the socialists' cause was not in a position to do well in the territory. She could see that the slogan, "Alaska for the Wealth Producers," did not have much pull.[7]

The subculture early Anchorageites created was not conducive to the pursuit of an airy utopia built on class struggle. The Bank of Anchorage and businessman Z. J. Loussac contributed to the construction of a Union Labor Hall because they were community-minded and wanted workers' business, not because they were interested in promoting an imaginary laborers' promised land.[8] Anchorage's residents were interested in making good lives for themselves and in creating an attractive community; they had less interest in abstractions that would help workers on their way toward "fulfillment of their destiny." Anchorageites did not want to denounce the "ruling class" as a gaggle of criminal "social-abortionists." And where rousing quotations from Karl Marx of the "workers of the world unite!" variety may have briefly warmed the blood in the last months of 1916, parents were more keen on seeing to their children's basic education, while shopkeepers only wanted to sell their wares.[9]

Alaska Labor Union building (1916). Anchorage Museum, B64.X.3.6

Even the language used to describe the building of the Union Hall took the theme of Alaska toughness a little too far. "What fitting tribute can we pay," the *Labor News* declared, to those courageous men who faced the severities of the rigorous winter, went out to the woods, felled the timber, dragged it to town, and

> erected the big hall, in order that their newly formed organization might have a permanent home.... If there are any disloyal to [our] cause, if there are any who are weak in seeking the enforcement of [our] rights, we do not believe such will be found among those who participated in the struggles that marked the opening chapters of [our] history.[10]

Anchorageites were as familiar with the language of Darwinian struggle as other Americans, but a simple life in early-twentieth-century Alaska offered challenges enough. Where the editor of the *Labor News* saw fools, cynics, exploiters, and agents of the "master class" acting according to evolutionary "biological principles" and advancing their interests at the expense of others, most Anchorageites just saw neighbors.[11]

As a newspaper, the *Labor News* gained a wide circulation with, according to its editor, some 1,500 readers. The paper editorialized that it aimed to provide material that a father would be glad to have his children read, though it seems doubtful that many wished their children to think of them, in the *News*'s words, as "wage slaves."[12] Anchorageites favored teaching immigrants English in night schools, and if the socialists organized the schools, that was fine. Few, however, would go along with the slogan "Educate, Agitate, Organize," and not many agreed that a chief purpose of a community night school should be to open workers' "eyes to the stupidity of…throwing away their votes" on Democrats or Republicans.[13] In any event, the night school idea was encouraged by the same government officials the socialists denounced. Alaska Engineering Official Andrew Christensen asked Lena Morrow Lewis if she would start a citizenship school for the foreign-born living in Anchorage. She said that she had already had some private pupils but had been unable to secure proper quarters for formal classes.[14] The original request for such a school had come from the Commissioner of Naturalization with the Department of Labor.[15] (The fate of this particular school is unclear, although such evening schools did form.)

In the election of 1916, Lewis, running for Delegate to Congress, gained 218 of Anchorage's votes, as compared to Republican James Wickersham's 432 and Democrat Charles Sulzer's 336.[16] This would be the socialists' high point in Alaska's newest city. But that somewhat impressive figure—about twenty-two percent of the vote—was deceptive. Socialism's failure to reemerge in any noticeable way following the First World War suggests that commitment to radical politics never ran deeply. It is true that in the United States, socialists and other radicals became objects of legal harassment and persecution. There is no record of this happening in Anchorage, primarily because there was no enduring radical movement to respond to there. One probable reason was that the radicals left Anchorage for work Outside during the war. Another is that the extremes of wealth and poverty that stoked radical agitation elsewhere did not exist in Anchorage.[17] (When President Harding passed through town in 1923, there was reportedly no embarrassing poverty to hide from his view).[18] The greatest reason, however, was lack of abiding interest.

Perhaps, as one writer put it, this dearth of interest was due to a lack of spiritual depth among Anchorage's residents. "Christ was a real socialist," Anchorageites read,

> and went out into the world to build himself a kingdom on earth but he
> soon found that the great mass of humanity is inclined not to vote his

ticket.... If Christ should come to Anchorage tomorrow and run for justice
of the peace..., he would be overwhelmingly defeated. Why? Because the
great mass of humanity don't want to be good.[19]

Or, perhaps a better response was that, while the settlers who had gone to Alaska
were less self-reliant than they might have thought, they simply were not attracted to appeals for the surrender of personal property in the interests of a glorious future seen only by a chosen few visionaries.

It has been said that early twentieth-century Alaskans were "anti-radical."[20] In
the case of Anchorage, perhaps it would be better to say that, on the whole, they
were simply nonradical.

CHAPTER THREE

War

THE MOST OBVIOUS THING ABOUT WAR is that it divides people. Sometimes the lines of division are plain. During the Second World War,
Americans achieved a level of unity they have not experienced during any
other conflict, or probably at any other time. By late 1941, when the United
States entered the war against Japan and Germany, levels of immigration had
been relatively low for more than a quarter of a century. And by that time,
the immigrants who had come to the United States before the tightening of
the immigration laws in the 1920s had, to employ a term used in the early
twentieth century, been "Americanized." This helped to make for national
and regional unity.

The First World War has been controversial from the beginning; some
young people involved in it claimed not to know what it was about and
doubted its justice.[1] And when the United States entered the war in 1917, the
hearts of a few immigrants remained overseas, in nations with which their
new country was now at war. This made for division and suspicion.

In large cities like New York and small ones like Anchorage, strange-
sounding languages could feel threatening. This made for frustration and
some tension. A not-easily-comprehended letter written to Helen Van
Campen by a miner in La Touche, Alaska, points to the linguistic challenges
faced by immigrants and Americans alike. "[I] hopp you...haf good healt
and good time," the letter begins:

> tinges her Ar as usle.... [The men in] the camp ar A beit sterd upp A but
> the war[.] Frank Ride nerly went insen he tore his heir and cursd the Ger-

mans & Austrian & Turk and gif notice to quvit and he hasent spoken A word to a German or Austran.[2]

Spurring feelings of belligerence in the months leading up to America's entry into the war in 1917 were antagonisms between the United States and Mexico. Deadly chaos on the international border, fear of an uprising among Mexicans living in the southwestern United States, and the seizure of American property in Mexico caused Anchorage's *Weekly Alaskan* to declare in 1916, "everything looks like WAR."[3] In the following January, the *Forty-Ninth Star* wondered about the loyalty of Anchorage's eastern European immigrants in the event of conflict with Mexico. If the Mexican outlaw Pancho Villa should attack Anchorage, the *Star* mused sarcastically, who would defend the city?

> The Americans who are out in the forests sawing wood and clearing home-steads would have to be called in to stand up in line to be shot by greasers, while gentlemen from Montenegro, Greece and Canada would be down at the pool rooms playing pool or at the Labor Temple playing basketball.[4]

Formal war with Mexico never came, but when the United States entered the First World War against Germany and its allies in April 1917, demonstrations of national loyalty became mandatory. Americans sought ways to demonstrate their commitment to the country's new cause. "Let us show the world that Anchorage, the newest city in Uncle Sam's greatest territory, is with the president in this fight for freedom."[5]

One way Americans in Alaska, including the young town of Anchorage, showed their loyalty was by not complaining about the hard times the war brought.[6] During the conflict, Alaska's non-Native population dropped from some 50,000 to about 36,000 residents. Among those who had gone were the three thousand Alaskans in the armed services. Others went to the states for well-paying jobs linked to war industries. This notable exodus had a marked economic impact on shops, services, and trades. Natives in southeastern Alaska, meantime, worried because the war reduced demand for furs. Ships that normally plied the seas between Seattle and Alaska were taken over for the war effort.[7] As a point of connection between Alaska's regions, Anchorage felt the impact of territorial economic hardship.

Before the war, the population of Anchorage was reported to be greater than 5,000. (Transience made pinning down a number difficult; Outside newspapers placed the figure at 6,000 and 8,000.)[8] By the end of the war, the city's population had dropped to less than 2,000.[9] This local decline mirrored the hardship throughout the territory. "Alaska has suffered intensely from the great war," the territory's governor Thomas Riggs wrote:

> We have none of the unnatural war industries, such as the giant shipyards or munitions plants, with their greatly increased scale of wages. Our young men have flocked to the colors in great numbers, either through the draft or enlistments; our mechanics have answered the call of the Government for skilled labor and a large proportion of the population … has left for the scenes of greater excitement and activity.

Consequently, Riggs continued, Alaska's normal productivity had become paralyzed.

Though eager to state the facts while making a case for government investment in Alaska, the governor took care not to complain, for Alaska's wartime loss was its "contribution to the welfare of humanity." Riggs looked forward to the day when the world would be liberated from the "Teutonic menace to civilization."[10] No one could doubt Governor Riggs' loyalty.

At first, the war seemed to present Anchorage, and Alaska generally, with opportunities to expand economically while also assisting the war effort. A few months after the global struggle had begun, and when the United States was still neutral, Riggs argued that Alaska's resources, if developed, could make up for the decline in goods from overseas.[11] Others said that if the coal in the Matanuska Valley could be shipped to the Pacific fleet via Anchorage, then more resources would be available for vessels fighting Germans and supplying allies in the Atlantic. The trains now used to take coal across the states to the Pacific would also be freed to more directly support work on the Atlantic coast.[12] But as war continued in Europe and drew close to the United States, Alaska's needs and interests ceased to be priorities for many Outside. At that time, the United States faced no serious threat in the north Pacific.

Observers did point to Alaska's long-term strategic importance, especially now that Anchorage was poised to help deliver Alaska coal to the U.S.

Navy. William Stephenson, who had served as U.S. Commissioner in Alaska, argued that the United States' second great concern (after winning the war in Europe) should be the defense of its Pacific coast, especially noncontiguous Alaska. "The Pacific Ocean is the great problem of the American people to-day and Alaska is the prize beyond compute of the Pacific Coast." Stephenson and others worried about Japan's growing power, and headlines like "Japan Makes New Record in Foreign Trade" made worrying easier.[13]

American strategists paid keen attention to Hawaii and the Philippines, assuming that Japan would take them if allowed.[14] That focus was justified, but Stephenson wondered if the falling of Dutch Harbor into Japan's hands would be akin to Britain's taking of Gibraltar from Spain centuries before—a humiliating blow and the mark of national decline in the face of a growing and ambitious military power. "There can be no question that in the event of a struggle for the possession of the Pacific the fate of Alaska will be exactly that which befell Korea in the Manchurian war [against Japan] of a decade or two ago."

The answer to this hypothetical disaster was government investment in Alaska. The railroad system under construction since 1914 needed to be expanded and more troops needed to be brought to the territory.[15] The Alaskans in Anchorage could prove their loyalty by serving as a bastion against rising powers in the Pacific.

In one way or another, Alaska's service to the United States was seen primarily in its usefulness to national security. The point had been made before the First World War and would be made continually until the attacks at Pearl Harbor, Guam and, soon after, Attu and Dutch Harbor made the case more eloquently than any American theorist might have. The Japanese Empire would eventually put Anchorage at the forefront of America's military "frontier of destiny."[16]

Against Anchorageites' hopes, the First World War ensured that little of the nation's wealth would be spent in the northern territory, even for purposes of defense. Recruitment of Anchorage's workers for a war-related railroad construction regiment further reduced the city's human resources. According to one report, a third of the laborers with the Alaska Engineering Commission (AEC) were drafted.[17] Among those leaving Anchorage to help build railroads in France was Frederick Mears, now Colonel Mears, who had supervised the AEC and presided over the establishment of Anchorage.[18] So thin had the employable ranks become by mid-1918 that women were hired to wait tables in the AEC and YMCA lunch rooms.[19] The availability of material and supplies for the railroad plummeted; activity on the road slowed.[20]

Still, as a center of trade within Alaska and as one of Alaska's larger population centers, Anchorage seemed to have much to offer. Governor Riggs noted in his report that the value of Alaska's imports and exports in 1917 stood at nearly $132 million, compared to the $127 million worth of goods that had come and gone from the much more greatly populated Philippine Islands.[21] And the *Anchorage Weekly Times* noted that "Alaska, the frontier wonderland, [had] become in the hour of national need the land of the world's cheapest food supply, and an important source of metals essential to the manufacture of munitions."[22] Some businessmen in Oregon saw Alaska's resources as the solution to their state's coal requirements, and observers of the international scene knew that the markets of East Asia were eager for American goods.[23]

> The people of the Far East are primarily fish consuming; Alaska fish is being sent forward under war conditions and the Oriental trade is going to become familiar with the Alaska sea product and when war conditions cease there will be a constant demand for Alaska fish as well as other Alaskan products.[24]

The *Forty Ninth Star* implausibly suggested that a well-developed Alaska could feed Europe's hungry millions. "Anchorage has back of her a wealth of soil upon which to raise food, and mountains of mineral wealth with which to supply the world."[25] In an optimistic moment Anchorage's *Alaska Labor News* made a similar point:

> Everything is coming to Anchorage, that favored town, situated amidst the most wonderful resources of Alaska. Like a queen on her throne she rests on the shore, her railroad and her steamship lines extending as two arms filled to overflowing with the abundance of the world's commerce and industry.[26]

The flat terrain on which Anchorage was situated, along with the city's modern amenities—electricity, a sewage system, a hospital, two theatres, and "city-owned tennis courts"—also suited it for prosperity.[27] Even as Anchorage's decline set in, readers of the *Philadelphia Inquirer* learned that Anchorage's Alaska was a "vast empire in the making."[28]

As the war progressed, Anchorage's experience was increasingly disheartening. A heightened demand for copper and fish led to growth in those industries in Alaska during the war, and gold was still shipped from the territory,[29] but other goods that could go to the states and contribute further to the war effort did not do so because many of the ships that had worked the North Pacific's trading lanes had been put into service on the East Coast. Even within Alaska itself, roads were insufficient to get fresh vegetables from the Matanuska Valley to homesteaders.[30]

Anchorageites would deride the governmental inattention they believed these problems represented, yet they were sure to cast their aspersions on individuals, not on the government generally (as they had done before, and would do after, the war). Certainly they would not rail against Woodrow Wilson, the wartime president. Anchorage's opinion leaders knew that their task now was to endure, contribute to the national cause in as many ways as possible, and wait for brighter days. "Things are a little slow in Anchorage during these war times.... But when the war is over, just watch for the big stampede to Alaska.... Anchorage property owners have no reason to feel dubious about the future."[31]

Throughout the United States the pressures of wartime loyalty led to friction. To an extent, this was also true of Anchorage. Some newcomers to the city responded to this more anxious atmosphere by attending night school—yes, to obtain a general education (by learning French or shorthand) but also, and perhaps primarily, to study English, American history, and American civics.[32] Of the Anchorage night school's 250 students in late 1918, nearly a third were foreign-born.[33]

The pressures of loyalty also drove articles in Greek and Italian, along with statements of political radicalism, from the city's newspapers. Antiwar sentiment was quickly pressed out of public existence.[34] Animosity toward apparent or actual disloyalty in Anchorage, however, was not directed at particular local ethnic groups. Indeed, the relative racial and ethnic equanimity that existed in the young city is notable, at least to the extent that it challenges the textbook narrative that focuses on anti-German outbursts.[35] Once the war came, Anchorageites hated the Germans *over there*. Germans over here, in Anchorage, were watched, but if they acted loyally they faced no problems. If they served in the American military, residents of German heritage received the same praise as any Mississippian or Michigander.[36]

As a class, noncitizens were not harassed. The preponderance of names like Dzarensoff, Kaboff, Bozaroff, and Geboff on the city's list of suspected military "shirkers" probably led longtime Americans to be suspicious of immigrant newcomers, particularly central and eastern Europeans.[37] But Anchorageites also cheered for noncitizens, such as "one of the prominent Greek boys," George Vlahos, who volunteered to fight with the United States. Anchorageites were as glad when volunteers of any ethnicity demonstrated loyalty to their adopted country, and they approved when these volunteers were given a fast track to citizenship.[38] The *Weekly Times* noted in late 1917 that no native-born Americans had yet been accused of avoiding military service—only Russians (mostly) and some Swedes, Italians, and Austrians.[39] The time soon came, though, when born and bred American draft dodgers and mutineers with names like Gooding and Connors and Parker and Booker were found out, and they were despised as much as any Zitoff, Zoldan, or Zukoff.[40]

Over two thousand names were entered into Alaska's enlistment files for delinquents and deserters. Some five hundred names appeared on the Anchorage military service board's final list. Reasons and excuses for delinquency varied. Helmer Wickberg, it turns out, died before the draft could get him. Sula Makela said that he had tried to register but his work hours conflicted with the registrant's.[41] Others had been working and living in remote spots and did not know a draft was on. A few had joined the military elsewhere in the United States or shown up late after a last prewar fling. Some were tracked down and forced into martial service.[42] Among the delinquents linked to Anchorage were an Adkins, Biluzzi, Churion, Del Piero, Evans, Franzioi, Gushovich, Hartman, Johnson, Kupoff, Lundberg, McCourt, Nelson, Ostberg, Pasquale, Radue, Sagoff, Toisoff, and Velisarakos. Among those fingered as enemy aliens (Austro-Hungarian and Germans nationalities) were a Ciszek, a Corak, a Deretich, and a Granc.[43]

Of course, Anchorageites wanted immigrants to fight with American forces—this was how the newcomers could show their appreciation to the nation that had given them employment. But the city's residents also honored, though perhaps somewhat mutely, the nationals from allied countries who went home to fight for their mother country. In late 1917 a Serbian flag was raised in Anchorage in honor of 15 Serbs and Russians who left the city for the war. "My prayer and prediction," their spokesman said, "is that the flag raised by you in Anchorage...will never be lowered or surrendered but will rise to the eminent height where it will lead a free and united people."[44]

Articles in Anchorage's newspapers referred positively to France's colonial African troops, and a leading *Weekly Times* article was titled "Colored Boys, Members of Pershing's Army, Are Heroes in Most Daring Feat of War."[45] Anchorage's papers also highlighted the contributions of Alaska's Natives to the war cause. Some Natives knitted to make ends meet in hard times, some raised money by selling furs and carving ivory, and some, like Newton Kaska, went into combat units.[46] "The Alaska native...has shown the most loyal and intense patriotism in helping the government in the present crisis."[47] Anchorage's opinion leaders saw the hardship the war had brought to Natives and praised their commitment to the war. "No baby in Belgium or France has suffered more than these untutored sons of Uncle Sam, and none have given to the war cause more patriotically than these."[48] The *Weekly Times* said that the American patriot was of "no particular race or color."[49]

Anchorage's Japanese residents also seemed to have had few if any problems on account of their heritage. Perhaps this was because the number of Japanese in Anchorage was small; in 1918 just one was enrolled in Anchorage's night school, and Mary Mikami, a first grader, was the only child of Japanese parents in Anchorage's public school.[50]

The best evidence that Japanese came under no particular pressure is found in a striking piece published in the *Weekly Times*. Subtitled "Sons of Japan Living Here Liberal in All Patriotic Movements," the article instructed readers that loyalty stemmed from actions not place of birth, and the "sons of the Mikado living in Anchorage have been ultra-loyal in purchasing liberty bonds and supporting the Red Cross." The *Times* derided the "bugbear of the yellow peril" and praised the loyalty of Japanese throughout the states. The paper pointed to the loyal example of J. G. Shinowara who ran Anchorage's Union Laundry and Bath House and who had "recently sent a liberal consignment of tobacco to the American boys in France."[51] Perhaps this article was written and published to counteract anti-Japanese feeling in Anchorage, but no record of such sentiments survives. Anchorageites knew that federal law prohibited Japanese immigrants from serving in the U.S. military.[52] This explained the presence of young Japanese men in town.

In Anchorage, then, racial and ethnic equanimity was the norm so long as one's wartime loyalty was unquestionable. A loyal German was preferable to a disloyal Canadian or Californian. This partly accounts for the failure of socialism in Anchorage, which, in the immediate prewar years, had been hard-edged, intolerant, and self-defeating. In the spring of 1917, for instance, the *Alaska Labor News* drew on Marxist categories, announcing the American entry into the war with headlines like: "U.S. Commerce to be Preserved at the Cost of Lives of Flower of Nation"—"Profiteers Plunge U.S. in Slaughter"—"Capitalism's Doom Pending!"—and "On with the Revolution!"[53] The Alaska Labor Union cabled a note of protest to President Wilson saying that its members were "opposed to being used as cannon fodder."[54]

Alaskans who felt this way soon learned to expect repercussions if they said so. At the war's beginning, the *Labor News* challenged readers not to mistake jingoism for patriotism, for criticism of country and love of country could coexist. But in 1918 such distinctions found few congenial quarters. The general mood leaned instead toward the musings of the evangelist Billy Sunday, who prayed that God would let America exterminate Germany the way ancient Israel had destroyed idolatrous Canaan. Anchorage's antiwar contingent, well represented among the small class of committed socialists, took notice. The *Labor News* was soon consumed by the *Weekly Times* and, by November of 1917, the labor pages in the *Times* argued that no one approved more of American workers striking for higher wages than the German Kaiser.[55] By mid-1919, the exercise of the Golden Rule seemed a better solution to labor's difficulties than revolution.[56] The socialist moment in Anchorage had passed.

Early in 1918, the Anchorage Council of Defense had agreed that it needed to take cognizance of "seditious remarks" brought to its attention.[57] One target was William Britt, an American serving as vice consul for Norway in Juneau. The defense council accused Britt of helping Norwegian immigrants avoid military service.[58] Britt denied the charge and the implication of disloyalty underpinning it, but the *Weekly Times* and other Alaska newspapers turned against Britt and he lost his job. Whether he actually was disloyal might have been debated. His mistake was in not avoiding what could be construed as disloyalty.[59]

The *Times* also went after lesser figures, such as Jack Love, "one of Sweden's offal," who had withdrawn a citizenship request to avoid military service. The United States was no place for slackers, and the *Times* suggested that Love should do the prison-sustaining taxpayers a favor by committing suicide.[60] Another unnamed foreigner who also had ended his bid for citizenship had had a yellow ribbon pinned on him (signifying cowardice) and locals deprived him of food and lodging.[61] The Alaska Engineering Commission, meanwhile, dismissed a worker who refused to donate to war aid projects. "We heartily approve of the discharge of this man," the *Weekly Times* editorialized. "[T]here is absolutely no excuse for a man who has had steady employment at a good wage to refuse to give a small donation."[62]

Then there was the case of a certain Bernard Hettel who was arrested for calling liberty bonds a "joke" and for saying that "what the United States needed was German discipline and the sooner it came the better."[63] Had Hettel not fled apprehension, he might have been given the same punishment meted to Dick Windmueller, who allegedly claimed that "America had broken her Monroe Doctrine by sending soldiers to Europe and that...all American soldiers who had gone to France should be killed and that Germany would clean them all."[64] Windmueller was found guilty of breaching the Espionage Act of 1917 and was sentenced to a year in the prison at Valdez and fined $250.

During Windmueller's trial, the government prosecutor's case was premised on the idea that the preservation of freedom of speech, and other freedoms, depended on the stamping out of antiwar speech. The prosecutor saw the potential paradox in the government's position but noted that while the Constitution had not changed, conditions had. Conditions had changed in part, he said, because for years "ignorant and fanatical persons" had abused their freedom, threatening to undo ordered liberty with the passions of anarchy. The prosecutor did not say so, but he knew that President McKinley had been assassinated by an anarchist, and he knew that many severe labor actions had been led by immigrants with radical leanings. Now, in Anchorage as elsewhere in the states and American territories, lines had to be drawn. At Windmueller's trial, the jury learned that his "treasonable utterances" had to be punished to prevent other German sympathizers from assisting Prussian militarism.

Prosecution for speech that was seditious but not apparently dangerous took place in the context of widespread misapprehensions about German conduct in the war. Wartime adversaries are always the Other, but fabricated or exaggerated stories about German atrocities against women, children, and prisoners of war made the Hun look peculiarly monstrous. Just recently, German had been the language of first-rate philosophical and biblical studies; children had studied it in Anchorage's school.[65] Now German was just guttural trash talk.[66] Not so long ago, Anchorageites had enjoyed Bach and Beethoven. Now one expressed his appreciation for those composers only with great care. "Frankfurters," sounding too German, were renamed "hot dogs."

Back in the summer of 1915, when the war seemed far away, heartstrings had been plucked by a story published in the *Cook Inlet Pioneer* relating the contents of a letter an Anchorage-area woman had received from a friend in Germany. The letter spoke of starvation in Germany as a result of Britain's coastal blockade.[67] But now Anchorageites, like Americans generally, were tempted to think of Germans as apelike brutes with an unusual passion for conquest and gore.[68]

Such ideas were accepted and passed along by Alaska soldiers writing letters home. "Hate the Germans?" one asked. "If you were over here and could know about the atrocities they commit you would agree with me that the best thing would be to have every one of them wiped out."[69] Newspaper articles claiming that Germans bombed hospital ships as a matter of policy were false but seemed credible thanks to the accidents and passions of combat.[70] The *Weekly Times* advocated Germany's "extermination" as a justifiable war measure.[71]

At the end of the war, some failed to see the value of a moderate peace—as President Wilson put it, "peace without victory." Germany needed to be imposed upon, "hog-tied," and reduced to second-rate status. The barbs needed to be extracted from the German war machine.[72] Anchorage's newspaper writers had no patience with the idea that the United States was at war with the German government rather than with the German people.[73] The *Weekly Times* encouraged Anchorage's bleeding hearts who wanted to help the destitute of postwar Germany instead to spend their money on needs closer to home.[74]

During the First World War, probably more than at any other time in the twentieth century, Americans eyed one another seeking signs of loyalty. The publication of the names of residents who bought liberty bonds rewarded the purchasers, giving them loyalty status while also applying pressure to everyone else not only to purchase liberty bonds but to "go over the top" in their financial contributions to the war effort.[75] In this environment, it seemed almost impossible to be too patriotic. One event in Anchorage—a "patriotic evening [where] patriotism was prevalent throughout"—was praised for its "intense patriotism"; a speech was said to have been "full of patriotic utterances"; and through the "courtesy and patriotism of the members of the Anchorage band, patriotic music was rendered."[76]

Most Anchorageites were content when the authorities rounded up the "slackers" who had failed to register for military service.[77] An October 3, 1917 headline in the *Weekly Times* declared, "Open Season on Slackers in Full Swing." The paper predicted that future generations would feel shame for the malcontents who could have joined the great new Grand Army of the Republic in the making but did not.[78] Nearly 70 slackers who attempted to sail for Alaska—thinking, perhaps, that the law did not reach into the final frontier—were arrested.[79] And when the federal order went out for male citizens of Germany 14 years and older to register at Anchorage's post office (and to supply four photographs of themselves), the affected knew to keep grumbling to themselves.[80] The registration of 35 Germans passed without a glitch.[81]

Though anti-German feeling in Anchorage never led to violence, it is not possible to know the extent to which Anchorageites disapproved of the harm inflicted on Germans and political radicals Outside. The *Weekly Times* reported without comment on seventeen members of the Industrial Workers of the World ("Wobblies") who had been gathered in Tulsa, Oklahoma, and then flogged, tarred, and feathered in the names of the "outraged women and children of Belgium."[82] Anchorageites read about counties in Illinois that stamped out disloyalty using the same method. "Several men were taken from their beds and, kneeling on the sidewalk, were forced to kiss every star in the flag."[83] In Ohio, thirty Germans under coercion chanted "to hell with the Kaiser."[84] In Seattle, timber workers merely expelled Wobblies from their union.[85] So far as the historical record shows, nothing like this happened in Anchorage.

As always in free societies, voices of moderation could be heard. Some observed that a heavy-handed pursuit of socialists made President Wilson's slogan about making the world safe for democracy less credible.[86] The president himself had warned against mob action, and the *Weekly Times* cautioned

Alaskans against using false patriotism as a cover for exacting revenge on personal adversaries via allegations of disloyalty: "retailing malicious gossip only hinders our efforts."[87] Even in tense war days, a report on a "well-devised plot on the part of German sea-raiders to raid Alaskan seaports" seemed too absurd to be mentioned more than once in the *Weekly Times*.[88]

And while residents who "knocked" the city's economic standing during the war were criticized and even persecuted, there were limits to how much the genuinely discontented could bottle up.[89] Once war came, Anchorage's "labor temple" was no longer a site to learn about the glories of radical socialism but it remained a gathering place for the disappointed. In late January 1918, some five hundred workers gathered in the city to express their opposition to the suspension of an eight-hour (maximum) workday as a war measure.[90] At the meeting, workers heard that patriotism did not necessitate submission to indignities, that railroad workers' pay in Anchorage was ten percent lower than it was in Seattle, and that each person who left Anchorage accounted for nearly $700 less spent per year in the local economy. Laborers, said the disgruntled, could stay in Alaska and freeze or go Outside and prosper, and if the government did not believe that railroad work was necessary, "they should shut it down and let the men go out to do their patriotic duty."[91] Notice that even these unhappy thoughts were linked to the virtue of loyalty.

Few could doubt the city's commitment. Anchorage's quota for the third Liberty Loan to finance the war was $59,000; residents subscribed $113,000. Anchorageites formed societies: the Alaska Women's Patriotic League; the Alaska Council of Defense; the Alaska Loyal League; and a chapter of a group devoted to helping the fatherless children of France.[92] And there was some personal deprivation for the sake of making resources available to combatants: Tuesdays and Fridays Anchorageites went without meat; on Saturdays they said no to pork; on Wednesdays they refused wheat. "I have come to the end of a wheatless day," a lighthearted poem in an Anchorage newspaper read,

> I have eaten no cookies or pie;
> I have had no bread that was made with wheat,
> It was made out of corn or rye.
> And I liked it so well that when war is past,

And glorious victory won
I'll keep observing "wheatless days"
And I'll eat "corn pone" for fun![93]

In the fields of battle, Anchorageites also played their part. The Rice family sent three sons—Thomas, Shirl, and Lee—to the war.[94] A. R. Kinsman wrote from France that the Alaskans he was with were the sort of "red-blooded men" he wanted at his side in battle, and he requested a moose steak for dinner when he returned home.[95] Howard Patten had given up his confectionary store in Anchorage to join the army.[96] Daniel Patterson helped provide the army with horses, and the "Anchorage girl" Mayme Byles enlisted in the Navy.[97] Reportedly, Richard Lander and two friends had been eager to get into the fight while most Alaskans were still willing to turn the other cheek in the face of the "German hordes...and their inhuman deeds of wantonness, cruelty and rape."[98]

When sixty-one recruits gathered at Fourth and "G" streets in March 1918 to begin their trek to Fort McDowell in California, some two thousand residents turned out to say goodbye—including school children and men with the Home Guard, the Pioneers of Alaska, members of the South Slavonic Defense League, workers with the Italian Relief Committee, the Boy Scouts, and the Camp Fire Girls.[99] "The thousands of persons at the station cheered as the train pulled out on what was for the enlisted men the first stage of their long journey to the battlefront in France."[100] In unusually awful prose, the *Weekly Times* noted that seeing the young men off had brought the war home to Anchorage:

> We know what it means to send the best blood of our community to face the unknown dangers of a ruthless war, and it is up to this community to bear in mind the fact that it is up to us and other similar communities, that the boys on the front look for support, and taking pattern from the brave ones who left this morning, exert every effort in our power to see that they will want for nothing which will tend to make their lot as safe and comfortable as possible.[101]

Outside newspapers said that many of the Anchorage men had been spurred to enlist upon learning of the sinking of the *Tuscania* by German submarines. After arriving in San Francisco the fresh Alaska warriors joined a demonstration for liberty bonds.[102]

Altogether, during the war some four hundred men marched out of Anchorage in uniform—some of them having lived in the city proper, others coming from the region. They trained at forts in Valdez and Haines, and in Kansas, Georgia, North Carolina, California, Washington, and Maryland.[103] Some fought alongside Oregonians and Washingtonians in Flanders, reportedly on one occasion advancing six miles in the face of machine gun fire.[104]

Occasional newspaper articles pointed Anchorageites to the horrors of war. One, titled "Machine Gun Is Effective War Weapon," used the familiar metaphor of a scythe cutting grass to describe what could be seen when men massed and charged an enemy's trenches.[105] In their letters home, Alaska soldiers wrote about the American warrior's prowess, the Germans' tenacity and, in vague ways, of the war's ugliness. Combatants wrote that they looked forward to returning to Alaska, while men who had gotten into the war late claimed to regret that they might miss combat.[106] Anchorageites Robert Blee,

Anchorage Museum general photograph file, AMRC-b69-22-1

Jack Henry, and James Meechan were killed in action; William Hooker died of influenza in an Army camp.[107]

After the fighting ended in November of 1918, Anchorageites felt free to hope again for prosperity. "With the conclusion of the peace…we may rest assured that Alaska will be looked to as a great storehouse."[108] Alaska needed wagon roads and navigation aids; its land needed to be developed; its fishing industry needed building up.

> In order that the industrial workers, going into Alaska after the war, may not be hindered in their work and may be afforded ample opportunity to improve their condition and thereby that of the territory, it should now become the purpose of the United States to launch upon a strong, constructive policy for Alaska backed by authority of Congress.[109]

After the war, servicemen who returned joined the newly-founded American Legion and met under the auspices of Anchorage's Elks Lodge.[110] Military officers who visited the city and soldiers from Anchorage said that they and others looked forward to carrying on with their lives.[111] The veterans did not want to talk about combat. Some felt motivated to make the world better than the one that had created such devastation. One of these wrote that the war veterans would form a "brotherhood of righteousness." Surely the world had learned its lesson, and the "modern soldier" had been trained for the "highest purposes of peace which will be lasting."[112]

During and immediately after the war, observers had said that Alaska's war veterans would turn their energies to the good of the community.[113] They said that after experiencing the rigors of war and European cosmopolitanism the country's warriors would be eager for the kinds of challenges Alaska presented. "They will be filled with a love of adventure; they will be filled with the spirit of conquest. Alaska will have no terrors for them now."[114]

But veterans would only go to the young city of Anchorage if the government gave them access to the territory's opportunities. Short of this, J. L. McPherson of the Seattle Chamber of Commerce said, the former soldiers would be tempted to settle elsewhere. Up-and-coming Anchorage, like Alaska generally, afforded the government an opportunity "not only to recompense its veterans, but also to prevent their migration to other countries."[115] Yet, as for Alaskans generally, the kind of transformative U.S. government investment Anchorageites sought would have to wait out a lackluster 1920s followed by the Great Depression.

Over the next couple decades, relations between the United States and Japan deteriorated. In 1924 immigration from Japan into the United States was halted and, the *Anchorage Weekly Alaskan* reported, anti-American feeling in Japan had come to a "threatening point."[116] But the general racial equanimity that had existed in Anchorage during the First World War continued to hold. As we will see in the next chapter, Mary Mikami, the first-grader mentioned above, would prosper, as would her siblings. "[A]ll my friends were Finnish, Swedish, German, Italian, Russian, and Natives," said William Kimura, also of Japanese heritage, reflecting on his youth in Anchorage in the late 1920s and early 1930s. "[W]e all got along together."[117]

During the Great War, loyalty to the nation's cause was essential. On that, there was no public space for diversity. But loyalty had nothing to do with accent, nation of origin, or skin tone.

INTERLUDE

Z. J. Loussac

I t is not possible to scan Anchorage's early newspapers and not gain some insight into the influence of Zachariah Joshua Loussac, a Russian Jew of democratic commitment who fled his country in the early twentieth century. At times he lived in Nome, Juneau, and other Alaska towns. He settled in Anchorage in 1916 and soon was recognized as an important businessman and community pillar. During both world conflicts, Loussac was an early purchaser of war bonds.[1] He was Anchorage's Chamber of Commerce president in 1943, the city manager in 1948, and mayor in the years 1948–1950. By then he had become a philanthropist, having established the Loussac Foundation in 1946.[2]

Probably few people can promote their own commercial interests with such openness and yet with as soft a touch as Loussac did. Whether or not he knew about a basic theory at the heart of Adam Smith's capitalist classic, *The Wealth of Nations*, he did clearly understand that if he could make the interests of others his own, and if he could meet those interests in a way that was satisfying to customers, then his chances for success would be enhanced and the community would benefit.

An advertisement made to look like a news article, published in July 1916, is not riveting, but it points to the business sense that made Loussac a success:

> Last boat brought Z. J. Loussac at the new drug store on 4th and D the largest and most complete stock of stationary for office, store and home use. There will be no shorts in this line from now on. We will be glad to show you our assortment. The Store That Has What You Want When You Want It.[3]

That last sentence became a Loussac slogan.

Parade in Anchorage (Loussac store in background). Anchorage Museum, AMRC-b83-146-245

By September of 1916, Loussac had decided to abandon his commercial efforts in Juneau to focus on his work in Anchorage. We know this because of "Loussac's Daily Gossip," a literary advertisement that appeared every day, for years, on the editorial page of the Anchorage Daily News. "While visiting in Seattle and Portland," Loussac wrote in one installment, "I added new lines to my stock and increased the others, giving the public a better opportunity for selection."[4] Loussac mentioned percolators, Victor phonographs, and his plans to start a circulating library.

That latter item will ring a bell with twenty-first-century Anchorageites who refer to the city's public library simply as "the Loussac." In 1954 the businessman donated $350,000, through his foundation, to build the library. "The people of Anchorage have been good to me," Loussac said at the foundation's outset. "Everything that I earned came from here and I want it used here."[5]

Loussac died in Seattle in 1965.

CHAPTER FOUR

Inside

ONE MIGHT HAVE DEVOTED separate, shorter essays to the 1920s and the ensuing decade of national economic crisis rather than take up the two decades in a single, longer chapter. The Great Depression of the 1930s certainly made a difference in Anchorage. Early in that decade about one-third of the town's employable residents were without work.[1] But the economy had been grim for some time before. The *Christian Science Monitor* referred to the early 1920s in Alaska as "years of depression," obviously unaware of what was to come.[2]

While it was true in 1929 that Anchorage possessed the amenities of an industrialized society—plumbing, electricity, radios—it was not true, as some claimed, that Alaska was "fast developing."[3] We know this in retrospect. Anchorageites and journalists who wrote about them possessed the usual human limitation of not knowing the future. So the *Monitor* told readers to look for Alaska's imminent rejuvenation. The *American Architect* also expected a renewal of railroad work and a surge in oil discovery, extraction, and transportation.[4]

Others were less cheerful. The writer Wilds P. Richardson encouraged the *Atlantic Monthly*'s readers to disregard all they had heard about Alaska's purchase from Russia in 1867 as a supposedly great business bargain. Predictions about the territory's speedy growth following the building of the railroad from Seward to Fairbanks had busted, Richardson wrote, claiming that in 1920 "the little state of Iowa alone produced...more than the total output of Alaska." Richardson offered little sympathy to the "credulous and

hopeful" Americans who had invested their money and energies in the government's faltering town of Anchorage.[5]

Other pessimists used animal metaphors to describe the Alaska project—
it was as doomed as the dodo, a hopeless "white elephant."[6] A bitter blow
came from Andrew Christensen, who had been a key figure with the Alaska
Engineering Commission in Anchorage's first years. By 1935 Christensen had
turned against the idea of settling the Anchorage region and he said so, quite
publicly, in the pages of *Time* magazine. "I happen to be the man who selected
the town site of Anchorage, surveyed it, laid out its streets and put in public
improvements," Christensen wrote. Now, however, he could speak of the
settlement of the Anchorage area only in terms of wasted money and impossible conditions. He offered to furnish *Time*'s editors with details on Alaska,
"if you are interested in exposing this fiasco."[7] Christensen's words echoed a
sentiment expressed in the 1920s by a manager for the Alaska Railroad. "The
town of Anchorage," he said, "has practically ceased to exist."[8] Even the up-
beat *Christian Science Monitor* had acknowledged that a reason for President
Warren Harding's visit to Alaska in 1923 was to determine whether Alaska
would be developed or "allowed to remain dormant."[9]

After the Great War, many inside and outside Alaska hoped to see the
territory boom. But many of the three thousand young men who left Alaska
for military service did not return to the territory. The same was true of many
who had left to work in war-related fields. In the 1920s, Anchorage grew by
only four hundred residents, its population rising to around 2,270.[10] The figure was about the same at the end of the 1930s. These numbers represented
a significant drop from the town's 1916 population of 6,000,[11] though they
accounted for nearly one quarter of Alaska's population growth since that
year.[12]

Some said that political red tape and nearly forty government agencies
with overlapping and competing jurisdictions in Alaska hampered Anchorage's growth. They said that natural resources could not be tapped without
the permission of "a jealous bureaucracy five thousand miles away."[13] Alaskans had little freedom to develop the territory's oil fields,[14] and the cost of
living and doing business in the territory was high. Ocean freight rates from
Seattle to Anchorage (about 1,500 miles) were five times the rates from Seattle
to Hong Kong (7,500 miles).[15] Moreover, Anchorage's diminished population
created a greater tax burden on those who stayed.[16]

Some said that if the government subsidized rail rates, thus making them cheaper, more settlers would come.[17] Businessmen, meantime, aimed to attract tourists. Anchorage guide Andy Simons published advertisements in the national magazine *Forest and Stream* offering organized big game hunts and glacier tours.[18]

Anchorageites who felt that their town was being belittled by outsiders were quick to offer corrections. Philip Laing, publicity chairman of the Anchorage Booster Club, recorded his bad feelings after being "slighted" by *Time*, which published a map of Alaska void of reference to Anchorage. Along with other letter writers, Laing put in print some of the things the small city had going for it. By 1935 some twenty civilian planes were based at Anchorage's airfield, and the city had become the territory's primary commercial air base. Anchorage had two canneries, was the headquarters of the Alaska Telegraph system, and the radio station KFQD, "the farthest north broadcasting station," was based there.[19] Anchorage was a modern town: radios had arrived there by 1923, and the Anchorage Radio Club had built the KFQD station. A local group, the Arctic Ice Worms, offered music and humor programs on the station twice weekly.[20] As of April 1931, KFQD offered 17 hours of entertainment each week.[21] Anchorageites had some reason to bristle at the construal of their town as an irrelevant backwater.

Yet the Great Depression was what it was. In 1936 at least one hundred laborers with the Alaska Railroad were laid off and, of course, this meant hardship for the men and their families. The *Anchorage Weekly Times* worried about the railroad "abandoning" Anchorage, which would have seemed like a betrayal since the city and the railroad had grown together in mutual reliance.[22] Government officials countered that Anchorage's merchants had turned from the railroad to private industry. "In view of the disloyalty by some of your merchants... in patronizing the Alaska Railroad competitors," a railroad agent wrote to Anchorage's Chamber of Commerce, "your demand to continue operation... at a loss is not well taken."[23] But the railroad stayed.

New Deal projects designed to mitigate the effects of the Depression came to Anchorage. The Public Works Administration built a new school, made $100,000 available to widen Fourth Avenue, and provided for upgraded telephone, water, and sewer systems. The Works Progress Administration made for the paving of Fourth Avenue,[24] and nearly $700,000 was appropriated for the construction of a road linking Anchorage and the Matanuska Valley.[25] By the fall of 1936, the Civilian Conservation Corps in Alaska had built nearly 150 bridges and 80 buildings of various kinds, along with some 4,000 yards of dikes and jetties.[26] (Some CCC workers used Anchorage's community building for athletics.)[27]

The federal government's reach was hard to miss. In a handful of issues, an Anchorage newspaper reported on the work of the U.S. Soil Conservation Service, the Federal Power Commission, the U.S. Geological Survey, the Engineer Corps, the Bureau of Indian Affairs, the Coast Guard, and the fire control service of the Department of the Interior.[28] In an address at the University of Alaska Fairbanks, future governor Ernest Gruening defended the New Deal against cries of socialism and praised the Home Owners' Loan Corporation and the Tennessee Valley Authority.[29] Anchorage's city hall, too, was a New Deal project.[30] But then again, no one would say that these works did much to create lasting wealth. As with the country generally, the American prosperity to come would be generated by the world's greatest war.

Anchorage's first government building had been the post office, the Montana Café its first business.[31] The Model Café promised service around the clock, and the proprietors of the Woodrow Café appealed to Alaska pride, claiming the status of old-time pioneers. Harry Tasaki opened the U.S. Restaurant promising "good eats" and quick service.[32] Anchorage's Catholics offered confession and attended Mass in a library. Father Shepherd came up from Seward.[33]

As Anchorage developed, the small settlement of Knik, across the Cook Inlet, faded. The Horning family published advertisements reminding Anchorageites that their general store in Knik still existed, though with little business success.[34] Newcomers with tongue-tricking names like Zookivick, Zhoocoirick, and Zpooconick tried their luck on the new frontier,[35] while Alaskans from other towns in the territory—Nome, Juneau, Fairbanks, Seward—moved in or came to see the federal government's new handiwork.[36] Newspaper editors who had seen settlements come and go predicted that Anchorage would be another "passing scene in the flight of time," while the *Cook Inlet Pioneer* called for the rapid organization of a clean water supply, public school, dance hall, and city government.[37]

The minutes of Anchorage's early council's meetings provide little to thrill even the devoted scholar, yet in them one observes a community taking form. Here the Committee on Streets, Alleys, Lights, and Buildings considers a petition for a light at Fifth and "F" streets; there the Police and Jail Committee report that gamblers infested the city's pool rooms and cigar stores. The new town's councilmen discussed the practical problems of garbage collection and snow disposal. They wondered about the propriety of "children under 16 found roaming around the Streets from 9 P.M. to 5 A.M." The councilors passed ordinances for the control of vicious dogs and "prohibiting stray cattle from roaming around the streets." They regulated telegraph and telephone poles. In February 1921, the Finance Committee reported that total property in Anchorage was valued at almost $2.4 million.[38]

Automobiles were a problem. The chairman of the Fire and Water committee "complained of the promiscuous driving of automobiles over the fire hose" near the site of a fire. And, reportedly, a little girl was nearly run over at the intersection of Fourth and "C" streets. On another day, a taxi driver asked permission to drive up to twenty miles per hour within city limits.[39]

Readers of the young town's newspapers kept up on the political and cultural issues of the day. Lengthy articles in the *Alaska Labor News* defended birth control, arguing, among other things, that available contraception would not lead to heightened sexual activity among the unmarried.[40] And moral concerns over problems related to alcohol led the territory to become "bone dry" on January 1, 1918. This movement was spurred by reports about debauchery in dark places. "Barbary coast in its palmiest days never presented such scenes as nightly are staged in the Mint Grill, of Anchorage," one writer complained.

> Although this city is presumably dry, and no liquor is sold within its limits, here nightly are to be seen men and women in various stages of intoxication reeling about the floor and conducting themselves in a manner that would have put a Dawson dance girl to shame.[41]

It was said that where the men of Alaska had seen the need for liquor in years past, such a requirement no longer existed, since civilization "has brought with it other and better means of keeping warm and in good spirits"—tennis, golf, music, dancing, and a "'chummy' feeling that seems to possess all the occupants of the land."[42]

The age of television and the Internet was far off; the town's residents talked and mingled. Among the clubs formed in Anchorage's first decades were the American Legion, an Anchorage Women's Club, the Daughters of the American Revolution, the Elks, the Campfire Girls, Boy Scouts, Girl Scouts, the Masons, a Women's Christian Temperance Union, and the YMCA, in addition to many others. In 1923 residents voluntarily cleared what would become the municipal airfield, and community groups regularly met tourists as they arrived in town. In 1935 Anchorageites greeted families from the upper Midwest who had decided, with government assistance, to settle in the Matanuska Valley.[43]

The city hosted beauty contests. In one of them, competitors were supposed to appear before judges in bathing or tennis suits, but several of the girls had received vaccinations in response to a scarlet fever scare and the injec-

Laying cornerstone of Odd Fellow's Temple, August 20, 1923. Marie Silverman clippings and photographs, Archives and Special Collections, Consortium Library, University of Alaska Anchorage, HMC-0778-4-352.

Aerial view of Anchorage, 1925. Anchorage Museum general photo file, AMRC-b65-2-6

tions had left unpleasant blemishes. The girls displayed themselves in evening gowns. At the end of February 1936, and after much multiple voting, Charlotte Manning was announced the winner with a total of 24,050 votes. Eileen Bagoy came in second with 11,325. In a field of nine contestants, Bonnie Bell got last place with a disheartening tally of 70.[44] For its part, the Liar's Club sponsored a contest for tall tales, the main proviso being that the lies sent in for consideration had to be "distinctly Alaskan."[45]

A degree of historical and cultural literacy was taken for granted. A single newspaper editorial from 1931 drew on biblical, historical, and classical sources, alluding in passing to Shadrach, Meshach, and Abednego (Hebrew Bible), the Sermon on the Mount (New Testament), the English population theorist Thomas Malthus, and Prometheus (ancient Greek).[46] Z. J. Loussac's drugstore sold cameras and golf clubs, but also books in the fields of philosophy, history, and science.[47] Articles that took evolutionary theory for granted didn't seem controversial.[48] In 1925 the *Anchorage Weekly Times* editorialized against political moves in the states to prevent the teaching of evolution.[49]

City administration was as tedious and necessary in the 1930s as it had always been. The fire department reminded residents to burn trash at least 25 feet from buildings; private drivers bid for contracts to bring children from Lake Spenard to the school in Anchorage; and the city council approved Ed Glover's application to build a service station at the corner of Fifth and "E" streets.[50] The council gave the Streets, Alleys and Buildings Committee permission to buy twelve manhole covers, and the committee on Law, Ordinance and Police called on parents "to warn children from hanging on to [moving] automobiles."[51] In 1936, a plumber brought his family up from Portland, saying that he had always heard of Anchorage as an "up-and-coming town."[52] The Oregonian was more right than he knew, but the city was not free of occasional apathy: a school play was lightly attended, interest in local elections was sometimes lackluster, and a 9:00 p.m. curfew for students went unenforced.[53]

On the other side of the ledger, residents supported local education. In the summer of 1930, Anchorageites purchased nearly $50,000 in bonds for the support of city's school. A law required men between the ages of 21 and 50 who were neither sailors, soldiers, firefighters, paupers, nor insane to pay a five-dollar school tax.[54]

By the end of 1917 Anchorage comprised some 1,350 buildings whose value the young school district assessed at over $2 million. The year before, Secretary of the Interior Franklin Lane had authorized funds for the building and maintenance of a school for children of railroad workers in unincorporated towns along the line.[55] Frederick Mears, chief supervisor of early Anchorage, soon handed direction of the school building to the town manager, Andrew Christensen. The Anchorage school board thanked Mears and the commission for his "foresight and constructive spirit."[56]

As far as Anchorage's school was concerned, some news was bad, some good. At the beginning of the 1930s, Anchorage's students were unhealthy. Of the 350 children in the city's school in the first fall term of the decade, 273 had not been immunized, 70 were underweight, and 151 had bad teeth.[57] And, as always in a world that includes boys, vandalism was a problem.[58] On the other hand, the director of the territory's schools, Anthony Karnes, said in 1936 that Alaska's teachers were more highly trained and more motivated than their colleagues Outside. Most of Anchorage's high school teachers had master's degrees.[59]

Public school. Alaska Railways Photo Album, Archives, University of Alaska Fairbanks, 1996-0190-1a

The educational process involves idealism. It also involves tedium and the organization of people and things. For Andrew Christensen, this meant arranging for the moving of the school's piano to a certain Mrs. Anderson's house, on the corner of Third and "H" streets, for safekeeping during the summer;[60] and it meant staying apprised of the school's humdrum development—the hanging of blackboards, the installment of a bell system, the placement of drinking fountains,[61] the acquisition of desks, a fire alarm, encyclopedias, chairs, and a "bucket with a mop ringer."[62] Christensen passed one question about what to do with inappropriately purchased chairs back up the chain of command to Mears.[63] In short order, *Peter Rabbit*, Franklin's *Autobiography*, *Jack and the Bean Stalk*, *Robinson Crusoe*, and dozens of other books disappeared from the school's shelves.[64]

In 1917, the city's education system handled some 206 pupils, already the largest student body in any Alaska school district.[65] At first the school's athletes lacked competition outside town, but in 1925, Anchorage's basketball team had won every game it played against Seward, Fairbanks, and other schools along the railroad belt.[66]

The young Anchorage scholars' poetry was pedestrian if well-meaning:

Of all the spires that point above,
Where the air is pure and bright,
McKinley's Mount is the one I love,
For its grandeur and it's [*sic*] height.[67]

Sometimes the students' troubled grammar pointed to academic work yet to be done:

No town has ever had a more remarkable growth and development, than has that of Anchorage, Alaska. One of the great factors that has kept pace with all the other institutions, which have done their share in making Anchorage what she is today, is the Public Schools.[68]

In 1925, seven boys and four girls graduated from Anchorage High School. Four of the boys and all of the girls intended to go to university—all but one to the University of Washington.[69]

Far more than to any other single college or university, graduates in 1933 and 1934—there were forty-four of them—went to the Alaska Agricultural College and School of Mines in Fairbanks, soon to be renamed the University of Alaska. Many others went to the University of Washington, four to Stanford University, and one to the Naval Academy. Others scattered to various colleges and universities, mainly in the western and midwestern states.[70]

In the early twentieth century, going to college was increasingly an American thing to do. Already by 1870, the United States hosted more colleges, medical schools, and law schools than all of Europe combined.[71] Yet, relative to American young people generally, Anchorage's students went to college in unusually high numbers. Between 1925 and 1930, nearly fifty percent of Anchorage's graduates went to college or university.[72] In 1934, five years into the Depression, this number fell to about forty percent, a figure that was still far above the national norm of eight percent.[73]

It is not certain why Anchorageites went to college in such high numbers, although the personality of Alaska's settlers must be considered. However clichéd references to Alaskans' special hardiness have become—one writer suggested that they put the sturdy Pilgrim Fathers in the shade—it remained true that the material and psychological challenges Alaskans faced were daunting.[74] Alaska was attractive to ambitious risk takers and to the possessors of a certain kind of fortitude. They also seemed to be intellectually curious.

Sherman Rogers, a correspondent for the *Outlook*, which published many articles on Alaska, commented on the territory's mental culture. Alaskans were, he said, well-mannered and well-read. "I make the carefully studied statement," he continued,

> that there is no part of the world where as many magazines are read.... I could engage in conversation with any one from the mayor of a town to a prospector forty miles from a railway, and they could put up an intelligent argument on any question concerning the public welfare that was receiving attention in American publications.[75]

Rogers praised the high quality of Alaska's newspapers, which still impress the researcher who recalls that they were prepared for miners, shopkeepers, innkeepers, and machinists. As of October 1930, the *Anchorage Daily Times* was producing 900 copies per issue.[76] A later claim that news coverage in Alaska was "poor" up to the Second World War does not apply to the journals published in Anchorage.[77] On his visit to Alaska, President Harding commented on the Alaska's "robust, educated families," and a journalist who chronicled the president's visit for *McClure's Magazine* asserted that Alaskans read more books and newspapers per capita in winter than any other Americans.[78]

Many who went to Anchorage in its first years had been on the move for some time. Fred Carlson had left Russia, gone to Canada, then to Seattle, and then to Anchorage. Michael Durback started in South Africa, emigrated to Argentina, thence to New York, Washington state, and, finally, to Anchorage. Ejnar Dybvik came to town via Norway, Nova Scotia, and Massachusetts.[79] A majority of the workers who went to Anchorage in the beginning did not have children, but many did, and surely some of these passed to the next generation an openness to risk and a desire to strive for a better life.[80] The average age of the immigrants in Anchorage who applied for citizenship in 1919 was thirty-nine.[81] Higher education was beyond their reach, but they passed a desire for learning and achievement to their children.

Early on, most settlers seemed to leave Anchorage before their children reached high school age. The largest class in 1933 was the fourth grade, with 48 students as compared to the sixteen twelfth graders.[82] Perhaps, then, the residents who stayed in town long enough to see their children through high school possessed a relatively high degree of a stick-to-it mentality that manifested itself in the high number of Anchorage graduates who went to university. This kind of outlook is hinted at in a letter some parents wrote to the territorial legislature asking for help with the maintenance of Anchorage's high school. They described their children as "the sons and daughters of parents who are reclaiming Alaska from its wilderness state."[83]

Of course, ambition did not always make for success. Some students excelled, but surviving grade reports from Anchorage's schools show that the academic bell curve also appeared on the far frontier. And, of course, some parents never rose to their basic duty. Kenneth Osier's mother made regular excuses for his frequent absences from school: his father was sick; the weather made for "bad walking"; a bridge was unsafe; the weather was too cold; and Kenneth, at various times, had a headache, a toothache, a cold, a sore throat, and a bad foot. One time Mrs. Osier said that Kenneth had needed to stay home with his brother while she was away. On another day the boy purportedly stayed home to help his parents with work. In one rare moment of candor, Mrs. Osier acknowledged that Kenneth had been "playing hooky." But on another day she wrote that the boy had a paper route that caused him to arrive home late, "and it get [sic] so dark these days." An exasperated school principal wrote in green ink below her latest excuse: "Yet Kenneth stays for the second show [at the theatre] and goes home at eleven o'clock, and later."[84]

Other students attended school regularly and caused no problems but still did not fare well. One ill-prepared Anchorage graduate received two grades of "C" and two of "D" in her first semester at Fullerton Junior College.[85] Another student in the high school put in a mediocre performance in shop, did poorly in his English class, and failed algebra while his brother stumbled in English and Latin, even earning a "C" for his work with the Glee Club (although he did do well in geometry).[86]

In 1932 the University of Washington assessed Alaska's high schools based on the grades the territory's graduates received in their first college semester. Only the school at Petersburg ranked highly, followed by the school at Juneau. Of the thirteen high schools studied, Anchorage came in tenth place and was labeled inadequate.[87] "It would appear," an education bureaucrat wrote laconically, "that many of the larger schools of the Territory should offer better preparation for college."[88]

Yet, given the very high number of Alaska students who went to university, perhaps it is not surprising that many (relative to other cohorts) did not do well at the outset. And it is true that some who started poorly finished well. One of them, John Erickson, served in the army's medical corps during the Second World War, gained a bachelor of science degree in 1950, and became a pharmacist in Anchorage.[89]

Faculty turnover was a problem. Anchorage's high school teachers came and went, few staying more than a couple years. Of the six high school teachers in 1931, just three remained the following year, and by 1935 all of them were gone. Of the high school's seven teachers in 1934, just three were still in place the following year. Alaska's commissioner of education made an obvious point in 1922: "[A] school system which is continuously changing administrative heads and teaching force cannot be efficient."[90] Students also came and went; few graduates had known their peers for more than a handful of years.[91] To the eve of the Second World War, observers commented on the "transitory nature" of residence in Alaska.[92]

Certainly the brevity of the teachers' tenure was linked to the difficulty of life in the territory. "I have already been in Alaska four seasons," wrote one agent with the Alaska Engineering Commission:

> [M]en who serve...in Alaska find it a hardship as soon as the novelty of newness and travel wears off.... [S]ervice in Alaska *is, in reality*, very much akin to foreign service in the army, and in view of this fact and the physical and social deprivations and hardships it entails, it is respectfully submitted that when [a man] has served four years he should reasonably be entitled to an honorable discharge from that line of service.[93]

The teacher turnover must also have been linked to the high number of single women who taught in the school. As the young teachers married, most left the classroom to tend to home and children. Alaska's department of education understood that a higher number of male teachers would probably mean more stability in the schools, and wages were increased with the hope of attracting more men to the classroom. Still, in 1922, even with war veterans returning to the job market, just sixteen percent of Alaska's school teachers were men.[94] This trend held into the 1930s. In 1931, four of the six teachers in Anchorage's school were women. Two years later, women comprised five of the seven teachers.

Where, in the eyes of the University of Washington, Anchorage's high school was deficient relative to the schools at Petersburg, Juneau, and several other towns, it was deemed superior to the schools at Nome, Valdez, and Wrangell.[95] On its own terms, Anchorage's school was neither very good nor very bad. Students could gain from it what they put into it, depending on personal motivation, parental involvement, and natural ability. In 2007, seventy-six years after her graduation from Anchorage High School, Alice Mikami Snodgrass's memories of the school were detailed and borne out by archival records. When asked about her teachers, she remembered that Ruth Glasier, who had taught English and algebra, was highly competent—she simply knew how to teach and how to control a classroom.

Alice had no complaints about any of the teachers she had had at the Anchorage school, and records show that as a student she had kept a busy schedule. In 1925 Alice, then in the second grade, won a prize for her essay "The Prevention of Fire."[96] In a high school play Alice took the part of a flapper named Pansy Prosser. She was a member of the high school's academically oriented "A" Club, and she assisted at the lunch counter during the high school's annual carnival. Alice was her class's treasurer, a member of the Glee Club, and in her senior year she was the elected "class prophet."[97]

At Alice's graduation ceremony, Mayor James Delaney urged Anchorage's students to go to college, to strive to learn something new each day, and to pray for challenges in life to rise to. At the ceremony, Alice and the five other graduating women "presented a charming picture in their pretty gowns" and figured as a "fine addition to the community's womanhood."[98]

Alice was the second oldest of the four Mikami children who graduated from the high school in Anchorage. All of them—in order of age, Mary, Alice, Harry, and Flora—finished high school as their class's valedictorian, although they differed in their academic abilities. Everyone seemed to agree that Mary and Harry were the most intellectually endowed. Their Ph.D.'s from Yale University, both acquired in the 1930s, made this perception concrete.

Mary's gifts were clear from the beginning. She was the only one of the Mikami children to show up at school in Anchorage unable to speak English, Japanese being her parents' tongue. Yet as a first grader, she made the school's honor roll, and in 1923, when she was ten years old, she won a $2.50 savings deposit as a second-place winner in an essay contest sponsored by the Bank of Alaska.[99]

Mary's high school resume has been lost but, in addition to being the first of the four Mikami valedictorians, she was the first Mikami to attend what would become the University of Alaska at Fairbanks. She graduated from there in 1934 with the highest honors and with the loftiest grade point average of any student who had studied at the college to that point.[100] After she died in August of 1999, she was remembered in the U.S. Senate by Alaska Senator Frank Murkowski as a person of "courage" and "tenacity."[101]

The Mikami children did well because their parents, especially their mother, required much of them. The historian almost wishes for a heroic tale involving the Mikamis' success in the face of the animosity they felt

"Class of 1929" (actually the class of 1930). John Bagoy Collection, Anchorage Museum, B96.32.66

from their classmates and other Anchorageites in an era when Americans of Japanese heritage were facing pressures and animosities in parts of the United States and Canada. But no such struggle is discernible in the historical record. Photographs published in the Anchorage school annual, *The Anchor*, often have Mary, Alice, and Flora at center stage (Harry seemed to shun cameras).[102] Other surviving photos show the Mikami girls, especially Alice and Mary, enjoying time with their friends, arm in arm, dressed fashionably, confident, one of the gang.[103] The Mikami kids joked around like others. In a note to a precocious classmate, Flora wrote, "Wish I was as studious as you.... But it kinda hurts me think hard."[104] A few years before, Mary had written to an underachieving schoolmate, calling her "the best of girls and a sweet friend." In another place Mary joked about her ability to argue with a teacher, but "only when in a tight fix."[105]

Interviewed near the end of the twentieth century, Alice, who still lived in the Anchorage area, could not remember ever being made to feel as if she were an outsider.[106] To be sure, assimilation came at a cost. In middle age Harry wrote to Alice saying that it was too bad that they knew so little about their Japanese heritage—so little, indeed, of their own parents' biographies.[107] But this was hardly unique to the Mikami family or to immigrants from Japan.

The Mikami children lived up to the stereotype of the Japanese academic overachiever, but in Anchorage this did not evince animus such as could be found, for example, in parts of California. "You came to care for our lawns— We stood for it," declared one piece of anti-Japanese propaganda from the Los Angeles.

> You sent your children to our public schools—
>   We stood for it.
> You moved a few families in our midst—
>   We stood for it.
> You propose to build a church in our neighborhood—
>   *We didn't and won't stand for it.*
> You impose more on us each day until you have gone your limit.
>   *We don't want you with us so, get busy, Japs, and move out of Hollywood!*[108]

Anchorage was too far removed from the agitations of more settled places where competition for resources or jobs was sometimes pronounced. In its first decades, Anchorage, like Alaska communities generally, wanted more settlers.[109] And, given the high number of immigrants in early Anchorage, the Mikami parents' accents were in plentiful company. One page from census information gathered in Anchorage in 1929 gives us a sense of the American and international diversity present in the town, for it lists a native Tennessean, Iowan, Kentuckian, Ohioan, two New Yorkers, a Scot, a Canadian, four Finns, a Swede, an Italian, two Norwegians, and a resident originally from the Balkans.[110] From 1928 until after the Second World War, the Alaska Railroad's manager, based in Anchorage, was a Cuban-cigar-smoking "doughty little Swede" named Otto Ohlson.[111] Anchoragites were not put off by leaders of non-American birth.

The gathering clouds of war in the Pacific had no discernible effect on Alice or Mary, on their studies, on their friendships in Anchorage or, later, in Fairbanks. Each of the Mikami children served on the staff of their school's yearbook. All joined the Torch Society, whose members had to maintain at least a grade average of "B." Harry joined the debate and science clubs; he played trumpet in the school orchestra. Flora was assistant editor for the high school's newspaper, *The Anchor Chain*, and played on the basketball team.[112]

Anchorageites, like Americans everywhere, were interested in the activities of the celebrity pilot Charles Lindbergh, although by 1936 the focus had turned to tragedy—the kidnapping and murder of his infant son. The *Weekly Times* criticized the trial of the boy's killer as a scandal worthy of "the more frivolous Roman Emperors," yet the paper and its paying readers could not bring themselves to avert their gaze from the misfortunes of so popular a figure.[113] Some Anchorageites were also interested in the exploits of George Hughes, a ninety-six-year-old Civil War veteran, who reportedly fathered a child with a woman sixty-eight years his junior.[114]

Anchorage's churchgoers may not have approved of Mr. Hughes, although surviving records do not point to a town marked by theological fervor. Churches filled their roles as social organizations, centers of civilization, and moral and spiritual uplift. Anchorage's first library was established in the Episcopal Church,[115] and the Episcopalians, along with the Christian Scientists, seemed philosophical. In one lecture published for Anchorage's readers, a Christian Scientist spoke about Christ the "revelator of God to man," turning later to the theme of Mary Baker Eddy as God's "revelator" in the modern age. The Episcopalians discussed the religious "instinct" and the benefits of spirituality. The local rector claimed that the best assurance for world peace was every person's acceptance of the principles of Christ.[116]

Children at Anchorage's Lutheran church dramatized the story of Daniel in the lion's den.[117] The First Presbyterian Church, attended by the Mikamis, demonstrated the greatest commitment to family outreach. It sent buses to pick up children who lived on Government Hill and invited residents to enjoy congregational singing and compelling sermons. One cantata put on by the church's girls promised "thrills and delights."[118] Prospective visitors were assured that services would not exceed seventy minutes.

The Presbyterians radio-broadcasted their evening service to towns throughout Alaska and offered public lectures for locals. One of these focused on the workings of communism in Russia.[119] The church grew.[120]

Anchorage's public culture shared the American civil religion that drew on general Christian categories. No one was surprised when American ministers worried aloud about family life being abandoned for the less elevating amusements found in theaters and dance halls, or when the *Daily Times* editorialized on Mother's Day that, after Jesus Christ, mothers were God's best

Presbyterian Church. AEC Collection, Anchorage Museum, AMRC-aec-9543

gift to men.[121] In late 1930, former president Calvin Coolidge predicted that in coming years the United States would experience a deepening of "national faith, an increasing reverence for holy things, and a more thorough, loyal devotion to God."[122]

A broadly shared commitment to cultural Christianity is probably among the factors that account for the general spirit of equanimity that existed among Anchorageites. To be sure, as is common, people saw race and ethnicity. The concept of social "colorblindness" was unheard-of. Thus Anchorage's newspapers noted that "Demos Guveles, a Greek," had been found dead near the cemetery as a result of suicide; that "David Morgan, a Negro," was being held in Ketchikan on charges of stabbing a girl; and that "Paulino Sembrano, Filipino cannery worker" was tried at Anchorage "for the fatal stabbing of Patty Stickwan, native." George Tanaka, a city dog-catcher, was presented as a "son of Nippon."[123] But the sentence construction that listed ethnicities was old and wide-ranging. In 1919, in a single short list, the *Daily Times* referred to "Techen Longcarp, a native," "W. Woerner, lineman employed by the Alaska Engineering Commission," and "F. H. Getchell, miner."[124]

Certainly, twenty-first-century readers looking through old newspapers find reasons to pause. The *Daily Times* published advertisements about movies with actors in blackface, and Tom Robertson won an award for "best black-face man" at an Elks Hall masquerade. (Another participant, Hilda Corey, masqueraded as Gandhi.)[125]

The striking thing is not that Anchorage's newspapers occasionally drew on the language of stereotype but that its editors wrote against it. In one of its numerous statements against the possibility of another world war, the *Daily Times* argued in 1931 that peace would be more possible if youth were taught to admire and trust people of other nations and races. An editorial noted that "many history textbooks in the schools contain deliberate falsifications inspired by a mistaken sense of patriotism, race hatred, national jealousy and envy."[126] And when the paper did editorialize about the threat some immigrants posed as a result of crime or competition for jobs, the threat was always somewhere beyond Anchorage.

Insofar as the pages of the *Daily Times* were concerned, local ethnic differences did not make for a lack of cohesion. Indeed, the city celebrated a week of public, multiethnic music. "There is no better medium for the establishment of harmony and unity of feeling in an organization or community than music," the paper noted, adding that "Americanization" was sometimes resisted among immigrants because they perceived it as stemming from bigotry. In Anchorage, the paper continued, things were different. At the festival, the music of at least eight nationalities was represented, and the enjoyment shared by people of different backgrounds helped to place Anchorage "among the progressive cities of the nation."[127]

Insofar as Alaska's Natives were concerned, the story was more complicated, although the general theme holds.[128] There was little news on Natives living within Anchorage before the Second World War because, aside from laborers with the railroad and New Deal work programs, relatively few Natives lived there before 1940.[129] One settler referred to the city as a "white man's paradise," but this was more descriptive than anything else.[130] In 1934, eighteen "full-blooded" Natives were reported to have lived in Anchorage, with an additional thirty-six designated as one-quarter or one-eighth Native. The large majority of these were related through marriage—husbands, wives, children.[131] (The census of 1930 showed some 131 Natives living in Anchorage, although many of these probably did not reside in the town proper.)[132]

Before Anchorage—or *Angits* in early-twentieth-century Dena'ina pronunciation—was founded, Native fishing camps existed in the area and were destroyed—depending on the situation, intentionally or inadvertently.[133] Certainly there was nothing in the Anchorage area akin to the large-scale territorial displacement that had been seen in the states from colonial times.

Information published about Natives in Anchorage's newspapers was often positive, at least from the perspective of the majority who took for granted the need for Natives' assimilation into American society. Most Anchorageites approved when they read that Native schools in southeastern Alaska, some of them operated by Natives, seemed full of material and spiritual promise, for the Natives were casting off tribalism and superstition in exchange for an introduction into mainstream American culture.[134]

By a later standard, the language used to convey enthusiasm for such schools seemed unfortunate, crass, or arrogant. The "Indian overnight was not willing to cast off his blanket and war paint," one writer said, but as time passed and as educational efforts succeeded, the "native people adjusted their living." Yet at the time, it seemed obvious that there was no way that Natives could thrive unless they learned to work within American cultural structures. Natives' best interests lay in access to good schools and, from there, in entry into American political and economic opportunities.[135] Except in po-etry, spiritual meditations, or utopian ideology, there would have been little point in longing for a never-existent Eden untroubled by the complications of a modernity that could not have been avoided.

So the focus was often on education. In 1917 a writer for the *Overland Monthly and Out West Magazine* observed that the system of education set up for Natives in Alaska was superior to what many Americans had in the states. The schools, the writer said, were devoted to preparing Native youth for the modern world; they emphasized instruction in cleanliness, nutrition, ethics, and civics; girls as well as boys voted in elections for school officers. "The entire scheme of educating the Alaska natives is to make them into self-supporting citizens, that when they leave school they may build up their social status and do their part in developing the territory of Alaska."[136]

The attention Anchorage's readers (or some of them) paid to education among Natives points to concern, even if some of the words used to discuss the topic ceased being acceptable in the latter twentieth century. In a letter to the *Daily Times*, three women wrote in praise of the work being done at the Eklutna industrial school, where "dusky heads bowed reverently while they stood by the table, chanting...'Grace' before meals." Lives that previously seemed erring and aimless were now in training for productivity, the letter said; students were learning about economics, horticulture, agriculture, "domestic science," and animal husbandry.[137]

Modernity would not go away; to prepare all children, Native and non-Native alike, for life in an industrialized economy was, it seemed, good work. Such was what people in Anchorage believed. "If opportunity for education and employment is offered [the Native]," a journalist who had spent time in Anchorage wrote, "he will aid materially in the development of Alaska."[138]

Sometimes Natives were seen as objects of jesting. A *Weekly Times* article published in 1918 about Native couples wanting to marry was friendly but demeaning, referring to the Natives as "dusky children of the wilds" and "brunette children of the mossy glades."[139] Another piece, written in praise of Native women in Teller donating their hair to the cause of winning the First World War, called the ladies "dusky belles of the midnight sun."[140] This was rudeness, not animosity. A short article published in another column on the same page told Anchorageites that the natives of Alaska were standing "shoulder to shoulder" with non-Natives in their support of the war effort.

Natives were also sometimes looked on as a kind of ornament. Romantic appeals to their folkways remained a staple of tourist brochures well into the twenty-first century. "I wanted to see Eskimos in their igloos," said a disappointed tourist dressed in a parka near Fairbanks in July of 1922.[141] But such things need not be seen only with a cynical eye. They can also point to a kind of real appreciation. When the Alaska Federation of Women's Clubs worried that Alaska was losing its mystique to the blandness of American popular culture, it called for the production of more Alaska poetry, but also for a stress on the "use of native handicrafts, such as basketry...and other crafts indigenous to Alaska." The territory would always have its wild wonders to commend it, but making its towns more "Alaskanesque" depended in part on recognizing the achievements of Alaska's Natives.[142] One writer, who likened Alaska's natural beauty to an "exquisite" Japanese sketch, praised the works of Skagway's Harriet Pullen who "is a member in blood brothership of many local tribes, and speaks the several Indian dialects of the coast."[143]

Some looked on Natives as a burden. Overcome and distracted by a powerful, energetic, and sometimes pushy and violent civilization, Natives could appear helpless and lacking moral power—easy prey to deception, alcoholism, poor diet, illiteracy, crime, and abuse. Professionals and others could see that candy, liquor, and cigarettes were having a deleterious effect on Natives' health. Efforts to suppress the sale of alcohol to Natives were long-standing and often unavailing.[144]

Concerns were various. Dr. Morton Myers of the Bureau of Indian Affairs wondered if dancing all night contributed to a Native's difficulty in fighting off disease,[145] and a dentist for the bureau worried about the impact of Western diets on Natives, noting that Yankees, too, might not be so devoted to tooth care if it meant going outdoors in subfreezing temperatures to get water for brushing.[146] Such arguments were not always compelling, but the general point seemed right: Natives benefited from the ways of the "whites," but the melding and clashing of cultures came with costs.

The Anchorage police department's reports from the late 1930s are replete with entries about drunkenness in general and drunkenness among Natives in particular. "I picked up a Native at 12.45 A.M.," one entry reads. "Carl Woods drunk [Native] laying in the snow at 3rd and C Street. Locked him up, City taxi used.... Released 7.30 A.M."[147] Agents for the Bureau of Indian Affairs noted similar problems while also, depending on the situation, noticing the absence of such problems. The Seller family, for example, made a "good type of home" and included Renee, a college graduate and teacher.[148]

Opportunities that might have been taken to slur Natives often were not. In 1915 the *Cook Inlet Pioneer* reported that "Indian Jim" killed another Native and went to prison but made no derogatory comment.[149]

The *Daily Times* published articles that expressed hopes for Native independence but also called on the government to ameliorate living conditions among Natives—for example, to end the dirty and slavelike conditions Natives faced in some canneries, and to take up the challenge presented by Natives' high rates of death from tuberculosis.[150] Anchorageites were eager for precautions to be taken against flu among Natives on the Seward Peninsula, and they read reports on Alaskans' use of new technologies—radios, aircraft, and medicines—to help Natives stricken by illness.[151]

If Natives were to succeed, let alone prosper, in an inevitably changing world, it seemed that Alaska's residents of European descent, or their government, would have to ensure assistance was available. This led, among some, to feelings of paternalism, which in turn led at times to cynicism and ill-will. Reflecting on three Natives who had been flown to Fairbanks to serve time in

Somersaulting in blanket toss. Russell Dow Collection, UA Anchorage, UAA-hmc-0396-14f-618

jail, the *Alaskan* noted that locking up the three was beneficial for all, since it "provides regular meals and comfortable living quarters for the redskins, puts fees in the pockets of commissioners and makes business for the air transport companies."[152]

Alongside reflections like this, however, we should place the numerous instances when Anchorageites showed a personal interest in Native individuals and their culture. The *Weekly Times* reported on the Camp Fire Girls at Nome who had named their club "Paneat Apunni" ("Daughters of the Snow") and whose members had taken individual Native names.[153] And the city council worked to organize the Fur Rendezvous, in which Native games figured prominently.[154] Anchorageites admired Native athletes' skill and strength in these games, and while the Native dress that some Anchorageites wore to the games in the 1930s was ornamental, this also pointed to a certain appreciation for Natives. One would not dress like a person one loathed.

Commentators denounced non-Natives who took advantage of a sometimes vulnerable population. In 1929 it seemed good that the "native is fast taking on civilized ways and adopting the white man's standards of morals," but, simultaneously, the writer regretted that "the white man's vices were…carried to [the Native] and have done much to retard his progress."[155]

Others romanticized Natives, speaking of them as being somehow naturally beyond moral blight, as "simple and guileless," as corrupted only

Miss Alaska and court. John Urban Collection, Anchorage Museum, AMRC-b64-2-508

90

by outsiders. This was a disservice to the obvious facts of the human condition, as well as to the historical record. A study conducted by Yale University's Peabody Museum in the 1930s into the history and life of Natives in the Cook Inlet region commented on the "pitiable disintegration" of Tanaina culture, although it also noted that violence had historically been part of that culture.

> The spear and bow and arrow were used [in battle] but dropped to depend wholly on the club in close encounter. The fighting continued until there were only two or three men left on one side.... Fighting was ... an honorable pursuit, from which prestige was gained.... At Iliamna the heads [of slain enemies] were cut off and hung up, the remainder of the body burned.[156]

It is difficult for the reflective person not to see that human history is universally problematic, yet it is also true that unscrupulous non-Natives brought to Alaska what, to Natives, would be novel ways of serving the dark side. Natives acquired some good things from non-Natives, but also some bad.[157] In addition to the problems noted above, we might add language loss, social and psychological disequilibrium, and cases of institutional abuse—intercultural phenomena as regrettable as they are ancient.[158]

In a post-civil-rights era, the racial segregation taken for granted in early-twentieth-century America is difficult to comprehend. But at the time, it seemed normal for Natives and non-Natives to have separate times for skating at a rink, such as was the case in Ketchikan.[159] Separate church services also were common, although seemingly contrary to basic New Testament teaching. A journalist from Outside opined somewhat enigmatically in the early 1920s that an "Eskimo walking down the streets of Fairbanks would cause a riot."[160] A well-known case of de facto segregation comes to us from Nome's Dream Theatre.[161] As for Anchorage, the only case of willful segregation uncovered for this study came after its period, in 1948, in the form of a covenant in the Airport Heights neighborhood prohibiting the sale of property to any nonwhite person.[162]

Bias obviously underlay these realities. But the complicated facts on the ground paint a broader picture. For example, Anchorage's first July Fourth celebrations saw Natives mixing with non-Natives and beating them in competitions, and Shem Pete, a Native who lived in the Anchorage area, reminisced late in life about his work on the railroad and as a mail carrier and barber. He remembered paying for flights in planes based in Anchorage.[163] All of this involved peaceable interaction with non-Natives. And while some in Alaska saw a 1925 law requiring literacy in order to vote as a measure designed to keep Natives from the polls, the *Weekly Times* editorialized that "this must not be the case" and that the "law must be made generally applicable to all voters."[164]

It is also worth noting that nondiscrimination legislation was passed in Alaska in 1945—a decade before the civil rights movement in the lower states gained traction. If nothing else, this points to a spirit of equanimity broader and deeper than existed in much of the United States.

The temperance of Anchorage's public culture also manifested itself in the city's politics. Aside from a brief, fervent, and relatively small socialist effort before the Great War, Anchorage was politically centrist. Through the period 1917–1941, Anchorage's representatives in the territorial legislature at Juneau were evenly divided, fifteen Democrats and fifteen Republicans.[165] In the town's first years, Anchorageites voted for Democrats, while through the 1920s the city's voters gave a majority of ballots to Republicans. In November 1930, Anchorageites voted almost evenly for the major political parties—376 for George Grigsby, the Democratic candidate for Alaska's delegate to Congress, to 317 for the Republican, James Wickersham.[166] (Wickersham won the territory-wide vote by a slim margin.) Political differences existed but they were not usually dressed in rancor.

As the Great Depression deepened, Anchorage, like the country generally, favored Franklin D. Roosevelt's Democratic Party. In the fall of 1936, Delegate Anthony Dimond, a Democrat, gained 578 Anchorage votes to the 169 votes of his Republican opponent. At the same time, the Democratic candidate for highway engineer won 222 votes—more than the total of the two Republicans running for the job. The *Weekly Times*, edited by a Republican, announced a Democratic "clean sweep in Anchorage," but the sweep did not involve heated partisanship.[167] In a small way, the victory probably also pointed to a more serious effort among Democrats for votes, which suggests a greater sense of organizational purpose and mission. One Democrat running for a seat in the territorial legislature claimed to be "deeply interested in the problems of the fisherman, the miner and the farmer of Alaska," while his

Republican counterpart sold himself with the uninspiring cliché, "a vote for me is a vote for progress."[168]

In the mid-1930s both major parties supported expansive government, though, holding power and, thus, greater responsibility, Democrats were more vigorous in calling for appropriations: "federal appropriations for road and trail building in Alaska," "liberal appropriations for the improvement of [the] rivers and harbors of Alaska," and "liberal appropriations for public schools in Alaska."[169] But if Republicans complained about the nearly three thousand Alaskans eligible for old-age pensions paid through the National Recovery Administration, few residents heard them. If anyone objected that nine hundred of the prospective recipients of the NRA benefit were Natives and that among the others were the vaunted trappers and traders of yore, few paid attention. At this moment, even some of Alaska's doughtiest residents lined up without censure for government goodies.[170]

For all the rhetoric about rugged individualism, Anchorageites wanted government. The point was made when Anton Anderson of Palmer criticized the idea of placing a statue of an old miner in front of Anchorage's city hall. Gold seekers had no part in city's history, Anderson said, but the federal government's role was central. The statue should depict Uncle Sam.[171]

Formal education in Anchorage had always involved government, but here, too, the presence of the state became more obvious as it acquired tasks previously seen to (or not) by family. The *Weekly Times* noticed that tasks once assumed to belong to parents were now being handled by public schools. "When Junior trudges off to school nowadays," an editorial said,

> he is not merely setting out to learn how to read and write and cipher. He is also going to be taught how to avoid the dangers of city traffic, how to keep his teeth and ears clean, how to read the newspapers and find out what is going on in the world, and how to get along with his fellows.... If he has bad tonsils, defective eyes, or poor teeth, the chances are that the school will learn about it before his parents do. If he is underweight, the parents are apt to learn about it from the school.[172]

Among the New Deal initiatives in Alaska was the settlement of the Matanuska Valley with economic immigrants from the upper Midwest. By the early twenty-first century the towns of the "Mat-Su" region had become bedroom communities for Anchorage, but in the 1930s, the Mat-Su seemed far away. It took one man twelve hours of driving to get his fifteen hundred pounds of turnips to Anchorage; he had to chop his way through a glacier near Eagle River.[173]

Like Anchorage, the small town of Palmer was birthed and raised by government. In the settlement and growth of the town Ernest Gruening saw old American ways melding with the new. Alaskans were passing through "the preparatory stage of the territories that have gone before," he said in 1936.

> You have seen right here in Alaska, in the government-fostered Matanuska colonization project, a blending of the old American ideas of self-help and the contemporary need sensed by our government today of making the opportunity for self-help available.[174]

For some, the colony was an inevitable "big government flop" foisted on tax-payers; for others it was a way to populate the territory. Critics drew dubious pictures of settlers living in ease on forty acres of land, in beautiful homes furnished with new rugs, overstuffed furniture, hot and cold running water, washing machines, and well-stocked grocery stores.[175] But Anchorageites were glad to have the valley's eggs and vegetables, even if a majority of these goods would continue to come from Outside.[176] By the end of February 1936, less than a year after their arrival, some forty-eight families that had gone to the Matanuska Valley had returned to the states. But other families took their place.[177]

Through the 1930s, colonization was spoken of partly in terms of defense, for the more people there were in Alaska the more difficult it would be for Japan to invade and conquer it. Colonization ideas floated around. Anchorage businessmen, for example, called for the settlement in Alaska of nearly a thousand refugees from Russia's civil war.[178] Others suggested colonizing the Aleutians with criminals.[179] "Three months after being placed in the colony, [thieves] would be raising reindeer and bandits would be breeding rabbits."[180]

Still others proposed opening Alaska to African Americans tired of living with segregation, or to Europe's persecuted Jews.[181] The latter scheme was criticized, not so much for ethnic reasons as because it seemed unlikely that

94

immigrants accustomed to urban life in Europe could adapt well to a more rugged existence in the far north.

As with other forms of freestanding prejudice, anti-Semitism had little pull in Anchorage. Among the town's first store owners were a Shapiro and Finkelstein, and the city's first mayor, Leopold David, was a Jew directly tied to the new immigration of the late nineteenth century. The same was true of Z. J. Loussac, chamber of commerce president in 1943 and mayor in the years 1948–1950.[182]

Aside from the Matanuska project, none of the colonization schemes led to settlement.

Anchorage was no paradise. Human realities are what they are, for good and ill. As we saw in chapter two, the town experienced some crime and embittered personal relationships. But not all American subcultures are the same, and context and environment matter. Life in Alaska was difficult, and the territory needed more people. When more residents were needed to help the town and territory prosper, it would have seemed ridiculous for Anchorageites to unnecessarily harm public relations between productive residents already on the scene. "[Newcomers] are welcome here," wrote Anchorage's first historian in the mid-1950s; they will "find little tradition or inertia that they must overcome. Cooperation and friendships are available on every hand so long as the individual moves ahead and his work is constructive."[183] There was overstatement and romance in the writer's generalization, but not too much.

INTERLUDE

Mikami Family Photos

While many Japanese came and went from Anchorage between 1915 and 1941, records point to only two families of Japanese heritage living in town through most of those years—the Kimuras and the Mikamis. Below are some of the many images Mary and Alice Mikami put into a photo album around 1935.

Alice (left), Mary (middle), and their mother and brother at their Anchorage home (c. 1927)

Flora leads her dolls in song at the Mikamis' Anchorage home (c. 1927)

Alice Mikami, about sixteen years old, with friends near Anchorage (c. 1928)

Alice with her mother and father, probably over Ship Creek (c. 1929)

Alice with her mother and father at their Anchorage home (c. 1929)

Flora Mikami (left) with friends in Anchorage. In the center is Louise Kimura (c. 1929)

Mary in style (c. 1933)

Mary (third from the left) and Alice at the University of Alaska Fairbanks (c. 1933)

Alice in Fairbanks (c. 1933)

Mary with a boyfriend in Fairbanks (c. 1934)

Harry with his mother, Miné, in California (c. 1940)

CHAPTER FIVE

Outside

From the time in the mid-nineteenth century when Japan began to engage the outside world, American interest in that mysterious country was high. For some Alaskans, their territory's relative proximity to Japan heightened this interest. Fellow feeling for the Japanese expressed itself in Anchorage in late 1930 when the city council called for funds to be raised for the Japanese victims of earthquake.[1] Some immigrants to Alaska from Japan, on the other hand, were eager to forget their mother country. The children of Japanese parents living in Anchorage would begin to learn about their ancestral nation only after they had become adults.[2]

Through the 1930s Anchorageites' interest in Japan was fostered by a steady stream of books and newspaper and magazine articles. The *Reader's Digest*, for example, printed articles about Japan's emperor and his nation's efforts to feed its population, and the *Anchorage Daily Times* stated its approval of the Japanese government's scheme to "eliminate unsound companies and amalgamate others" as a response to the Great Depression. The paper offered no opinion on a report about the relatively high tax rates imposed on Japan's wealthiest citizens.[3]

A spirit of competition colored much of the news from or about Japan. This was not surprising since Japan and the United States had only recently risen to importance as major powers in the Pacific. And it was difficult not to be impressed by Japan. Anchorageites read about Japanese chemists looking for ways to develop synthetic sake as part of a rice conservation effort, and they learned that the first woman to parachute from a plane was Japanese.[4] There were many stories about Japanese and American fliers competing for honors.[5]

Anchorageites kept track of Charles and Anne Morrow Lindbergh's August 1931 flight to Japan from the United States via Alaska, where Natives at Barrow received them as celebrities.[5] In Japan, the Lindberghs were glad to find "[s]ubways, soda fountains and modernistic hotels as well as rice fields, paper houses and kimonos."[7] The next month a Japanese news agency gave American pilots $2,500 as a reward for their courage in taking up a challenge to fly to Seattle from Japan.[8]

Much of the binational jousting was friendly, yet there was also something unpleasant on or just under the surface. In one minor international case, Japanese police imprisoned American pilots who had flown over Japanese fortifications with a camera in their plane. The row passed quickly; U.S. authorities convinced the Japanese that the flight path had been inadvertent and, after a month, the pilots were free to fly home.[9] But there were always points of tension: Japanese fisherman taking crab from the Bering Sea; Japanese economic developments in Manchuria that looked more and more like imperial depredation; the execution of some 80 "head-hunters" on Taiwan; a campaign of political disruption and assassination orchestrated by Japanese nationalists.[10] Japan's political life seemed unstable and sinister. Anchorageites learned that suicide had an honorable place in Japanese culture.[11]

Since the late nineteenth century American strategists had seen Japan as a threat, chiefly to Hawaii and the Philippines. Now, with the advent of air travel, Alaska seemed vulnerable. By the fall of 1931 observers surmised that one day Japan could invade Alaska, set up bases, and launch attacks from them onto the U.S. mainland. This led to calls for the building of airbases in the territory, although everyone aware of Alaska's vast remoteness could see how difficult it would be to defend against a committed adversary.[12]

Estimations of Japanese military capacities were high. "The Japanese have learned much from the west since Admiral Perry opened the doors of Japan [in 1854]," an article in the *Anchorage Weekly Times* noted. "She has mastered western science, eclipsed western industry in low cost production, made herself the military equal of the west on land, at sea and in the air."[13]

Lending weight to such conclusions was the growing recognition that things were increasingly unwell in the wide world. In the early 1930s, Anchorageites read about Germany and the extreme parties, left and right, that were on the ascendancy there.[14] The Nazis, especially, seemed to be growing in strength among a beleaguered German electorate.[15] Anchorageites were also made aware of Benito Mussolini's first official visit to Germany, and they learned about hostile Japanese action in Manchuria.[16] "Thirteen Chinamen and two Japs are reported to have been killed as a result of the encounters," the *Daily Times* reported.[17] An editorial in the same paper asserted that the world's dictators were building houses on sand and that the human desire for freedom—a legacy of the American Revolution—would eventually topple tyrants and military swashbucklers.[18]

Early in the 1930s, calls for war preparation were not yet much heard among Alaskans. Indeed, the *Daily Times*, like many American newspapers, hoped for peace, sometimes in almost dreamily pacifistic tones. At various times the paper wondered if the marvels of chemistry were worth the perils of poison gas used in war, or whether aviation was really so desirable in light of its wartime potentialities.[19] The *Daily Times* denounced thug politicians who had returned the "tiger law of life" to the fore in a demon-possessed world, and published a letter arguing for Esperanto as an international language.[20] If Esperanto had been spoken at the peace talks following the First World War, the writer implausibly suggested, there would have been fewer postwar difficulties.[21]

Most antiwar criticism was reserved for the home front. The *Daily Times* denounced "navy and army war lords" who relied on "preparedness propaganda" to coax a strapped federal government to spend on the military; it critiqued American war hawks committed to dragging "peace-loving, non-imperialistic America" into another war.[22] The paper thought well of proposals to eliminate the federal government's department of war and to abolish conscription. If such ideas took hold generally, European wars would cease and the United States would have no need to maintain a costly military force.[23] In an editorial, the *Daily Times* sarcastically supported the idea of sending women into combat. It was true that such a thing seemed to go against old codes of chivalry, but modern warfare had become completely uncivilized and the idea that women could serve as combatants simply recognized that fact.[24] "If the people of the nations want peace they can have it," the paper said on another occasion.

> If they are content to keep on buying, selling, eating, drinking, and leaving their affairs in the hands of cheap politicians and men anxious to get rich

out of war, then they can have war, and war they will have, and war they will deserve.[25]

The next war would be "incomparably more terrible than the last," the *Daily Times* correctly predicted. "It is impossible to humanize war. When it is started it is out of control. The only way to check the barbarities of war is to check war itself."[26] The paper warned readers about the "menace of the war profiteer" and noted that given the hardship the country was experiencing in the Depression, it was amazing that America's hustlers of carnage had not moved to improve the economic situation by instigating a fight with some small nation.[27]

Anchorage's journalistic spokesmen had moved some distance from the image of the leather-skinned, Arctic tough guy of lore. The *Daily Times* ran editorials praising the Indian nationalist Mahatma Gandhi's commitment to nonviolence, an approach the importance of which could hardly be over-stated "in a world that has almost invariably used force to gain its ends."[28] The Wild West, after all, had become less wild when men put their weapons away.[29]

The paper even offered an editorial decrying the condition of captured and caged animals, noting that Alaska's territorial flower, the forget-me-not, was an appropriate emblem for all the creatures in the world that suffered from neglect, abuse, mangling, trapping, vivisection, and captivity.[30]

Early in the 1930s, the *Daily Times*' lack of interest in building the na-tion's capacity for war was broadly shared. The Navy took less than twenty percent of enlistment applicants, and reduced the Pacific fleet from 42 to 30 vessels. In 1930, the Marine Corps closed recruiting offices in Seattle, St. Paul, Denver, and Dallas.[31] Meantime, Italy sought to build a new African empire, while news about the political successes of an Austrian named Adolph Hitler began to appear in Anchorage's newsprint, and Japan's military was showing what it could do against a vaster but less well-organized Chinese popula-tion.[32] An ominous cartoon the *Daily Times* published in November 1931 showed the forces of war—greed, imperialism, conquest, and the develop-ing Sino-Japanese crisis—contending for preeminence against the forces of "world peace sentiment," supported by, among other entities, the League of Nations.[33] As 1931 drew to an end, angry clouds knitted on the far horizon. "Japs Attack Chink Troops," a headline read in early November. "Feared War Close at Hand."[34]

The concerned might have found some assurance in the American destroyers that stopped at British Columbian and Alaska ports as part of ordinary patrols, or they might have recalled the words of a few who wanted dirigible bases to be set up on the west coast, arguing that hostile forces could creep up on Puget Sound via the Aleutian Islands.[35] Others sought to see things from the Japanese point of view. A month after the attack on Manchuria, the Japanese consul in Seattle likened his country's action to America's sending of troops into Nicaragua, Haiti, and Mexico for the protection of U.S. property and citizens. Japan had built hospitals and schools in Manchuria, the consul said; Japan had improved sanitation and, above all, was promoting peace and order.[36]

At the time, the consul's words may have seemed plausible. With growing news of Japanese atrocities, however, doubts about the dark nature of the Japanese war machine would give way to loathing. By the mid-1930s, it was less creditable to put off thinking about the possibility of another large war. In January 1936, the new U.S. aircraft carrier *Ranger* conducted training operations off the Alaska coast.[37] Planes from the ship landed at Merrill Field outside Anchorage, the only Alaska airfield not hampered at the moment by snow.[38]

Probably no one sounded the call for Alaska defense more loudly and consistently than the territory's delegate to the U.S. House of Representatives, Anthony Dimond. With a record as an Alaska miner, lawyer, U.S. commissioner, mayor (of Valdez), and member of the territorial senate, Dimond knew Alaska and its vulnerabilities well. In 1935 Dimond informed Congress that in years past the distance between Alaska and the American states would have discouraged any potential enemy from thinking that he could invade Alaska and use it as a base from which to bomb American cities. But now, with the advent of warplanes, "an enemy in possession of Alaska is within easy striking distance of the continental United States, and the rich cities and vast forests of the Pacific Coast would be open to attack."[39] This would be Dimond's primary theme: the defense of Alaska was essential to American defense.

Dimond provided Congressional colleagues with numbers and figures showing that if one sailed directly from Seattle to the Japanese port city of Yokohama following the shortest route, the traveler would pass through the Aleutian Islands.[40] The point was that in the event of attacks on the U.S.

mainland, it would be in Japan's strategic interests to take, hold, and develop Alaska territory. Dimond saw, as did many others, the importance of Hawaii to national defense, but he wondered at the blindness of those who could not see how easily Japan could take Alaska. "Is it not obvious," he asked

> that an enemy moving across the Pacific would not come by way of Honolulu...but would rather strike first, invade, and take Alaska at one gulp,...Once the enemy is in possession of Alaska, Hawaii could be ignored, because Alaska would be on the inside strategic line. I think it will be admitted that if a foreign power should take possession of Alaska, billions in money and probably thousands upon thousands of lives would be required to expel him.[41]

Defense against the bombing of the American mainland was Dimond's primary argument for a military buildup in Alaska. There was also a need for American pilots to be trained in subarctic conditions and, he further noted, the loss of Alaska's natural resources to another nation would be keenly felt in the states. He offered statistics on salmon, timber, copper, iron, coal, and gold production to make his point. "Considering the really illimitable resources of Alaska, one can well understand how it might be a temptation to the avarice of a country much poorer in natural resources, limited in territorial extent and practically overflowing with people."[42] Dimond was obviously speaking of Japan, which was already proving that its small size as a nation did not stop it from imposing its will on a much larger nation like China.

Where some hoped the world's leading militaristic nations could be appeased, Dimond spoke of Japan's "aggression" and the "falsehoods" it offered to countries critical of its grasping for territory and influence.[43] Japan had not invented "heartless conquest," he knew, "but we can truly say...that Japan has exemplified all of the graceless scoundrelisms in foreign policy so commended by Niccolo Machiavelli."[44] Dimond understood that Japan faced serious challenges, chiefly, shortages in natural resources—and these, in part, were what Japan was after in China. And there were no grounds for hating the Japanese people. Dimond claimed to admire them. "But," he continued

> there is a point, there is a sound reasoning for calmly considering what the Japanese have done [in China] and to picture their actions truly in our

own minds. The fact—and I think no one can doubt that it is a fact—that we have on the other side of the Pacific a nation whose territories are within 700 miles of ours [in Alaska], ruthlessly bent upon expansion, upon the acquisition of other lands rich in resources—these facts, I say, ought to impel us to take proper measures to defend what is our own.[45]

It was true, Dimond said, that Hawaii was a door through which any power with sites on the American West Coast or the Panama Canal would have to pass. That door was well defended. But there was another door, the undefended Alaska one. "What is the use of locking one door and leaving the other open?"[46]

Dimond offered these thoughts in February 1935, the same year Italy, the first of the fascist nations, invaded Ethiopia. In August the Congress passed, and President Franklin Roosevelt signed, the first of a series of Neutrality Acts, which sought to keep the United States out of foreign wars.

The *Weekly Times*, like its daily counterpart, expressed the isolationist sentiment that prevailed in the country. It did not think much of "the fuss" in Ethiopia. Alaskans could get misty-eyed over stories about the "pitiful plight of the bombed Ethiopians," and they could hope that Britain would confront Mussolini, but the cynical result, the paper said, would only be the extension of England's empire.[47] At the same time, the *Weekly Times* criticized the ineffectual League of Nations, "a high-powered debating society, ornamental, but impractical," which roundly condemned Hitler's growing depredations in Europe without actually taking effective action.[48] The League's inability or unwillingness to force Mussolini or Hitler to stand down revealed that it was "washed up," which only proved that the United States should not entangle itself in problems overseas.[49] "Europe is going to have a new war one of these days; then the old problems of [the First World War] will come up again, and we shall have to try once more to dodge pitfalls which grow progressively bigger and more numerous."[50] The *Weekly Times'* editorials were sometimes world-weary and bitter:

While the nations of Europe are spending their money on bomb-proof dugouts, against the day when it will be necessary to do battle once more for the sacred principles of human liberty, manifest destiny, and profits for [weapons] makers, it might be a sound idea for us in America to devise some new defenses against propaganda.... For when a man's moral indignation is once stirred, he ceases to think; after that, he will swallow anything and everything, content to feel rather than to use his gray matter.[51]

At the end of the First World War, some Anchorageites had looked for the annihilation of the German nation, perhaps even the German people. Now, in a less fervent day, the *Weekly Times* expressed the sense, shared even by Britain's hawkish Winston Churchill, that Germany had legitimate grievances stemming from the war-ending Treaty of Versailles. The vindictive French, Anchorageites read, were primarily to blame for giving a "revenge-monger" like Hitler a platform to shout from. The Versailles Treaty had been "one-sided," and Germany, which had experienced international humiliation, had a "right" to rearm and to be treated as an equal among nations. The result of Allied pressure on Germany was Nazi rule, for Hitler had promised to return strength and dignity to the German people. "Today Hitler can proudly point to achievements which are highly important in German eyes; when he talks about the lost colonies, the victors of 1918 have got to listen— no matter how uneasy it makes them."[52]

Near the end of 1936 the *Weekly Times* brushed aside the suggestion that Mussolini or Hitler would be to blame if war came. The burden of responsibility lay with the democratic powers.[53] If the injustices of the Versailles Treaty could be altered, the paper argued, Hitler could be appeased and war averted.[54] And, anyway, if war came, the United States should stay out of it.

Events unfolded. Anchorageites read about Charles Lindbergh's visit with Nazi leaders and about the aviator's hope that Germany would use its weapons responsibly, noting that combat aircraft had "abolished what we call defensive warfare." Then a Czechoslovakian journalist killed himself during a League of Nations meeting to bring attention to the worsening plight of Jews in Germany.[55] Multiple articles appeared on Japanese spies and their American accomplices.[56] In July 1936, Harry Thompson, a U.S. navy veteran, was sentenced to fifteen years in prison for "conspiring to sell secrets of the country's defenses to a high ranking officer of the Imperial Japanese Navy."[57] And Spain's civil war, beginning in 1936, brought to light the grim possibilities of modern warfare. The concept of "civilized warfare" was dead.[58]

As news from overseas worsened, the focus on Anchorage as a center for American defense sharpened. City leaders lobbied for military funds to be spent in the city and its region, and Anchorageites knew about the farming colony established in the Matanuska Valley—its purpose in part being to serve as a bulwark, albeit a very thin one, of American defense.[59] The "good people" of the Valley, Congressman Francis Culkin of New York sarcastically said, were expected "not only to bare their breasts to the Arctic breezes but also to any Japanese bayonets that came along."[60]

In the nation's capital, in the spring of 1937, Anthony Dimond called again for the preparation of the nation's defenses. He said he wanted to "insure peace by tending to make it impossible for any potential enemy to attack us."[61] In his extended remarks, Dimond restated many of the points he had made two years before, although now the conflicts in Ethiopia and Spain lent urgency to his appeals. The "speed and deadly destructiveness of modern aircraft" drove home to him to need for air defenses hundreds or even thousands of miles from the appealing targets of the American west coast.

> Modern aircraft during the recent years have attained performances which make flights between the mainland of the United States and Hawaii, and between Hawaii and Alaska, and between Alaska and the continental United States, and to the Panama Canal entirely feasible, even though they may be carrying heavy military loads.[62]

Alaska needed to be as thoroughly defended as Hawaii was, and Alaska and the Panama Canal now needed to be seen in a similar light, as they had been when Anchorage was founded. In 1915, the Canal and the effort at Anchorage both pointed to the United States' reach into the Pacific. Now they represented what needed to be kept safe from that other great Pacific power, or perhaps even the Soviet Union.

But as things were in 1937, Alaska was without any form of defense. "Fewer than 300 soldiers and no other armed military or naval forces of any kind are stationed in the Territory," Dimond said.

> In the event of a foreign assault, the few infantry could do nothing but surrender. Alaska could be taken almost overnight by a hostile force... and once in, that hostile power would have a perfect line of support from the Asian Continent through the Aleutians, and by placing submarines in the principal inlets and bays on the Alaska coast, and by stationing a defensive air force in Alaska, the task of recapturing the Territory would be

tremendous, involving billions of dollars and probably the loss of thousands of lives.[63]

Dimond appreciated the "golden sentiments," "exalted opinions," and "pious gesture[s]" that isolationists and appeasers offered on behalf of "universal and everlasting peace." But "the only thing that restrains the national 'wolves' of the world is fear."[64] Dimond wanted to give potential aggressors something to fear in Alaska.

Dimond cited backing from Alaska's branch of the American Legion. But his claims lacked support among his congressional colleagues. Congress passed its Neutrality Acts, and in the summer of 1937 Japan extended its war against China. At the end of that year, the Chinese civilians of Nanking would experience profound atrocities at the hands of Japanese soldiers.

Articles in influential journals like the *American Mercury* dismissed the possibility of war with Japan. One writer, William Henry Chamberlain, agreed with Dimond that America's western defensive frontier was in Alaska and Hawaii, though he was unable to see why Japan would ever threaten either.[65] Another writer argued that America was impregnable. "From the American Aleutians and Alaska to Hawaii and southwards...to the Pacific Coast and Panama, our fleet has naval and air predominance."[66] The *Weekly Times* published articles pointing to American military superiority over Japan. One graph, for example, showed that U.S. warships amounted to some 288,000 tons as compared to Japan's 94,000.[67] And Father Bernard Hubbard, the "Glacier Priest" who had studied Alaska geography for fifteen years, said that even if Japan invaded the territory, "it would be most ludicrous for them to attempt to use Alaska as a base of operations."[68]

But less rosy titles also appeared in the *Mercury*—"Japan's Secret Navy" and "Japan Takes over the Philippines," for example; and while the Soviet Union had been seen as a possible threat to Alaska from the time of the Bolshevik Revolution of 1917, some now looked on the communist empire with an increasingly wary eye. The Soviets' increased activity in eastern Siberia in the late 1930s was explainable in terms of Russia's longstanding rivalry with Japan, but once those tensions were settled, how might the communists look on their former colony, sold so cheaply to the United States in 1867? The concern was not merely hypothetical: at the time, Russian nationalists were calling for the retrieval of land earlier sold to other nations, a clear reference to Alaska. Delegate Dimond declared himself "almost forced to conclude that the military activity of Russia [in eastern Siberia] has relation to Alaska and not to Japan."[69] Others envisioned a Soviet-Japanese alliance for control of Asia. Senator J. Hamilton Lewis of Illinois surmised that the alliance's first move against the United States would come via Alaska.[70]

Dimond took the podium again in the spring of 1938. He pointed to a map to show that Alaska provided an Asian invader with the surest route to bombardment or invasion of the Pacific Northwest. In an earlier statement, he had recounted the story of Marco Polo's reaction to "the taking of the city of Baghdad by the Tartar prince Alau." (If the United States did not look to the defense of its natural wealth in Alaska, Dimond surmised, "we shall be almost certain to meet the same fate which overtook the Caliph of the great city of ancient times."[71]) On another occasion, Dimond discussed the examples of ancient Persia's King Cyrus, Genghis Khan, and Napoleon.[72] Now he raised the old Greek story of Achilles and wondered if Alaska, "which is just as much a part of the United States as . . . Maine or . . . Texas . . . or California, is not the Achilles heel of our national defense situation."[73]

Again Dimond pointed out that Alaska's only defense could be found in a few hundred soldiers based at Haines. He noted that increasingly Congress and the army recognized the need for greater defenses in Alaska. He asserted that, anywhere else in the world, a region as wealthy in natural resources as Alaska would have been the site of "half a dozen wars."[74] He said that "some of the land-hungry and resource-hungry nations of the world would consider themselves as economic royalists if they had Alaska."[75] How much more natural wealth did Alaska possess when compared to China, with its vast population? How quickly had large parts of China fallen to the Japanese? How much more quickly might the Japanese take portions of a thinly populated Alaska, which was "as lacking in defensive works and facilities as babe in arms." This was "a serious matter for the people of Alaska, and it is 10 times as serious for the people of the United States," Dimond continued, rehearsing his theme:

> for if a hostile foreign power were to get possession of Alaska we would be obliged to then expend in the defense of the main body of the United States more billions of dollars than it would now take millions to install adequate defense works in Alaska, including, first of all, the Army air base.[76]

Dimond wanted an air base capable of accommodating at least a thousand warplanes.

The general response was the same. Longstanding misperceptions of Alaska as a mostly irrelevant block of ice and a bias against projects that could be construed as fiscal "pork" worked against the delegate's efforts.[77] Representative Luecke of Michigan said that the Congress was speaking too much of external affairs and disregarding conditions in the United States, where economic depression prevailed. Luecke said that he did not like "the idea of building a wall of steel around this Nation and have it decay in the center."[78]

Other potential problems vied for congressional attention and resources. In September 1940, Pennsylvania Senator James Davis called his colleagues' attention to the possibility of a German occupation of Canada, followed by the Nazi power's bombing of the American steel industry at Pittsburgh.[79] The prospect of a Nazi attack on Pennsylvania seemed implausible, but so had France's stunning collapse in the face of German strength a few months before.

But Dimond also had allies. In 1937 General William Mitchell, hero of the First World War, all but asserted that Alaska was destined to be attacked, for it was "the most strategic place in the world."[80] The year before the *Weekly Times* had quoted Mitchell as saying that if the Japanese were able to set up operations in an undefended Alaska, they could fly from there, "destroy" New York City, Washington, DC, or Chicago and then return to safety in America's captured final frontier.[81]

While an invasion of Alaska territory might have seemed far off in the late 1930s, Japanese fishing in Alaska waters had been a source of long-standing tension. And as time went by, some doubted that the fishing vessels were strictly devoted to catching seafood. Senator Homer Bone from Washington state claimed that a Japanese vessel supposedly fishing in the Bering Sea was really a navy ship, and it "is reported that that the Japanese have taken very careful soundings of all the Alaska waters."[82] Bone wondered why some congressional "hotheads" were calling for firm American action against Japan in China when America's own sea resources were being jeopardized. Meantime, Dimond raised the specter of incendiary bombs dropped in the forests of the west coast from enemy planes based in Alaska.[83]

Global events forced the issue. In 1939 work began on what would become Fort Wainwright at Fairbanks. Early in the next year, senators from California, Washington state, and Alabama stated their support for the building of another Alaska air base at Anchorage. General George Marshall, the future secretary of state, agreed that the base at Fairbanks was insufficient, and the *Washington Post* criticized members of the House of Representatives who let an admirable commitment to budgetary economy "ride roughshod over [the] vital necessity" of a second air base in Alaska.[84]

President Roosevelt set aside fifty thousand acres near Anchorage for use as an air base. Congress appropriated nearly $13 million to provide for the building of the base.[85] In the summer of 1940, work on Fort Richardson and Elmendorf Field outside Anchorage began. The first on-duty soldiers to come to town since a small detachment had left in 1926 arrived in late June.

For the first time since the beginning, Anchorage boomed. The edition of *Time* magazine published just before the attack at Pearl Harbor reported on the "big job" underway in Alaska. This involved an envisioned string of fortifications from mainland Alaska into the Aleutians—"a 2,000-mile flagstone path toward Asia and a natural rampart bristling with man-made ramparts."[86]

While journalistic opinion in Anchorage had been antiwar, hardly anyone was opposed to the idea of a military base near town. Events had shown that war was probably coming, and so defense was necessary. But, perhaps more importantly in personal conversation, bases meant jobs, population growth, and the creation of local prosperity.

Anchorageites had long sought this. In 1934 the *Weekly Times* editorialized on the importance of building a new city hall with the future in mind, for no other Alaska town held the resources or the promise that Anchorage possessed.[87] Two years later the city's chamber of commerce compiled twenty-two reasons why Anchorage was an ideal site for an air base. The chamber noted the town's access to the sea, its relatively temperate climate, its inaccessibility to large enemy warships, the coal and vegetable supplies from the Matanuska Valley, and, perhaps less plausibly, the absence of mosquitoes and "annoying flies." Anchorage also had geographic advantages, such as a high mountain range to the north that militated against air attack from that direction. Air power based in the city could protect fishing fleets in the north Pacific. And then there was Anchorage's proximity to the harbors and gateways to the interior of Alaska at Seward, Valdez, and Cordova.[88] When they learned that a base was coming to town, some wondered if Anchorage's residents were enthusiastic enough about the new conditions that had been created "almost overnight, by realization at Washington that Alaska holds the key to adequate national defense."[89]

By late 1940 Germany had overrun Poland, Belgium, the Netherlands, Norway, France, and Denmark; the battle for Britain was on; and Japan's grim hold on much of China remained, while countries throughout East Asia were threatened. The United States demanded that Japan leave China and placed a complete embargo on Japan, depriving the nation of scrap metal, fuel, and other resources necessary to modern warfare. Japan correctly saw the United States as the primary block to its ambitions in the Pacific; the United States correctly saw Japan as a threat to its Pacific empire.

Anchorage's newspapers were less hopeful about the possibility of avoiding war. An article in the *Alaskan* offered the thought that "man is, always has been, and always will be predatory." And the *Weekly Times* now saw that the Axis powers, primarily Germany, had "destroyed the illusion in the United States that so great a people can remain indifferent to what goes on in the rest of the world."[90] Meantime, Robert Mills, commander of Anchorage's American Legion post, reminded residents that his organization had long been a "champion of militant Americanism and...an adequate national defense."[91]

Come early December 1941, conflict between the United States and Japan was almost taken for granted. Anchorage's Home Guard units met and drilled in the evenings and put out calls for more volunteers. The local Red Cross made preparations and also appealed for help.[92] The most prominent headline of the December 6 edition of the *Daily Times* declared, "Far East Gets Ready for War with Japan." No one in Anchorage knew that the Japanese operation that supported the attack on the U.S. naval base at Pearl Harbor, Hawaii, was well under way.

On that day, news related to the military and potential war was prominent: the Army Air Corps wanted more men; four ships previously used for Alaska commerce were being drafted into defense work; Japanese diplomats in the United States and Mexico were being called home; and Japanese militarists were reported to have said that war with the United States would mean that "a billion people in east Asia would become bombs." One political cartoon mocked isolationists; another featured a young man in uniform. A small article encouraged people to walk instead of driving, since walking conserved gasoline needed for national defense.

But normal life continued. The Elks club planned to broadcast a memorial service for their deceased members over KFQD. Other programs included songs from the Air Corps Quartet and a Sunday show, "Your Hymns and Mine."[93] The police department advertised for a dogcatcher who "must love dogs and be sober." Koslosky's store advertised potential Christmas gifts—rayon robes, mukluks, shirts, and ties.

At Providence Hospital, Mr. and Mrs. Dan Zivinich welcomed their baby girl of nearly seven pounds into the world. They might have wondered what the future held for their daughter. Perhaps they thought that war might not come. A local newspaper quoted a Japanese government spokesman as saying that his country and the United States should "continue with sincerity to try to find a common formula for a peaceful situation of the Pacific."[94]

It was cold. At noon on Anchorage's last day in the old dispensation, the temperature registered at four degrees Fahrenheit.

CHAPTER SIX

Transition

B Y THE EARLY AFTERNOON of Sunday, December 7, 1941, the people of Anchorage knew that their little world was on the point of change, although they could not know what changes were to come. Soon, some would not like what was happening. "The old Alaska is gone; she's wrecked."[1]

In the years before the Second World War, the nearly eighty Anchorageites who subscribed to *Time* magazine must have noticed that Alaska gained more attention as U.S. relations with Japan deteriorated. In the late summer of 1940, *Time* reported that Alaska, along with Hawaii, was among America's "most important outposts against invasion from the Pacific."[2] Weeks later, another article reflected on Alaska's vulnerability and potential use to Japanese forces intent on bombing American targets. An invader "intending to attack the west coast of the U.S. would find it a great advantage to snaffle Alaska and use it as an advance base for operations by air and sea against the U.S. proper."[3] Titles of scholarly articles published in 1940—"New Air Service to Alaska Follows Line of Hemisphere Defense," "Alaska in Relation to National Defense"—also pointed to a heightened national interest in Alaska, as had the statements of a sophisticated guest in the city who predicted that strategically located Anchorage had a more promising future than any other place in Alaska.[4]

The town had been growing in status for some time. The Army Signal Corps had established its Alaska headquarters there in 1931;[5] by the fall of 1940 weather reports from throughout Alaska were gathered in Anchorage and then passed on to Seattle; and now Anchorage was on the point of becoming the seat of Alaska's third judicial district.[6] Just outside town there were large centers for the army and its air corps. More soldiers were coming to town. Now Anchorage was where military men and civilians linked to defense work were "[s]pending money in large gobs."[7] It was a boomtown, a place of nightclubs, steak joints, and jukeboxes. If it had been true in 1922, as a writer for *Outlook* said, that Alaska's nightlife was as upright as "the most straight-laced New England towns," the observation no longer applied to Anchorage.[8]

The city's rapid growth had begun in 1939. As we have seen, in the U.S. Congress Alaska's delegate Anthony Dimond had been naming Anchorage as a chief site for a military base. Now that war with Japan seemed likely, some moved there in anticipation of the growth to come. In July of 1939 a new weekly newspaper, *The Alaskan*, set up shop, claiming to be nonpartisan and dedicating itself to encouraging the "continued growth and prosperity of Anchorage and of the Territory generally."[9] The new paper called for resident Alaskans to be given the first chance at defense-related work and argued against an ill-fated Congressional proposal to settle European immigrants in the territory.[10]

In June 1915, the editor of the *Cook Inlet Pioneer* had addressed Secretary of the Interior Franklin Lane from "Anchorage, Alaska, a prospective commercial center of importance."[11] Already, the infant town threatened Knik, where merchants felt the need to remind settlers across the Cook Inlet that they were still open for business.[12] In the same year the *Pioneer* said that Anchorage was getting "so big and important...that we can laugh and enjoy the vain efforts of our small rivals."[13] Now, in late 1941, Anchorage really was becoming Alaska's primary economic engine.

Into the late 1930s the towns of the Matanuska Valley seemed far away; the *Anchorage Weekly Times* noted that there was little cooperation between Palmer and Anchorage.[14] Now, the stage was being set for a day when residents of Palmer would make daily commutes into the big city.

Five years before the war, only about 70 miles of roads led cars to and from Anchorage.[15] By war's end, the city would be tied by road with Fairbanks and, indeed, with the Outside via the Alaska–Canada Highway.

In the early days, each person who stepped off a steamer or a train and settled in Anchorage boosted confidence in the community's permanence.[16] The more who came and stayed, the better earlier settlers felt. In that era,

Charles Herron, publisher of the *Anchorage Daily Times*, had offered reflections on the economic value of a military post in Anchorage. He guessed that a fort would bring about three hundred more people to the new town and that this would be "quite an aid to the community."[17] Now Anchorage faced far more than a few hundred newcomers. Already in August 1941, about 3,400 workers—a number slightly less than the city's resident population—had arrived to build Fort Richardson.[18] The year before the United States entered the Second World War, *Alaska Life* magazine surmised that within fifty years Anchorage would be home to twenty thousand people.[19] Within only three years the city and its surroundings hosted some five thousand more than that.[20]

Crowds bring trouble. The housing shortage that this peaceful invasion made inevitable led to soldiers living in tent cities and to homelessness, a rising crime rate, and "slums."[21] In the late summer of 1940 the city's police chief encouraged residents to stop leaving keys in their parked cars. The following year the Salvation Army opened its first Anchorage mission.[22] On the other hand, Anchorage's stores faced the happy Christmastide challenge of meeting a skyrocketing demand for merchandise.[23]

Army truck arriving in Anchorage. Russell Dow Papers, University of Alaska Anchorage, UAA-hmc-0396-14f-713

Downtown Anchorage circa 1940. Anchorage Museum, B01.2.23

In the fall of 1941, the city's army inductees, based at Fort Richardson, were said to have been "busy, happy, comfortable and having as much fun as a bunch of kids on a camping trip." Domestic builders were also happy, as were bartenders, ministers, and civic club leaders. The *Daily Times* noted that the number of liquor establishments in Anchorage had grown with the influx of defense workers but, the paper argued, the city was "far from the dank cesspool of sin some would make it in their thoughtless mouthings." Critics needed also to see the brighter cultural and spiritual side of things, such as the rising number of church attendees and the lodges and clubs that now had more members who could occupy themselves doing good deeds.[24] Anchorage's schools were now the largest in the territory, even without a kindergarten.[25]

When Anchorage was just getting started, local writers penned verses on federal government neglect: "we want to be loved...Sam," wrote one poet, while others noted that Anchorage already was the "government's town."[26] Now, at the end of 1941, there could be no doubt that Anchorage was a government entity—a city born, weaned, nurtured, and fed at the table of the Feds.[27]

Residents of other parts of Alaska—among them farmers associated with the New Deal–sponsored colony in the Matanuska Valley—moved to

Anchorage to take advantage of the economic boom and, in the process, helped to bring the colony experiment there to an end.[28]

Journalists from Outside came to take a look. "Here in the middle of a wilderness is a city, a living exciting city." Anchorage was a place in "breathless" transformation—a place with "plenty of room for expansion"; it was "roaring" and "charging ahead like a steamer plunging down the Yukon."[29] In August 1943, *Time* contrasted "blood-soaked Attu," where more than five hundred Americans died retaking the frigid Aleutian island from the Japanese—with "brisk, modern Anchorage."[30]

The high temperature on December 7 was three degrees Fahrenheit. The sun had risen to a cloudy day at 8:55 a.m., just a few minutes before the attack on faraway Pearl Harbor began. Anchorageites may not have known at precisely what time they heard the news; the clock outside city hall was usually wrong, and in November the city telephone exchange had discontinued announcing the time to callers.[31] But by the time the sun dropped below the horizon again at 2:45 p.m., everyone in town knew war had come.[32] Orville Herning of Wasilla wrote in his diary: "WAR finally on with Japan. This morning Japan bombed Honolulu, Guam, and the Philippines…while talking peace at D.C."[33]

Some were in church when the first announcements were made. Congregants at the 11:00 a.m. Christian Science Church service were listening to a sermon titled "God the Only Cause and Creator." Parishioners at the Church of Christ celebrated the Lord's Supper at 10:45, followed by a message from the pulpit.[34] If the evening services at the Anchorage Gospel Tabernacle and the Praise Chapel Church of God were not cancelled, they must have focused on the themes of duty and sacrifice, or prayer for the nation. Sunday lessons from the Sermon on the Mount must have seemed slightly irrelevant now. From Washington, DC, Alaska Congressional Delegate Anthony Dimond stated his lack of surprise. "If we had done what we should have done years ago in Alaska and established adequate defense Japan would not have attacked," he said. "All we can do now is fight and win."[35]

Within a few hours three hundred Anchorageites had volunteered to guard the city against sabotage. The *Daily Times* cautioned residents to stay out of alleys, where saboteurs might lurk; they were told to freeze in place if a member of the home guard ordered them to halt. Most in the city readily understood the need to conserve electricity and to use telephones only when necessary.[36] General Simon Bolivar Buckner, commander of the Alaska Defense Command, called for all outside lights to be extinguished between 5:00 p.m. and sunrise, when air raids on the city were most likely.[37] Soon Buckner extended those hours.

In its first edition after the United States's entry into the war, the *Alaskan* offered a summary of the city's response. "Anchorage was quick to respond to the emergency brought about last Sunday by Japan's surprise attack," the paper recounted.

> Immediately following the receipt of word that the little brown men of the Orient had launched an offensive against the United States in the Pacific, all local defense and Red Cross disaster units made ready for whatever service the emergency might demand of them. Department heads gathered in the [city] Council chambers for a general conference and while they were deliberating, the Home Guard companies were hurriedly gathering at the Community Building for assignment to posts of duty.[38]

Soldiers marching through Anchorage, "Anchorage" file, Anchorage Museum, B88.53.8

Elsewhere in the same edition, the paper encouraged residents not to feel "down" or to let "the Japs bluff you into losing your grip on the Spirit of Christmas." There was something a little incongruous in that statement, though probably no one noticed at the time.

In the early fall of 1916, the *Daily Times* had reflected on the young town's moral character. Employing the kind of hyperbole common then, the writer insisted that there was not "a more delightful community in which to live than Anchorage on the face of the globe." He wrote that Anchorage's public spaces experienced little "bitterness, less strife, less petty jealousies, less of all things that go to make a bickering, grouchy community." The claim was not that Anchorage was some kind of heaven on earth. But the writer did mean to say that the people of Anchorage "live at peace with one another and that they do pull together in aid and support of the town."[39] Decades later, Anchorageites who had lived in the city before the events of late 1941 remembered it as a friendly place. Everyone knew everyone and shared the hardships that came with their town's remoteness.[40] Disincentives against unnecessary animosity or tension were strong.

Would this spirit of public evenhandedness persist insofar as Anchorage's residents of Japanese birth and descent were concerned? It might have seemed unlikely.

The America into which Anchorage was born had been of mixed minds about a sometimes mysterious and romantic, sometimes sinister and crafty Japan. A story published in Anchorage early in the century about Japan's plans to build a naval base near the Panama Canal was bogus, and in the days following the beginning of this war in the Pacific many false reports would be filed, such as that Japanese planes were flying information-gathering missions over San Francisco.[41] But the anxiety such stories raised in peoples' minds came to the fore on the morning Anchorageites heard that Japanese bombs had fallen on American territory.

Soon after news of the attacks on Hawaii, Guam, and other American holdings arrived in Anchorage, the Kimura family, whose roots in Anchorage reached to the city's first years, penned a short article to be run the following day in the *Daily Times*. "In this hour of crisis of our country with Japan," the message began, "we feel that as loyal Americans we should publicly reaffirm our loyalty to the country of our adoption and of our birth." The notice went on to recount the family's ties to the United States and to Anchorage: Harry had emigrated to the United States twenty-five years before, had served as a cook aboard the *U.S.S. Albany*, and later, along with his wife, had made Anchorage his home. All of the Kimura children had been born in the United States, and their son, George, was a soldier based at Fort Richardson. "We are all 100% Americans," the Kimuras wrote.

> We never have had and have now no connection whatsoever with any person, organization or thing representing Japan or any other foreign country whose policies are opposed to the democratic ideals of the United States. We publicly denounce the attack and invasion by Japanese armed forces upon possessions and territories of the United States today. We all rise and once more pledge allegiance to Our Flag and to the Country for which it stands.

The first names printed beneath the advertisement were hardly foreign to Anchorage's readers: Harry, Frank, George, Louise, and Sam.[42]

The reason the Kimuras felt compelled to run such a public message in a hometown newspaper the day after Japan's attacks seems obvious. As we have seen, hostile sentiment between the United States and Japan had waxed and waned since the late nineteenth century, though it had never been far below the surface. The American and Japanese governments saw one another as territorial and imperial competitors, and therefore as potential enemies; and the two nations possessed conflicting metahistorical narratives—the United States as the agent of a providentially blessed manifest destiny, Japan as the sacred soil of the gods.[43]

Since at least the late nineteenth century, moreover, scholars, politicians, and military leaders had been fixated on "race." This obsession obviously informed Hitler's agenda in Europe, but it played itself out in the Pacific as well. Japanese propaganda centered on ousting the inferior peoples of European origin from Asia. A few weeks after the attacks of early December 1941, the *Times* noted that the internment of American Japanese would unfortunately lump good residents together with potential saboteurs, but "races are involved in this war and special attention must be given to the Japanese."[44] Coincidentally, *Reader's Digest* published an article titled "Japanese Saboteurs in Our Midst" just before the attack on Pearl Harbor.[45] "Japan," the article said, "is ready to hit us hard from the inside."

For several decades before the war, the tensions between Japan and the United States had manifested themselves in both countries' streets, with attacks on property and persons.[46] Now, the Kimuras worried that the kind of stresses that had led to unhappy episodes in San Francisco and Tokyo might manifest themselves on the streets of their small Alaska city.

There was no question that local sentiment, like sentiment nationally, would exhibit a profound antipathy for the Japanese overseas. But whereas in some places on the American and Canadian west coasts feelings of profound ill will were directed against local Japanese, this did not happen in Anchorage. During the Second World War, books had appeared describing Japan's persistent interest in Alaska—its fishing waters, its mineral and metal resources, its potential for military bases. "For years the Alaskans have felt uncomfortably close to Japan," one writer reported, and then leapt to equate the Japanese residential presence in Alaska with espionage.[47] There is no evidence to suggest that the people of Anchorage ever made such a leap insofar as their neighbors of Japanese heritage were concerned.

Anchorage had been founded with Japan in mind. The town's primary purpose had been to serve as a railroad center from which Alaska coal could be delivered to the U.S. Navy, whose mission in the Pacific was all the more important now that the American and Japanese empires were extending their reach.[48] We also know that at the same time, Japanese immigrants helped to build and sustain Anchorage. Early immigrants to Anchorage were named Tasaki, Tanaka, Kamada, Yokota, and Kemota. And where the Japanese families that settled in Anchorage—the Kimuras and the Mikamis—would accomplish enough to provoke animosity, no animosity emerged.

Like Harry Kimura, George Mikami had been the first of his family to arrive in the United States. Initially he settled in Seattle. Family correspondence written decades after the Second World War suggests that George worked for the U.S. Coast Guard and at some point studied English at the University of California at Berkeley.[49] After several years of work, George returned to Japan and married Miné (sometimes written as Minnie), a "liberated" woman who, her daughter Alice remembered, would never voluntarily live again in Japan, where women were "kept down."

In chapter four we met Miné and George's four children: Mary and Alice, born in Seattle; Harry, born in Seward; and Flora, born in Anchorage. Miné insisted that each of the Mikami children take advantage of American opportunity and go to college. She never became completely proficient in spoken English, although a touching letter she wrote to her children in 1949 demonstrates a high level of comfort with the written language. Miné watched, perhaps with some approval, as all but her oldest child Mary lost the ability to speak Japanese, for they mixed easily with other children in Anchorage's schools and neighborhoods. The Mikami children spoke only English with one another.[50] In middle and old age Mary, Harry, and Alice would correspond about their interest in learning Japanese, but only Mary would master it, making its study part of her professional work at Yale University.[51]

Photographs of Miné reveal a diminutive but attractive women, gentle but intense. Alice recalled seeing her mother cry as she read Hugo's *Les Misérables* (in Japanese translation), but also remembered her toughly insisting that her children practice mathematics in summertime while other Anchorage kids played in the Mikamis' own backyard. "You know how the Japanese are."[52] A few years after the war, Miné wrote to her children: "all of you have succeeded in your various pathways of life…far exceeding my expectations [and that] touches me deeply."[53]

Working through the archival materials, the researcher almost hopes for a story about the young Mikamis' heroic success in the face of the animosity they faced from classmates and fellow Anchorageites. But no such animosity is discernible in the record. In photographs published in *The Anchor*, the high school annual, the Mikamis take center stage.[54] Other surviving photos show the Mikami girls, especially Mary and Alice, enjoying time with friends—arm in arm, dressed fashionably, confident, snuggling with non-Japanese boyfriends, one of the gang. In a note to a fellow student, Mary joked about her ability to argue with a teacher, but "only when in a tight fix."[55]

The Mikamis proved correct the claim of some social commentators that American-born Japanese were perfectly capable of assimilating the "ideas, customs, and ideals of America." Each of the Mikami girls married non-Japanese men, also helping to prove untrue a bizarre social Darwinian theory, current in the 1920s, which suggested that Japanese and Westerners could not physically "blend."[56] In 2009, Mary's son, the thoroughly blended Peter Rouse, went to the White House as a senior advisor to President Barack Obama.[57]

Interviewed near the end of the twentieth century, Alice Mikami, who lived in Palmer, could not remember ever being made to feel as if she or her family were outsiders. William Kimura, who had lived in Anchorage in the decades before the war, had the same memory. Sam Kimura said that, until his internment in Idaho as a teenager in 1942, he had "never realized that I was any different from my friends. We shared the same dreams and ideals, admired the great men in American history and hardly gave a thought to my ancestry or physical appearance."

Sam went on to make a telling mistake. "Until World War II," he said, "I had never seen another child of Japanese descent."[58] But surely in so small a community he had seen the Mikamis. This lapse of memory affirms the point: the Japanese physical characteristics he possessed were not the object of attention; he had no reason to seek racial solidarity.

Indeed, surviving records of the Japanese presence in Anchorage in the years 1915–1941 are remarkable, historically speaking, precisely because they are unremarkable. The most compelling story is that there is not much of a story—only evidence of people making their way in life. Through the summer of 1930, Kay Hirano ran advertisements for his Chop Suey and Noodle House at 5th and "C" streets.[59] In the summer of 1937, Harry Kimura was denied a liquor license because he was not a citizen, but, this federal law notwithstanding, he had no sense that the local decks were stacked against him. The following year, he applied to open a restaurant and a "beverage dispensary."[60] By 1941, Frank and George Kimura's business, the Snow White Laundry, employed non-Japanese workers, and the family attended Anchorage's Presbyterian Church, as did the Mikamis. [61]

A clear example of Anchorage's Japanese and non-Japanese residents working together in a voluntary and coordinated way comes from a document written in 1934. Five years into the Great Depression, "members of the local Laundry trade of the District known as Anchorage" petitioned the federal government for assistance. The committee chosen to petition the government comprised seven members, three of them Japanese: George Sazuki, G. S. Sato, and George Mikami. Harry Kimura, not on the committee, signed the petition.[62]

At times mistakes, crimes, and allegations got in the way of personal progress, but here, too, no anti-Japanese bias was discernible. If someone wanted to criticize K. Tanaka for tax delinquency in 1919, they would also have to criticize the two hundred other residents in the same position—from an Anderson to a Nyberg to a Zoecovich.[63] In 1927 a certain T. Tanaka was indicted for selling a pint of whiskey for two dollars. He was convicted but, on appeal, the case was dismissed.[64] George Tanaka, once one of the city's dogcatchers, was arrested in 1930 and imprisoned for selling liquor to Natives. Later, he was sent from prison to the Anchorage hospital for an emergency operation for appendicitis.[65] The *Daily Times* might have taken reports on Tanaka's misadventures as an opportunity to inject a slur into the news, but it did not do so—and it is worth noting that the city had hired Tanaka in the first place. When the *Daily Times* reported Tanaka's death in July 1941, it referred to him only as a "well-known Japanese resident."[66]

A more involved case had arisen in May 1939, when the U.S. attorney in Anchorage, Joseph W. Kehoe, brought a civil suit against Miné Mikami, who owned the Globe Rooms in Anchorage, where Ora Estella Linder lived. The attorney alleged that, with Mikami's knowledge and consent, Linder had used the Globe "for the purposes of lewdness, assignation and prostitution." Mikami denied the charges and, perhaps for lack of evidence, the case was dropped.[67]

By itself, the case does not tell us much, although its aftermath does. Apparently, the Globe Rooms continued to be used for prostitution. The second case against Mikami, and now also against her husband, came in July 1941. This time, Kehoe brought six witnesses against the Mikamis, five of them men. The Mikamis were found guilty of the charges.[68] They left Anchorage feeling the weight of the judgment and, perhaps, the burden of the ongoing financial difficulty that had led them to rent the Globe Rooms in the first place.

In seems that during the Depression the Mikamis' tailor shop had not thrived. In September 1930 George had been listed, with dozens of others, as being delinquent in his taxes. He owed $172.54. He was able to pay fifty dollars immediately. The remainder went unpaid, and Mikami lost property valued at $121 dollars in January of the following year. Of the some fifty tax delinquencies publicly listed along with Mikami's, just two were of higher value.[69] This was the kind of thing Miné Mikami must have had in mind when she wrote to her children in 1949 that she remembered "with great emotion the struggling days of the past with the entire family—and "yet," she continued, "what a happy time that was."[70]

The thing to notice is that the legal proceedings against the Mikamis were not any different from those involving others. And neither economic hardship nor references to the Globe Rooms appear in a short outline of George Mikami's life, written a few weeks after his death in late 1948. Mikami "was all the time emphasizing his 60 years staying in America as his only pride," the Reverend Seizo Abe wrote, "and it was really so."[71]

Before and after the attacks on American territory, Anchorageites knew about anti-Japanese feeling elsewhere on the American west coast. They read about labor groups preparing for "war" with Japanese labor.[72] But in Anchorage, unlike in large western cities like Seattle, there were no Japanese-American tourist bureaus, Japanese churches, Japanese neighborhoods, or Japanese-language schools. No one could seriously say that American culture in Anchorage was jeopardized. And there were no sectors in the economy in which residents of European origin had been displaced by Japanese laborers, as was the case with California agriculture.[73] Anchorage was far removed from the agitations of more settled places where competition for resources or jobs was sometimes pronounced. We know that Anchorage, like Alaska communities generally, had always wanted more settlers.[74] And, given the high number of immigrants in early Anchorage, Japanese accents were in plentiful company. Life in Anchorage had always been challenging, so building and maintaining the community required a relatively easygoing public life combined with a willingness to work hard.

The only existing public statement specifically about Anchorage's Japanese residents in general terms complimented them. The surprising piece was discussed in chapter three but merits a second notice. Published in the *Weekly Times* during the First World War, the article argued that loyalty stemmed from actions not place of birth, and the Japanese living in Anchorage had shown themselves to be first-class Americans.[75]

Given all this, the question arises as to why the Kimura family felt compelled to write an address to the residents of Anchorage, on the day of the attack on Pearl Harbor, with the intent of having it published the following day. Obviously, in the absence of real concern, it seems that there would be little need to expend the time and energy.

A few pieces of evidence point to hostile elements in Anchorage. In January 1939, an angry miner named L. C. Doheny wrote to the secretary of the interior, Harold Ickes. The content of the eight-page letter, which Doheny himself acknowledged was "vitriolic, bitter, and on the fight," is not germane here, except for its last sentence. "I might even be here [in Alaska]," Doheny wrote of his work in the territory, "when the slant eyed Asiatics take over, but I'll be here fighting for this, God's country."[76] The reference clearly points to the mounting tensions in the Pacific, but maybe Doheny, seeing Japanese in Anchorage, felt more threatened.

Or perhaps it was anti-Japanese bias that spurred a civil case against Frank and George Kimura in 1941. On December 30, William and Dorothy Goodman brought a workman's compensation case against the Snow White Laundry. They claimed that Dorothy had been injured on the job and that the Kimuras owed her back wages and compensation for doctor and hospital bills.

The case's timing is curious. Dorothy had recovered in mid-September but had not filed the case until a few weeks after the attacks of December 1941. It is hard not to think that she and her husband hoped to tap into whatever feeling then existed against Anchorage's Japanese. But in April 1942, for unknown reasons, the Goodmans asked for the case to be dismissed.[77] They may have realized that the ill will they hoped would rise against the Kimuras personally would not materialize. Or it may be that the process of internment trumped the case. The thing to notice is that the Kimuras were not railroaded in court. There was no hint here of anti-Japanese hysteria. No other sources, including the Kimuras' own memoirs about the weeks leading up to internment, mention the case.

The one unambiguous statement against local Japanese comes from a letter to the editor of the *Times*. In his note, published on January 20, 1942, Anchorageite John Lentz argued that "the Japs are a race of sneaky, treacherous, backstabbers and are not to be trusted in any capacity."[78] Yet, even here, the bleakness is mitigated, for Lentz was responding to an earlier letter to the *Times* that denounced "the injustice of the treatment of the Japanese in our country.... We complain about the manner in which Americans are being treated in Manila," the earlier writer continued, "[but] what about Seattle and San Francisco?"[79]

One might point to the frequent use of the word "Japs" in the years before the war as indicating bias, but that would be a mistake. The term took on a completely pejorative meaning only with the advent of war. Before then, it was similar to the word "Brits" (for the British)—sometimes meant to be demeaning but often simply a form of shorthand. Japanese in Alaska themselves used the term, such as when M. Terama, writing to a federal judge in Valdez, referred to the "Jap language" and a "Jap boy."[80] In any case, the day after the news of Pearl Harbor, the *Times* opted for the full noun, noting that "the Japanese [had] made their first surprise raids on American life and property."[81] The following day an article on the FBI's rounding up of some residents in Seward was titled "Japanese in Seward Held."[82] Near the end of December 1941, fearing the loss of his Japanese workforce, cannery manager Early Ohmer wrote to Governor Ernest Gruening saying that "[t]he Japs that I have in my cannery are by far the best workers I have," not an obviously derogatory statement.[83]

A few weeks before the attacks in early December 1941, the *Daily Times* published a striking photograph showing a handful of the 350 Japanese Americans who had recently arrived in San Francisco from Japan. The caption read that the kids "just couldn't stop grinning as they realized they were home."[84] The message was indirect but clear: the Japanese *among us* are friends. The point was made again the next day in a *Daily Times* editorial on immigration. It said that America had "a habit of making loyal Americans out of the vast majority of those who come to these shores."[85] The claim was relevant in Anchorage, where young men with names as various as VanZanten, Hicks, Froemke, Welfelt, Thompson, Petroff, Thorgaard, and Kimura had recently been inducted into the army.[86]

The *Daily Times*, reflecting Anchorage's general sentiment, made distinctions. A few days after the U.S. Congress had declared war on Japan, the paper editorialized against the "Yellow Rats" that had struck fear in residents' minds while simultaneously calling for community solidarity. "Being a resident of Anchorage, whether temporary or permanent," the paper noted, "is like membership in a fraternity.... We are together in our present plight and we will face it together and united."[87] Nothing was said to suggest that Anchorage's residents of Japanese heritage were excluded from this outlook.

But, of course, all of Anchorage's residents would not face the war's home front together. In all, 14 Japanese residents of Anchorage and its environs were interned.[88] This included the Kimura family. The Mikami parents had moved to California before the war and were interned from there. When the war began, Mary and Harry Mikami lived on the east coast, while Alice and Flora were married to non-Japanese Americans and, thus, were not required to be interned.[89]

It was more to the spirit of the times than to Anchorage's own residents to which the Kimuras' open declaration of loyalty was directed. But if they really did worry that the community they had lived in so long would now turn on them, their worries were not realized. On their way to internment in the spring of 1942, the Kimura family thanked the "people of Anchorage for their long and faithful patronage and for their kindness and sympathy in these trying times."[90] Frank Kimura reminded the community that Anchorage was where his family's friends were.[91] For its part, the *Daily Times* put on notice "unscrupulous citizens" who might want to take advantage of the "perplexed state of mind of the evacuees."[92]

One needs to read with care reports from Japanese briefly interned at Fort Richardson; one is skeptical when they speak of the temporary camp's "eminently satisfactory" conditions.[93] Yet the claim suggests a lack of open hostility. All of the unhappy memories William Kimura reported of the internment process, such as being "herded into a train . . . at gunpoint," came as the result of policies set by federal authorities. William Kimura reported that the first personal discrimination he faced was in Idaho.[94] And private correspondence from Miné Mikami a few years after the war alludes to an internment camp and friends made there while relating no sense of bitterness. "Worrying does not help in any way," she wrote. "I wish to live my remaining days acknowledging God as my Savior."[95]

Was Anchorage's acceptance of the internment of their neighbors of Japanese descent driven by racial bias? There certainly was a racial component to the *Daily Times*' rationale for supporting internment: "races are involved in this war." Yet the paper, probably representing broad feeling, saw the detainment of Japanese Americans as an unfortunate but understandable wartime measure that certainly would negatively affect the "economy of the sections which have absorbed the Japanese into the system of production." The paper saw that internment would catch within its wide net the "many . . . Orientals [who] are loyal to the United States and would be worthy citizens were citizenship open to them." Indeed, internment would "work hardships on many who [deserved] nothing but the best." Still, the measure needed to be taken "in the best interests of national defense."[96]

Post facto, it is obvious that the federal government's internment policy employed a chainsaw, so to speak, where a scalpel would have done. But this was not obvious in early 1942, and the facts on the ground need to be observed. If there was any anti-Japanese "hysteria" in Anchorage, none of the Japanese living there remembered it.[97] Alice Mikami, who by 1941 had been married to Roland Snodgrass and had lived in Palmer for several years, recounted that even on the day after Pearl Harbor she did not sense any animosity directed against her.[98]

Flora Mikami's experience was similar. A few months after the strike on Pearl Harbor, the University of Alaska published its annual, the *Denali*. Included in the book was a photo of Flora, then a senior, dancing with other students who seemed to be enjoying themselves.[99]

Congressional delegate Anthony Dimond's predictions about what would come to a vulnerable Alaska were partly realized. The Japanese occupied the Aleutian islands of Attu and Kiska; Dutch Harbor was raided from the air. But the Japanese made no attempt to occupy mainland Alaska, just as they would make no attempts to land on the Mexican, American, or Canadian coasts.

In the first weeks of war, it was not possible to know that no attacks would come. Anchorageites blacked out all lights at night so as not to give targets to enemy bombers. Residents who let lights shine, by neglect or accident, heard about it from neighbors. The staff at Providence Hospital were said to have done an especially good job of darkening their windows.[100] On the other hand, and rather surprisingly, lights were seen coming from the homes of army officers.[101]

Authorities reminded Anchorageites not to share military information in letters or conversation:

> There is always plenty to write about in Alaska without repeating rumors or revealing details of civilian defense or military activities.... What the folks back home many not know and what they would like to hear is that Alaskans are playing the game because they know it is worth playing and that they are calm, cheerful, determined, neighborly, and alert.[102]

In the days following the destruction at Pearl Harbor, American warplanes patrolled Anchorage's skies. Upon receipt of word about incoming phantom Japanese planes, boats tied up at the city's docks set sail, hoping to make themselves more difficult targets.[103] Captain Paul E. Stockard of Fort Richardson gave a talk to Anchorage's veterans' organizations on how to handle damage created by incendiary bombs. The city's high school students joined the Red Cross in creating a stretcher corps.[104] Although the world, and along with it the little American outpost of Anchorage, was on the point of dramatic change, everyday life carried on. Merchants advertised, renters rented.

In the wake of the events of early December, crime rates in Anchorage fell thanks, probably, to the heightened vigilance of the citizenry. "Even the drunks are cooperating," a police officer said. But at least one prowler still prowled.[105]

Already by December 15, General Buckner was saying that Anchorage-ites could get back to their normal routines, so long as they remained keen. If the enemy came, they would not be looking to bomb Anchorage, "but this city could serve as a guiding beacon to steer the enemy to our military stronghold."[105] Soon, jokes helped to lighten the mood. Someone contributed an anonymous "rumor" to the *Daily Times*: the U.S. army had recently invented an artillery piece to provide for "Alaskan defense against mosquitoes next spring."[107]

Into the twenty-first century, Anchorage remained an American military stronghold. On any day of the week one could see warplanes in the skies over the city, and service personnel in uniform were so common in town that one failed to notice them.

When Alaska first became a site for the projection of American power, the United States possessed an empire. Whether the United States remained an imperial power in the next century was a matter of debate, usually focusing on the meaning of "empire." But there was no question that from Anchorage, as well as from points in Hawaii, Guam, and other sites, the United States continued to project vast power into the Pacific and beyond.

A study of the city published in 1953 made a claim that remained relevant decades after the Second World War's end:

> Victory over Germany and Japan [in 1945] did not spell retrogression for Anchorage. The city continued to grow. The hot war was traded for the Cold War. New concepts of polar strategy, new technological developments further emphasized Alaska's value in the defense scheme. Uncle Sam was pouring millions upon millions of dollars into the area.[108]

Such had been the dream of many Alaskans in many towns.

Anchorage by 1940. Anchorage Museum, B79.1.156

In the beginning, the *Cook Inlet Pioneer* had commented on the "jealousy" of some in other places in the territory that hoped to strip Anchorage of its potential and promise. Whether other settlements could actually do that might have been an open question before 1941. Not after. From that year, Anchorageites could really say, as their town's first newspaper had said twenty-six years before, that their city was "big and important."[109]

Appendix

T HE FOLLOWING ARTICLES from Alaska newspapers were published mostly in Anchorage's first few years. Their primary purpose is to provide readers with some of the raw materials of history. In the articles, we see people responding to events as they happened. The articles have been lightly edited by the book's author.

Document 1

Many saw Alaska in the broad context of American expansion dating to the early 1600s. In 1914, with the passage of legislation in Washington, DC, providing for the Alaska Railroad, Alaskans set to benefit believed that the settlement and development of Alaska were around the corner. That is this article's key interest. It also describes the kind of people Alaska needed.

Alaska's New Era
The Alaska Citizen (Fairbanks)
October 12, 1914

All history shows that human progress is ever traveling westward. Ancient civilization, such as it was, started in Asia. Then it went westward throughout Europe. Then crossed the Atlantic and took foot in New England. For more than one hundred years, the settlement and development of North America has been slowly working westward, and now the only remaining frontier is Alaska.

This westward movement of civilized humanity which follows the course of the sun is always promoted by men and women of more than ordinary energy and enterprise. It is their superabundant vitality that urges them restlessly to search for greater opportunity in underdeveloped countries such as Alaska.

Until now, the opportunities offered by Alaska to people in the thickly settled sections have been limited practically to a few placer mines of a richness that would make their development possible under adverse conditions. But the new government railroad is the magic wand that is promising to change it all and make of this neglected land a country of almost unlimited opportunities.

One worthy thing promotes another and the new government railroad is certain to be the cause of other important public enterprises. It can be expected that the coal mines that the government will control will be utilized in a hundred different ways to make more available the rich resources of Alaska. There will be power plants from which will radiate feed wires to a thousand industrial undertakings. There will be further railroad extension as population and industry grows. There will be factories that will convert the raw products of the Territory into articles of commerce, and there will be farms and homes and cities where there are now only trees and underbrush and wasted vegetation.

The men who come to Alaska now and take part in its initial development will be the men of local importance a few years hence. Thus the young men of energy will find in Alaska opportunities that, if taken advantage of now, will mean riches and good social standing in time to come.

What we need to do now is to let the world know what Alaska has to offer to the proper kind of people. We want to keep out of Alaska the men who are habitual faultfinders and encourage boosters to come.

Much of Alaska's present population is made up of men who are doing everything in their power to promote the Territory's best interests. It is to be expected that they will attract many others of their kind.

Document 2

Before Anchorage was established, the people of Knik, across the Cook Inlet, hoped to see their own town prosper. Like many towns that boomed and busted in early-twentieth-century Alaska—Dyea and Council, for example—Knik did not thrive. As Nome squelched Council on the Seward Peninsula, so Anchorage overtook Knik.¹

New Conditions
The Knik News
May 1, 1915

The building of the government railway system will bring about a radical change in business conditions. The Knik arm country will manifestly be the chief beneficiary because the larger part of the big appropriation will be expected in construction work in this locality or contiguous thereto. Now that the preliminary work has already begun, so...the process of evolution will keep step with the railway building and the development of the country which will logically follow transportation facilities.

Take, for instance, this little [newspaper]. Since its initial publication, it has been all and more than this settlement warranted, from a business stand-point. It has been operated at a loss since it began publication. But under the changing conditions, a paper of this size will no longer be tolerated. As business expands and increases—as expand and increase it will by leaps and bounds—so too must this paper grow and enlarge—or be left far behind the race for business. And we're going to have competition, too. Before six months shall elapse, there will be a half dozen or so newspapers at various points on the Arm where settlements will spring up with the rapid growth of the proverbial mushroom. We're not any longer going to be "the whole thing" in the newspaper business in this locality.

And what happens to the *News* applies to all other business concerns, big or little, in the Knik arm country. Competition will be keen in all lines. But to offset the competition will be an enormous increase in the volume of business.

So far as the *News* is concerned, it hails with elation the new order of things. We believe it means increased prosperity for all of us. We concede the right of any man to come among us and engage in any legitimate business he...may desire. We who have lived in these parts for many years gain no special privilege because of this fact. The newcomer has as much right as we who came before.

Hence, we should welcome the strangers. Population is the crying need of Alaska.

Document 3

The document below comprises the first editorial about Anchorage published in the new settlement.

Anchorage
Cook Inlet Pioneer (Anchorage)
June 5, 1915

Anchorage, the coal terminal for the Matanuska coalfields, owes its birth and being primarily to the great Alaska government railway project now in course of construction. Anchorage enjoys the distinction of being the starting point of this huge commercial enterprise, which means so much toward the opening of the dormant mining and agricultural resources along its prospective course to the Yukon River.

Anchorage is now little better than a city of tents, although there are several pretentious wood structures. This inchoate state of affairs is due to the fact that the permanent townsite recently selected by agents of the land department, is not available to the public, and will not be in all probability, before another sixty days.

The present status of Anchorage, which reached almost to the limits of a city within a month after the railway work was inaugurated, speaks volumes for the enterprise, faith and abounding activity of the inhabitants. Nearly all lines of business are here represented. Living expenses are not greater than in the coast towns of Alaska.

The permanent townsite is located across Ship creek from the present townsite. It is beautifully situated, with frontage on both the waters of Knik Arm and Ship Creek. Opened to location under proper auspices and conditions, as now seems highly probable, there is no reason to doubt but that Anchorage will evolve into one of the important commercial centers of Alaska. This view is accepted by business and professional men and people generally now living here. Given the coal terminus, and logic and common sense agree that it shall become such, the future of Anchorage is assured.

Document 4

From the late 1800s American strategists were concerned about the possibility of war with Japan. During the First World War, when Japan and the United States were nominal allies, relations improved and many glowing articles on Japan's efforts related to the war appeared in Anchorage's newspapers. Soon after that war, however, old tensions reemerged.

The document below was published the year before the United States entered the First World War. The report about the Japanese purchase of land near the Panama Canal was false, as the writer surmises. The sense of anxiety the article points to, however, was real.

The Japanese Menace
Anchorage Daily Times
August 22, 1916

The dispatches today inform us that the Japanese government has acquired 60,000 acres of land on the Atlantic seaboard, located near the Panama Canal, to be used as a naval base. Japan has no territorial interests in the western hemisphere that demand protection and there can be no logical reason assigned for the acquisition of this naval site other than a design against the interests of the United States.

It is probable that the state department is not unmindful of the activities of Japan and will successfully protest against the carrying out of the plans of the little men of Nippon. It would seem that the acquisition of this naval base would be directly in opposition to the Monroe Doctrine, a well established policy on the part of the United States, and one which the people of the country demand shall be applied in this instance, assuming that the Japanese have in fact acquired the land in question.

Document 5

Some Alaska towns failed. Anchorage eventually grew to unexpected proportions. Other towns succeeded, but not to the extent that their boosters hoped.

Alaska newspapers are full of editorials in which local writers attack other towns. Editorialists in Seward and early Anchorage went at one another. The article below is fairly tame. Another one, published the next year, called Seward a "dirty little cur," and claimed that the people of Anchorage had "a supreme contempt for the activities of the small, disgruntled clique in Seward."[2] Somewhat paradoxically, the article below describes Anchorageites as easygoing. As far as interpersonal relations within the town went, that was mostly true.

Applies to Resurrection Bay
Anchorage Daily Times
September 15, 1916

The Seward Gateway appears to be considerably exercised over the condition of affairs in Anchorage. It takes occasion to say editorially that the town is divided into two separate parts; that factional strifes are bitter, and that altogether the situation here is far from being desirable. These are not the exact words employed, but the meaning is about the same. If our esteemed contemporary would substitute the word "Seward" for "Anchorage" in its article, it would be the strict truth, which all who have ever lived there will agree. As a matter of fact, there is not a more delightful community in which to live than Anchorage on the face of the globe. There is less bitterness, less strife, less petty jealousies, less of all things that go to make a bickering, grouchy community here than in any town we have had occasion to live in or hear about.

We do not mean to say that Anchorage is a heaven on earth or anything of that sort. We do mean to assert that the people here, as a whole, live at peace with one another and that they do pull together in aid and support of the town. One may appreciate this state of affairs more when they have, once upon a time, lived in the Resurrection Bay town.

Document 6

Early twentieth-century Alaskans, or at least the thinkers among them, wanted to know not only how to live in Alaska. They wanted to know what it meant that they lived in Alaska. What were Alaskans like? What was the stuff of Alaskan identity? The article below offers some early Anchorageite thoughts on the topic. The combativeness and factionalism referred to seems to be the kind seen in document 5.

Alaskans Form Type
Anchorage Daily Times
Aug. 23, 1916

Alaskans are said to form a distinct type.... It is just as pronounced as is that of the Southerner, the Westerner or the down-east Yankee. Environments undoubtedly have a great deal to do in forging type. In an earlier stage of embryo civilization, or advanced savagery, the Indian tribes of the North American continent were distinctive according to local climatic and geographical conditions. The Alaskan type carries with it the idea of bigness, of self-confidence, of wide charity, of quickened sympathies, of direct honesty and of impatience with petty conventions and the placing of money value above everything else. The Alaskan is a strong individualist. His opinions are positive and expressed sometimes without regard to that of the other fellow. Hence the bitter factional fights often engendered.

The Alaskan is never of the cringing sort. President Wilson or Roosevelt...could walk the streets of any of the towns of Alaska without creating any more excitement than the arrival of some sourdough from the hills. Indeed, should either one of those persons be making a speech and a miner come to town with news of a new strike the whole crowd would stampede to the mines and forget the existence of the celebrity.

In short, the makeup of the average Alaskan is the characteristic of the country—the pure, free air, not tainted with the city's breath which sweeps over wide distances of mountains and plain, the nearness to nature where wonderful sermons are preached, the close association of dangers which teach confidence and self-reliance, and a wide charity for the poor devil who gets up against it. Everywhere Outside, the term Alaskan is beginning to convey a meaning thoroughly distinctive of a type of empire builders of a large caliber.

Document 7

The following article—actually it is an advertisement—is short but rich. It points to an immigrant's enthusiasm (Z. J. Loussac was a Russian Jew), to a sense of American providentialism, to imperial competition, and to a civil religion that was taken for granted in early-twentieth-century America.

Loussac's Daily Gossip
Anchorage Daily Times
November 29, 1916 (day before Thanksgiving)

For what we have left behind us—
For what we see ahead—
Let us all this day
BE THANKFUL.

The spirit of America in 1916 is the same as the spirit of 1621, the year of our first Thanksgiving—for which let us all be thankful.

From American chimneys come vast clouds of smoke—call them not the palls of gloom—for they are the banners of prosperity.
For this let us all be thankful.

Financial Supremacy, World Commerce, Record prices of our crops and manufactured products, highest wages paid to labor and everywhere the people of our country at work and in peace—all of these make us proud and happy to be Americans. For this last, the greatest of all, let every one of us be everlastingly offering a PRAYER OF THANKSGIVING.

Document 8

A paradox of twentieth-century Alaska, and perhaps still, is that Alaskans liked to think of themselves as great individualists while at the same time relying very much on government. Document 6 makes the point about individualism. The poem below points to the feeling that Alaskans were not sufficiently cared for by an inept or indifferent government. The poem does not rise to the level of litera-ture. It is typical of the kind of verse that appeared frequently in Alaska's news-papers. The Labor News *was Anchorage's short-lived socialist newspaper.*

"The Orphan's Complaint"
Alaska Labor News
December 23, 1916

This land is an orphan kiddie,
Of the group with the star in their flag;

She is looked upon back home as an alien,
Where her treatment makes honest men gag.
She's treated the same as a harlot
Who barters her body for pelf
And carries it home to her master
And's told to look after herself.
Of course, we are an orphan adopted,
When cast off by the great Russian Bear
And our lot's been the lot of an orphan,
And we've had a stage orphan's care.
Our coal land was grabbed by our Uncle,
Our copper and furs by the Jews,
While another gang grabbed all the salmon
And corrupted our natives with booze.
Our Uncle took all our townsites,
Each harbor and naval reserve,
And the water that runs down the hillside
Has been grabbed by statesmen with nerve.
Our gold goes to pay off Sam's taxes
Till there is damn little left here, you bet.
And after the gang gets their rakeoff,
Pray, what does the poor orphan get?
Sam gave us an army commission,
And told it to build us a trail,
But all that he gave was permission,
Same didn't come through with the kale.
Now, that trail in Alaska costs money,
And when Dick tries to get a bill through,
Some jackass from Maine reads his figures
And moves the amount cut in two.
Our Uncle Sam owns all the cables,
And the prices he gets are a sin.
It costs more for a word to Seattle
Than it does from Salt Lake to Berlin.
Our coast lines are rugged and broken
And a menace to all ships that sail;

Yet Sam has no money for coast lights,
They get the same treatment as the trails.
And Alaska is some husky orphan.
We could reach from the Gulf to B.C.
We could stand with one foot in Kansas,
While the other was washed by the sea;
Yet, we have only one voice there in congress
And that one is bereft of a vote
And has to gain their permission,
Ere he loose his protest from his throat.

Document 9

This short article points to at least three themes—the hardship brought to Natives by the advent in Alaska of American society; the concern some non-Natives had for the welfare of Natives facing hardship; and the unity of sentiment created by the First World War.

Natives and World War One
Anchorage Weekly Times
June 13, 1918

The natives of Alaska suffered intensely this winter from cold and hunger, their supply of fish foods being shut off by building canneries in front of or on the streams to which they look for their winter's supply of food. No baby in Belgium or France has suffered more than these untutored sons of Uncle Sam, and none have given to the war cause more patriotically than these. Steps should be taken before next winter to provide for the destitute or there will be many deaths.

Document 10

Where document 4 above points to the anxieties the nation of Japan raised, this article points to the amicable relations that existed in Anchorage between residents of Japanese birth and others. During the First World War this spirit was assisted greatly by the fact that the United States and Japan were nominal allies. The article also provides a little insight into the soldier's experience during the war.

Sons of Japan Living Here Liberal in All Patriotic Movements
Anchorage Weekly Times
August 22, 1918

A man does not necessarily have to be born an American to be a patriot and support movements fostered by the administration. The sons of the Mikado living in Anchorage have been ultra-loyal in purchasing liberty bonds and supporting the Red Cross and other loyal issues that pertain to the war. They realize that Japan as well as America is in the great war fighting against a common enemy.

The bugbear of the yellow peril has proven another myth and dream of the pessimist and today the natives of Japan living in America are considered allies. This is especially true in regard to the young men running the Union Laundry and Bath house in Anchorage. They have subscribed liberally to all causes but particularly to the tobacco fund.

J.G. Shinowara, one of the proprietors, recently sent a liberal consignment of tobacco to the American boys in France and the following is the acknowledgement received on the last steamer:

Written from somewhere in France the writer, Sgt. J.T. Lincoln, of a South Carolina regiment, writes: "Dear Friend: Your liberal donation of tobacco and cigarettes were received this morning and it will be impossible for you to realize how much they were appreciated. The package came just at the right time, for we were all out of real American tobacco, which has no equal. We are at the front now giving the Huns hell, and believe me, they know that Uncle Sam's soldier boys are in this war to win. We are anxious for a chance to try our skill against them in a hand-to-hand engagement and from the report received from our commanding officer this morning the time is not far distant. Things are quite lively in this section of France. The people of this country have taken us in like brothers and you would never know but that we have known each other all of our lives. I am sergeant in a Carolina company but we have boys in our ranks from most every state in the union. The people at home have certainly been thoughtful in sending us many presents, but the good, old American tobacco is the best of all. The boys all join me in thanking you and your friends for your donation, which filled a long-felt want. We would be very glad to receive a letter from you telling us about your far-away country. Again thanking you, I am for Company "C", your well-wisher, Sgt. J. T. Lincon."

Document 11

Anchorage was open to all settlers willing to work hard and be productive. While the topic of the editorial below pertains to immigration policy generally, many Anchorageites would have agreed with the editorial's theme if applied to their town. Immigrants, yes; but not any and all. Well-functioning economies required particular skills and personal attributes.

Immigration
Anchorage Weekly Alaskan
March 30, 1924

A great deal of caustic comment is printed regarding the proposed restrictions of immigration, registration of aliens and the attempt to secure quality rather than quantity of incomers from the old world. Their arguments, boiled down, usually read "America should hold out a welcome to all; the country is big enough for all; we are all sons and daughters of immigrants, immigrants made this country; we need immigrants for labor; to restrict or register is Czaristic, not American."

It is true we are all "sons and daughters" of immigrants; it is true that the immigrants we have had have done much to develop this country. But as times change, so must methods.... When we needed pioneers, farmers, laborers, tillers of the soil, we received the best Europe has to offer. Not often does such an opportunity come; a new country, a new freedom, land for the asking. Of course the yeomanry of Europe seized the chance and the land, came, went west, grew up with the country, helped make America, America.

But today good land cannot be had for the asking. The pioneer days are over. American civilization has grown complicated. It takes more than willing hands and a stout heart to succeed here now. There must be a measure of education as well. Meanwhile, Europe is an impossible place for the diseased, the ignorant, the uneducated, the vicious, to live. The best equipped have none too easy a time; the worst equipped want to get out—out anywhere—but especially "out to America."

We still need, want, and welcome good men and women, who can and do become good Americans. But the time has passed when we can get them only by opening wide the door. The door must be shut, to keep out those who hurt, not help the nation and only put a little ajar for that thinning stream of the best kind of men and women, who are able to take advantage of the modern opportunities of modern America, as their forbearers were able to take advantage of the opportunities of American pioneer days.

Document 11

Like document 10, the one below is concerned with immigration, although the focus is on internal American movement to Alaska. Alaska needed more residents, but of the right kind.

No Room for Job Hunters
Anchorage Daily Times
May 12, 1931

Alaska needs population. Everyone who is at all familiar with Alaska conditions knows that. The last of the nation's wide open spaces are in Alaska and there is room in the territory for many millions of people, with wonderful opportunities for the development of the northland's natural resources.

Residents of the states should know about Alaska; they should be invited to come west and north.... But the invitation of the government should not leave too much to the imagination of those who are attracted by the publicity. Alaska needs young men to take the places of the old pioneers who rapidly are stepping aside as the years render them unable longer to carry on their arduous toil of trailblazing, but that does not mean that the territory will be benefited by opening wide the gates to an influx of uninformed and unprepared fortune seekers who have not been able to make a go of it in the states. Too many of that class already have drifted to Alaska this year because of the unfavorable conditions outside, with the result that Alaskans are finding it increasingly difficult to obtain sufficient employment to maintain themselves through the lean months of the year.

The invitation to "go west and north to Alaska"...should not be directed to those in quest of employment. It should be made plain that there is not enough employment in Alaska to keep permanent residents of the territory regularly employed; the invitation should carry with it a warning to stay away from Alaska unless the desire to come north is backed by a willingness to engage in real pioneering and by sufficient funds to carry on for at least a season in the hills. If any good is to result in...an invasion [of settlers], the invaders should come prepared, just as the stampeders of a generation ago came, with a grubstake and a determination to make good. There are opportunities for such as they. There are lodes and placers awaiting the coming of the prospector; there are agricultural lands which need only the courage and industry of the pioneer homesteader to transform them into productive fields; there are opportunities for capital investment which offer rich returns; there is a vast playground in Alaska for vacationists; there is paradise for sportsmen who delight in big game hunting.

Alaska does not lack opportunities but in its present stage of development there is need of caution in encouraging people to come to the territory. With all its more than half million square miles of area, Alaska is not big enough to take care of an influx of job hunters, and attention should be directed to that fact before the country becomes further over-run with men who are not interested in Alaska beyond obtaining employment to tide them over the dull period in the states.

Document 13

Underpinning the article below is the assumption that Alaska's Natives would benefit from western-style education. The reference to a "vanishing race" seems to be ironic, but alludes to the social Darwinian language that was common at the time. Note the reference to feelings of regret about past treatment of Natives.

Eklutna Industrial School
Anchorage Daily Times
September 25, 1931

A day spent in the Eklutna industrial school cannot fail to impress one with a feeling of gratitude that something worthwhile, even though tardy, is being done by our government, for the remnants of "A Vanishing Race."

Here, [young Natives] are being trained for better things, and already the evidence is manifested in many instances where human derelicts have been made over and started out on a life of usefulness and independence.

Whatever the people of our great commonwealth may have to regret in the treatment of the aboriginal inhabitants of the country in the past, there is at least a measure of satisfaction that this work is being done today in Alaska for a people trained for generations in endurance, rather than independence and industry.

The Eklutna school is truly an Industrial institution, not only equipped with an efficient corps of teachers for the usual study courses, but manual training, domestic sciences, economy, horticulture, agriculture, stock and poultry raising is being stressed, and one has but to see the satin-skinned livestock in the well-kept yards and stalls, and to inspect the flower and vegetable gardens, cannery, workshops and store rooms and see the class of work that is being turned out by the student body, to know that the lessons are being well taught and mastered.

The new school buildings are a credit to the community, and to Alaska as well. Especially interesting is the knowledge of the advantages the school will enjoy when the new dormitory is complete. Instead of the present crowded condition, there will be a separate room for every two girls. Every girl will have her separate bed with its snowy spread and linens, and a large closet fitted with shelves and racks for all personal belongings. The rooms are large, well ventilated, and lighted. The furnishings will consist largely of articles made in the shops by the students and the floors covered by the pretty colorful rugs the girls have made from old clothing and scraps, "that nothing might be wasted" and their new quarters will doubtless be further brightened and individualized by the really splendid needlework, embroidery, table scarves and pillows, work in which many of the other girls have become remarkably proficient.

The students take great pride in their work, but accept praise with a modest and quiet dignity that is refreshing to see.

We were deeply impressed with the manner of the student body when we saw the long rows of dusky heads bowed reverently while they stood by the table, chanting in their musical staccato their "Grace" before meals, and their orderly, praiseworthy manners would do credit to an older and higher civilization as they marched with solemn dignity from the hall at a sign or motion from the matron.

Everything seemed to move along like a piece of new, well-oiled machinery in operation, in this big, well ordered household, but we know that this condition is reached and maintained only through earnest and painstaking effort on the part of the supervisors and teachers, to whom great credit is due.

Mrs. J.S. Truitt,
Edith H. Miller,
Mrs. Winfield Ervin

Document 14

It may surprise Alaskans that Anchorage's newspapers took an almost pacifistic stance as the world's problems of the 1930s accumulated. Anchorage was hardly unique in this respect. Through the 1930s, American opinion was opposed to involvement in another European war.

Problems in the Pacific were less of a national preoccupation through the 1930s, although Alaskans were keenly aware of Japan's growth as a serious potential enemy. Still, the prevailing hope was that war could be avoided.

The article below, which comments on the Spanish Civil War, provides some insight into how Anchorageites saw modern warfare. The memory of the disaster of the First World War was very much in most people's minds. Of course, five years after this article was published, Anchorageites would find themselves involved in the greatest and deadliest war in history.

Civilization Is Menaced by Spanish Savagery
Anchorage Weekly Times
December 26, 1936

The airplane bombings of Madrid ought to make it perfectly clear, by now, that that kind of warfare is an ugly, inhuman, and unrelieved throwback to absolute savagery.

No plea of military necessity can excuse this long-continued bombardment of a populous city. The military mind which demands such measures is the sort of mind that sees in every bed-ridden cripple, every baby in arms, every housewife, and every school child an enemy as important as the soldier at the front.

For it is obvious that when an army showers flame and explosives on a city, as the rebel army has been showering them on Madrid, it is out to break, by any means, the populace's will to resistance.

To that end it can count the murder of an infant, the burning of a hospital full of expectant mothers, or the destruction of a school building and its pupils as an achievement equal to the capture of a trench or the destruction of an airdrome.

It may be that this frightful philosophy can exist only in a bitter civil war, where to the ordinary brutality of war there is added a fierce personal hatred, a bias which makes the opposition look like fiends against whom any form of frightfulness is permissible.

The war in Spain may end in rebel victory, and it may not. That, at the moment, is not the point.

The point is that savagery has been loosed which, if not disavowed and discarded by the conscience of mankind, means the beginnings of the end of European civilization.

But even there the excuse is a poor one. For warfare of this kind is the fruit of a mental attitude which can have no place in a world calling itself civilized. The mere existence of armies and governments which can fight in this way is a threat to the well-being of the entire world.

For a world which fights like this is not civilized. It is on a level with the ancient world in which Assyrian armies put the inhabitants to the sword after capturing a city. The only difference would be that the modern world put them to the sword before capturing the city, not afterward.

Document 15

The following document, discussed and contextualized in chapter six, provides some insight into how well-integrated the Kimura family, of Japanese heritage, had become in Anchorage. While the Kimuras were obviously concerned that sentiment would turn against them following Japan's attacks of December 7, 1941, that did not happen. Yet, like thousands of other Japanese-Americans many in the Kimura family were interned as a result of federal and military policy.

A Message from the Kimura Family
Anchorage Daily Times
December 8, 1941

In this hour of crisis of our country with Japan, we feel that as loyal Americans we should publicly reaffirm our loyalty to the country of our adoption and our birth.

Forty years ago Harry Kimura was an employee of the United States Navy aboard the *U.S.S. Albany.* Twenty-five years ago he came with his wife and small family to Anchorage where he lived and, to a small degree, prospered. It has been his life-long regret that having been born in Japan he is not eligible for United States citizenship. All his children were born in this country and are proud to be its citizens. George Kimura is now a soldier at Fort Richardson.

We are all 100% Americans. We never have had and have now no sympathy for and no connection whatsoever with any person, organization or thing representing Japan or any other foreign country whose policies are opposed to the democratic ideals of the United States. We publicly denounce the attack and invasion by Japanese forces upon the possessions and territories of the United States today. We all rise and once more pledge allegiance to Our Flag and the Country for which it stands.

Harry Y. Kimura
Mrs. Harry Y. Kimura
Frank Kimura
Mrs. Frank Kimura
George Kimura
Mrs. George Kimura
Louise Kimura
Sam Kimura

Document 16

Probably more than any war in American history, the Second World War was won as a result of concerted effort on the part of civilians and military personnel alike. Everyone had his or her part to play. The article below gave Anchorageites some ideas about ways they could aid the war cause.

Good Advice
The Alaskan (Anchorage)
Dec. 19, 1941

Some sound advice came out of the Public Relations office at Fort Richardson this week with regard to writing letters.

There should be avoidance of mention of anything that might be helpful to the enemy or disturbing to the folks at home. Write all the personal news that goes in the peace-time letter but omit all dangerous details. Tell how life goes on in Alaska, how everyone is making ready for normal observance of the Yule season: with stores open, clubs and lodges meeting regularly, schools in regular session and everyone giving enthusiastic support to the home defense program.

The folks back home will be glad to know that nothing has gone out of Alaskan life—that the common emergency has brought a new, vital, determined spirit here just as it has everywhere under the Stars and Stripes.

No loyal Alaskan would think of writing anything that might aid or encourage the enemy, anything that might injure the morale of the men in uniform, anything of a misleading nature that might endanger any Alaskan.

There is always plenty to write about in Alaska without repeating rumors or revealing details of civilian defense or military activities. And besides, what is going on in Alaska these days in the way of defense preparations is very much the same as it is in every American community where there is need of defense preparations.

What the folks back home may not know and what they would like to hear is that Alaskans are playing the game because they know it is worth playing and that they are calm, cheerful, determined, neighborly and alert.

NOTES

Note: *ADT = Anchorage Daily Times, AWT = Anchorage Weekly Times*

INTRODUCTION

1. *The New Encyclopædia Britannica* vol. 1 (Chicago: Encyclopædia Britannica, Inc., 2003), 378; Stephen Haycox, "Anchorage" in *The World Book Encyclopedia* vol. 1 (Chicago: World Book, Inc., 2007), 449–50; Bernard Johnston, editor in chief, *Collier's Encyclopedia* vol. 2 (New York: Macmillan Educational Company, 1988), 176–77; Phyllis D. Carlson, "Anchorage" in *The Encyclopedia Americana* vol. 1 (Danbury, CT: Grolier Incorporated, 1990), 802.
2. Haycox, "Anchorage," 450.
3. The *ADT*, April 4, 1923, refers to "Anchorageites and other Alaskan folks."
4. James Wilford Garner and Henry Cabot Lodge, *The History of the United States* vol. 4 (Philadelphia: John D. Morris and Company, 1906), 1437.
5. Archibald Cary Coolidge, *The United States as a World Power* (New York: The Macmillan Company, 1908), 38, 251. "[I]t must be remembered," Coolidge writes in another passage, "that in the 1867, when Alaska was purchased, most Americans believed that Canada would shortly come into the Union, after which Alaska would cease to be a detached fragment, and become the natural northwestern frontier of the country" (138).
6. Nathaniel Wright Stephenson, *History of the American People* vol. 2 (New York: Charles Scribner's Sons, 1934), 307.
7. Arthur Schlesinger, *Political and Social Growth of the American People, 1865–1940* (New York: Macmillan Company, 1941), 34, 374
8. Samuel Eliot Morison and Henry Steele Commager, *The Growth of the American Republic* vol. 2 (London: Oxford University Press, 1942), 60–61, 316.
9. The American Commonwealth, including, for example, Guam and Puerto Rico, still exists, of course. Some argue that the United States still operates as an imperial power. This book has nothing to say on that question. For an early statement on the U.S. Empire in the time period considered here, see Julius W. Pratt, *America's Colonial Experiment: How the United States Gained, Governed, and In Part Gave Away a Colonial Empire* (New York: Prentice-Hall Inc., 1950).

10. See Pitman B. Potter, "The Nature of American Territorial Expansion," *American Journal of International Law* 15:2 (April 1921), 193, 196, 197.
11. Roger Daniels quoted in Claus-M. Naske, "The Relocation of Alaska's Japanese Residents," *Pacific Northwest Quarterly* (July 1983), 124. The statement is irresponsible because it claims to know too much while taking into account too little. As these pages show, albeit in a limited context, the United States' actual historical experience was much more varied than the quote suggests.
12. Introduction to Stephen W. Haycox, "Racism, Indians and Territorial Politics" in Mary Childers Mangusso and Stephen W. Haycox, eds., *Interpreting Alaska's History: An Anthology* (Seattle University of Washington Press, 1995), 288.

CHAPTER ONE

1. Wilson quoted in the *Charlotte* (North Carolina) *Daily Observer*, March 3, 1914.
2. *Bellingham* (Washington) *Herald*, February 19, 1914.
3. *Grand Forks* (North Dakota) *Daily Herald*, March 22, 1914.
4. Ibid.
5. Ralph S. Tarr, "The Alaska Problem," *North American Review* (January 1912), 40.
6. *Fort Worth Star-Telegram*, August 13, 1914.
7. *Miami Herald*, January 26, 1914.
8. *Aberdeen* (South Dakota) *Daily News*, March 19, 1914.
9. *Fort Worth Star-Telegram*, February 1, 1914.
10. *Charlotte Daily Observer*, January 15, 1914. Also see Ella Higginson, *Alaska: The Great Land* (New York: Macmillan Company, 1926), 308–10.
11. *Fort Worth Star-Telegram*, February 12, 1914; and "Keys to Alaska's Wealth," *Outlook* (June 7, 1913), 267–68.
12. *San Jose* (California) *Mercury News*, January 29, 1914.
13. *Charlotte Daily Observer*, January 15, 1914; *Fort Worth Star-Telegram*, February 1, 1914.
14. Ralph S. Tarr, "The Alaska Problem," *North American Review* (January 1912), 49.
15. Theodore Roosevelt, "The New Nationalism" in Brian MacArthur, ed., *The Penguin Book of Twentieth-Century Speeches* (New York: Penguin Books, 1999), 30.
16. Schlesinger, *Political and Social Growth of the American People*, 375.
17. Morison and Commager, *Growth of the American Republic*, 439.
18. Kenneth Gideon, *Wandering Boy: Alaska—1913–1918* (Fairfax, VA: East Publishing Co., 1967), 33.
19. Frederick L. Hoffman, "The Economic Progress of the United States during the Last Seventy-Five Years," *American Statistical Association* 14: 108 (1914), 306.
20. Ibid., 298, 300, 301, 302, 306.
21. Ibid., 303–4, 310,
22. Ibid., 317.

23. Ibid., 313.

24. Lothrop Stoddard, *Re-Forging America: The Story of Our Nationhood* (New York: Charles Scribner's Sons, 1927), 380.

25. Ernst Troeltsch, *Protestantism and Progress: A Historical Study of the Relation of Protestantism to the Modern World*, trans. W. Montgomery (Boston: Beacon Press, 1958 [repr. 1912]), 206.

26. Woodrow Wilson, *The New Freedom* (Englewood Cliffs, NJ: Prentice-Hall, 1961), 151–52, 160. The papers collected in this volume were originally published serially in 1913.

27. *ADT*, May 7, 1930.

28. Thomas J. Schlereth, *Victorian America: Transformations in Everyday Life* (New York: HarperCollins, 1991), 243–50, 253, 257, 269.

29. C. E. M. Joad, *The Babbit Warren* (New York: Harper Brothers, 1927), *passim*.

30. Sisley Huddleston, *What's Right with America* (Philadelphia: J.B. Lippincott Co., 1930), 241–45.

31. *Fort Worth Star-Telegram*, September 13, 1914.

32. *Forty-Ninth Star* (Anchorage), February 18, 1917.

33. Ibid.

34. *ADT*, August 15, 1930.

35. Samuel P. Orth, *Our Foreigners: A Chronicle of Americans in the Making* (New Haven: Yale University Press, 1921), 33, 34, 35, 37, 42, 45, 65, 122, 124, 139, 168, 176, 178, 179, 182.

36. Angus Hamilton et al., *Korea: Its History, Its People, and Its Commerce* (Boston and Tokyo: J. B. Millet Company, 1910), 173, 178.

37. Isabel Ambler Gilman, *Alaskaland: A Curious Contradiction* (New York: Alice Harriman Company, 1914), 103. On a similar theme, some argued against making contraception available, since a declining birthrate among Americans would lead to "race suicide." See *Alaska Labor News* (Anchorage) February 10, 1917.

38. Winthrop Talbot, ed., *Americanization: Principles of Americanism, Essentials of Americanization, Technic of Race-Assimilation* (New York: H.W. Wilson Company, 1917), 141, 145.

39. Apparently because of melting due to climate change, the Native village of New-tok, Alaska, is threatened. In May 2007 a scheme was underway to move the village. In the course of the conversation about this scheme, the Newtok tribal administrator said: "The federal government, they're the ones who came into our lives and took away some of our values. They came in and said, 'You aren't civilized. We're going to educate you." See *Anchorage Daily News*, June 3, 2007.

40. Pitman B. Potter, "The Nature of American Territorial Expansion," *American Journal of International Law* 15:2 (April 1921), 195–96.

41. Diamond Jenness, "The Eskimos of Alaska: A Study in the Effect of Civilization," *Geographical Review* 5:2 (February 1918), quotations on 98, 100.

42. Stoddard, *Re-Forging America*, 258.

43. Orth, *Our Foreigners*, 46.

44. See, for example, Ellsworth Faris, "The Mental Capacity of Savages," *American Journal of Sociology* 23:5 (March 1918), 603–19.

45. Talbot, *Americanization*, 157, 162.

46. "The Mastery of the Far East," *North American Review* (July 1919), 135.

47. See J. B. Bury, "Progress in the Light of Evolution" in *The Idea of Progress* (New York: Dover Publications, 1932).

48. *Knik News*, May 1, 1915.

49. *Forty-Ninth Star*, February 11, 1917.

50. Phebe A. Hanaford, *Daughters of America; or, Women of the Century* (Augusta, ME: True and Company, 1882), 21.

51. Ibid., 55, 186, 698.

52. Benson Lossing, *Eminent Americans* (New York: John B. Alden, 1890), 333, 384, 418, 443.

53. Frederick Houk Law, *Modern Great Americans* (New York: The Century Company, 1926), 6.

54. *ADT*, May 12, 1930.

55. Ibid., July 3, 1930.

56. See, for example, Walter McDougall, *Let the Sea Make a Noise: Four Hundred Years of Cataclysm, Conquest, War and Folly in the North Pacific* (New York: Avon Books, 1993), 383–611; and Jean Heffer, *The United States and the Pacific: History of a Frontier* trans. W. Donald Wilson (Notre Dame, IN: University of Notre Dame Press, 2002), 219–47.

57. Hearn quoted in Christopher Benfey, *The Great Wave: Gilded Age Misfits, Japanese Eccentrics, and the Opening of Japan* (New York: Random House, 2003), 260.

58. Ernest Samuels, ed., *The Education of Henry Adams* (Boston: Houghton Mifflin Company, 1973 [repr., 1918]), 463.

59. See William Bruce Wheeler and Susan D. Becker, *Discovering the American Past: A Look at the Evidence*, vol. 2 (Boston: Houghton Mifflin, 1998), 115.

60. See Preston Jones, *Empire's Edge: American Society in Nome Alaska, 1898–1934* (Fairbanks: University of Alaska Press, 2007), 13.

61. Lafcadio Hearn, *Glimpses of Unfamiliar Japan*, vol. I (Boston: Houghton Mifflin Company, 1894), vii.

62. Grace A. Hill, "Along the Alaska Coast," *Overland Monthly and Out West Magazine* (September 1917), 10.

63. Otis Cary, *Japan and Its Regeneration* (New York: Student Volunteer Movement, 1904), 123.

64. "Japan's Proposed Entry into Siberia—An Invasion or a Rescue?" *Current Opinion* (April 1918), 234.

65. Basil Hall Chamberlain, *Things Japanese* (London: John Murray, 1902), 9.

66. Galen M. Fisher, *Creative Forces in Japan* (West Medford, MA: Missionary Education Movement of the United States and Canada, 1923), 218.
67. *San Jose Mercury News*, July, 29, 1906.
68. Ibid., September 18, 1906.
69. Orth, *Our Foreigners*, 203–4.
70. Bigelow quoted in Benfey, *Great Wave*, 270.
71. *AWT*, March 13, 1936. (Hereafter AWT)
72. Roosevelt quoted in McDougall, *Let the Sea Make a Noise*, 448. On Roosevelt and judo, see Benfey, *Great Wave*, 239–40.
73. AWT, January 3, 1936.
74. The point is made by Archibald Cary Coolidge, *The United States as a World Power* (New York: The Macmillan Company, 1908), 361.
75. Kiyoshi K. Kawakami, *American-Japanese Relations: An Inside View of Japan's Policies and Purposes* (New York: Fleming H. Revell Company, 1912), 14.
76. McDougall, *Let the Sea Make a Noise*, 391–95, 396, 426–28, 452, 455; and Benfey, *Great Wave*, 243, 255
77. Hoffman, "Economic Progress of the United States," 299.
78. McDougall, *Let the Sea Make a Noise*, 480.
79. Kevin Starr, *Embattled Dreams: California in War and Peace, 1940–1950* (Oxford: University Press, 2002), 42.
80. *Dallas Morning News*, November 19, 1904; and *Bellingham Herald*, November 22, 1905.
81. *ADT*, May 22, 1930.
82. McDougall, *Let the Sea Make a Noise*, 479.
83. Kawakami, *American-Japanese Relations*, 13.
84. "The Week Reviewed," *Barron's*, April 21, 1924.
85. Kawakami, *American-Japanese Relations*, 214–17.
86. Hamilton, *Korea: Its History, Its People, and Its Commerce* (Boston and Tokyo: J. B. Millet Company, 1910), 159, 170, 172, 173, 174.
87. "The Mastery of the Far East," *North American Review* (July 1919), 135.
88. James S. Gale, *Korean Sketches* (Nashville: Publishing House of the Methodist Episcopal Church South, 1898), 195, 196, 199.
89. Henry Chung, *The Case of Korea* (London: Fleming H. Revell Company, 1921), 226.
90. See, for example, Gwen Dew, "Horrors in Hong Kong," *The American Mercury* (November 1942), 559–63.
91. Cynthia Rose, ed., *American Decades: Primary Sources, 1910–1919* (Detroit: The Gale Group, 2004), 313; and Cynthia Rose, ed., *American Decades: Primary Sources, 1920–1929* (Detroit: The Gale Group, 2004), 265.
92. *The State* (South Carolina), January 1, 1914. This article claims that 43 blacks and 1 white were lynched in 1913. In 1921, the *Charlotte Sunday Observer* (January 1) claimed that 64 Americans had been lynched the previous year.

93. *AWT*, January 24, 1918.

94. See, for example, *ADT*, September 30, October 1, October 14, 1930.

95. *AWT*, July 2, 30, 1936.

96. In the *AWT*, January 4, 1918, is a rare very reference to an African American woman in Anchorage. Anna West had been arrested and imprisoned for violating the city's prohibition law.

97. On Buckner, see Terrance Cole, "Jim Crow in Alaska: The Passage of the Equal Rights Act of 1945," *Western Historical Quarterly* 23:4 (November 1992), 437–38. Also see Charles Hendricks, "Race Relations and the Contributions of Minority Troops in Alaska: A Challenge to the Status Quo?" in Fern Chandonnet, ed., *Alaska at War, 1941–1945: The Forgotten War Remembered* (Fairbanks: University of Alaska Press, 2008). Hendricks sees a complicated picture. Buckner said many appalling things about Natives and African Americans, but he also helped to create "an atmosphere comparatively conducive to the success of. . . the African-American soldiers" working for the Alaska Defense Command (287).

98. Banks quoted in Outten Jones Clinard, *Japan's Influence on American Naval Power* (Berkeley: University of California Press, 1947), 4.

99. See Jones, *Empire's Edge*, 83–91.

100. *Forty-Ninth Star*, June 21, 1917.

101. *Weekly Alaskan* (Anchorge) May 13, 1916.

102. Gilman, *Alaskaland*, 105, 107.

103. *Philadelphia Inquirer*, February 4, 1914. The pronoun beginning the third sentence is referring specifically of the Philippines, but the logic of the article applies it to all possessions then in American control.

104. Vreeland cited in *San Jose Mercury News*, January 29, 1914.

105. Jones, *Empire's Edge*, 48.

106. *Bellingham Herald*, October 30, 1906.

107. *The State*, April 17, 1910.

108. Ibid.

109. McDougall, *Let the Sea Make a Noise*, 427.

110. Schlereth, *Victorian America*, 243.

111. *ADT*, August 23, 1916.

INTERLUDE: NATURE

1. Anya Sostek, "Low budget trip to Juneau turns out to be capital idea," *Arkansas Democrat Gazette* January 27, 2008.

2. Joe Mitchell Chapple, "Discovering Alaska with President Harding," *McClure's Magazine* (October 1923), 8–26.

3. Ernest Gruening, "Colonialism in Alaska," *Current History* (December 1955), 349.

4. Grace A. Hill, "Along the Alaska Coast," *Overland Monthly and Out West Magazine* (September 1917), 6–17.
5. *AWT*, June 18 and 25, 1936.
6. *ADT*, August 15, 1930; September 4, 1930.
7. Ibid., July 10, 1930.
8. See the advertisement in *Forest and Stream* (September 1929), 693.
9. *ADT*, May 19, 1931.
10. Ibid., July 31, 1930.
11. *Anchorage Weekly Alaskan*, November 4, 1923.
12. *ADT*, July 28, 1930.
13. Ibid., July 25, 1930.
14. Ibid., April 3, 1931.
15. Ibid., April 3 and 4, 1931.
16. Ibid., September 3, 1930.
17. Mary Lee Davis, *Uncle Sam's Attic: The Intimate Story of Alaska* (Boston: W.A. Wilde Co., 1930), 2, 4, 14.

CHAPTER TWO

1. "Self-Government for Alaska," *Outlook* (June 15, 1912), 320.
2. "An Alaska Programme," *Nation* (January 1, 1914), 7.
3. "Developing the Nation's Treasure House in Alaska," *Current Opinion* (February 1914), 95.
4. William Harding Carter, "Public Opinion and Defense," *North American Review* (August 1916), 203–4.
5. George E. Chamberlain, "The Future of Alaska," *Independent* (March 16, 1914), 373.
6. "A United World," *Outlook* (July 27, 1912), 684.
7. William C. Redfield, "Rebuilding Our Foreign Trade" *Forum* (January 1919), 36.
8. *Philadelphia Inquirer*, December 23, 1915. See Katharine Carson Crittenden, *Get Mears! Frederick Mears: Builder of the Alaska Railroad* (Portland, OR: Binford and Mort Publishing, 2002), chapters 3–7; and Elizabeth Tower, *Anchorage: From Its Humble Origins as a Railroad Construction Camp* (Fairbanks: Epicenter Press, 1999), 28.
9. Crittenden, *Get Mears*, 51.
10. Ibid., 73, 76.
11. "Alaska's Resources Neglected," *Independent* (August 21, 1913), 425.
12. "Railroads for Alaska," *Independent* (January 26, 1914), 116. One Navy admiral was reported to have said that tests from the Matanuska fields had been "surprisingly successful" and this seemed to "assure an adequate supply of fuel on the Pacific coast." See "A Review of the World," *Current Opinion* (January 1915), 2.
13. *Knik News*, April 10, 1915.

14. Harry Albert Austin, "The United States Unprepared for War," *Forum* (April 1914), 534; and Edward Lyell Fox, "Menaces to American Peace," *McBride's Magazine* (November 1915), 108.
15. Carrington Weems, "Government Railroads in Alaska," *North American Review* (April 1914), 574.
16. Daniels quoted in Clinard, *Japan's Influence on American Naval Power*, 110.
17. Wilson quoted in Clinard, ibid., 111.
18. *Philadelphia Inquirer*, December 17, 1915.
19. Humphrey quoted in Clinard, *Japan's Influence on American Naval Power*, 111.
20. Albert Johnson, "Government Railroad in Alaska—An Inevitable Step" (Washington: Government Printing Office, 1914), 3.
21. Lyman A. Cotton, "Our Naval Problem," *North American Review* (March 1917), 371.
22. Alice V. Morrill, "Alaska—The Coming Country," *Herald of Gospel Liberty* (February 11, 1915), 172.
23. *Miami Herald*, April 12, 1915.
24. *Knik News*, January 9, 1915. In the issue of March 6, 1915, the *News* reported on Japanese warships operating in the South Pacific.
25. See, for example, *Knik News*, April 10, 1915.
26. *Weekly Alaskan*, May 13, 1916.
27. *Forty-Ninth Star* July 23, 1916.
28. *Knik News*, March 6 and 27, 1915.
29. *Cook Inlet Pioneer*, June 26, 1915.
30. Tower, *Anchorage*, 29. The lots were sold at auction and none sold for less than $75. See Crittenden, *Get Mears*, 92.
31. *Cook Inlet Pioneer*, June 19, 1915.
32. Ibid., June 12, 1915.
33. *Manatee* (Florida) *River Journal*, September 2, 1915.
34. *Philadelphia Inquirer*, July 24, 1915.
35. *San Jose Mercury News*, November 28, 1915; and *Philadelphia Inquirer*, December 23, 1915.
36. Federal Commissioners of Conciliation to Frederick Mears, May 2, 1916, "Labor-Wages" file, Records of the Alaska Railroad, Accession no. 322-69-0966, box 63, National Archives and Records Administration, Pacific-Alaska Region (Anchorage). Hereafter NARA-PAR.
37. Memo dated March 26, 1917, "Regulations for Anchorage Townsite" file, Records of the Alaska Railroad, Accession no. 322-69-0966, box 63, NARA-PAR.
38. *Knik News*, January 9, 1915.
39. See, for example, *Manatee River Journal*, September 2, 1915; *Evening News* (San Jose, California), December 30, 1915; and *Belleville* (Illinois) *News Democrat*, February 3, 1916.

40. *Philadelphia Inquirer*, December, 23, 1915.

41. Memos dated February 19 and April 14, 1917, "Regulations for Anchorage Townsite" file, Records of the Alaska Railroad, Accession no. 322-69-0966, box 63, NARA-PAR.

42. Undated memo draft in "Regulations for Anchorage Townsite" file, Records of the Alaska Railroad, Accession no. 322-69-0966, box 63, NARA-PAR.

43. Tower, *Anchorage*, 54.

44. "Uncle Sam's Newest Town," *Outlook* (October 25, 1916), 458.

45. *Miami Herald Record*, January 8, 1916.

46. Ibid.

47. Anchorage High School, *The Anchor* (1925), 30.

48. Andrieus Jones to A. Christensen, January 29, 1916, "Forfeiture of City Lots (Selling Liquor)" file, Record Group 322, Records of the Alaska Railroad, Accession no. 322-69-0966, box 64, NARA-PAR; *Knik News* April 10, 1915.

49. *Evening News*, November 17, 1915 and January 29, 1916.

50. Ibid., November 24, 1915.

51. Letter from Clay Tallman, January 3, 1917, "Forfeiture of City Lots (Selling Liquor)" file, Record Group 322, Records of the Alaska Railroad, Accession no. 322-69-0966, box 64, NARA-PAR.

52. U.S.A. vs. One Hundred and Ninety Packages of Whiskey, Beer, Alcohol, Wine, Cider, and Alcoholic Extracts, U.S. District Courts Alaska (Anchorage), Civil Case Files, 1915–1960, box 3, case no. A00075, NARA-PAR.

53. Letter to C. R. Arundel, January 16, 1917, "Coal Land Investigations" file, Records of the Alaska Railroad, Accession no. 322-69-0966, box 65, NARA-PAR.

54. Letter to Mr. Christensen, July 2, 1917, "Public School" file, Records of the Alaska Railroad, Accession no. 322-69-0966, box 64, NARA-PAR.

55. Gideon, *Wandering Boy*, 33.

56. Franklin K. Lane, "Freeing Alaska from Red-Tape," *North American Review* (June 1915), 892.

57. William H. Wilson, "The Urban Frontier in the North" in *Interpreting Alaska's History*, eds. Mangusso and Haycox, 249.

58. Governor Strong called on the city's residents to come up with a name with "more significance and local associations." A vote was held in the summer of 1915, 535 votes were cast, and the highest number, 146, went to Alaska City. The name of Anchorage received 101 votes. The city's Chamber of Commerce passed a resolution in favor of Alaska City, which Christensen also preferred. Mears and Lane were against the change, partly because some businessmen thought the name Anchorage had taken hold. Other options were Matanuska (54 votes), Ship Creek (48), Winalaska (18), Gateway (10), Terminal (16), Homestead (9), and Lane (129). See "Resolution to Change Name of Anchorage, 1915" file, Records of the Alaska Rail-

road, accession no. 322-69-0966, box 67, NARA-PAR. For a brief time, Anchorage was referred to as "the Anchorage." See *Knik News*, May 1, 1915.

59. *Cook Inlet Pioneer*, July 17, 1915.

60. "San Francisco," *Banker's Magazine* (September 1915), 347.

61. *Forty-Ninth Star*, January 21, 1917.

62. Weems, "Government Railroads in Alaska," 575; *Knik News*, May 1, 1915.

63. Crittenden, *Get Mears*, 60, 79.

64. See the letterhead in the file "Alaska Bureau, Seattle Chamber of Commerce, 1915–1916," Record Group 322, Records of the Alaska Railroad, Accession no. 322-69-0966, box 63, NARA-PAR.

65. Ibid., unsigned letter dated January 6, 1916.

66. "Seattle's Important Position," *Banker's Magazine* (September 1915), 3.

67. Crittenden, *Get Mears*, 61.

68. "Seattle Commercial Club," *Banker's Magazine* (September 1915), 333.

69. *Bellingham* (Washington) *Herald*, August 10, 1915.

70. *Knik News*, January 9, 1915.

71. Letter to Frederick Mears, May 29, 1917, "Public School" file, Records of the Alaska Railroad, Accession no. 322-69-0966, box 64, NARA-PAR.

72. Ibid., letter to Lowman and Hanford Company, January 11, 1917; *Cook Inlet Pioneer* June 5, 1915.

73. *Anchorage Weekly Alaskan*, November 4, 1923.

74. *Forty-Ninth Star*, July 30, 1916.

75. For formal documents on this scheme, see *Alaska Panhandle: Its Proposed Cession to Canada* (Washington, DC: Judd and Detweiler, 1915).

76. Forty-Ninth Star, December 10, 1916. Seattle's importance in the Alaskan economy has been an enduring theme. Nearly a century after Anchorage's founding a journalist called Alaska and Washington "symbiotically linked states" and an Alaska state senator denounced Washington legislation that added costs to Alaskan commerce an "act of aggression from our southern neighbor." See the *Anchorage Daily News*, June 5, 2007.

77. *Manatee River Journal*, September 23, 1915; and *Bellingham Herald*, August 31, 1915.

78. *Miami Herald*, November 4, 1915.

79. Letter to A. Christensen, May 23, 1917; and letter to Falcon Joslin, June 7, 1917, "Public School" file. In this file see the letters of application from the women referred to.

80. *Anchorage City Directory* (1917), 2; *Forty-Ninth Star*, February 18, 1917.

81. *Miami Herald*, November 4, 1915.

82. *Forty-Ninth Star*, January 28, 1917.

83. William B. Stephenson, *The Land of Tomorrow* (New York: George H. Doran Company, 1919), 202.

84. "Employee Info." File, Records of the Alaska Railroad.

85. See, for example, *Alaska Labor News*, December 23, 1916.

86. *Anchorage City Directory*, 7, 10, 11, 41, 42, 43, 60.

87. Records of the District Courts of the United States, District of Alaska, Third Division, Anchorage, Alaska. Petitions for Naturalization, May 5, 1916–September 14, 1920, volume 1, box 1, NARA-PAR.

88. Ibid., petition date: September 18, 1917.

89. Ibid., petition date: June 9, 1916.

90. *Anchorage City Directory*, 42, 43, 67, 74, 82.

91. *Cook Inlet Pioneer*, June 12, 1915.

92. *Alaska Labor News*, October 14, 1916.

93. Ibid., December 13, 1916; and January 13, 1917. See the photo that captures the U.S. Restaurant in Claus-M. Naske and L. J. Rowinski, *Anchorage: A Pictorial History* (Norfolk: The Donning Company, 1981), 41.

94. *Anchorage City Directory* (1921), 27.

95. Gideon, *Wandering Boy*, 38.

96. Ibid., 32.

97. The nicknames are given in Wilson, "Urban Frontier," 253; and Gideon, *Wandering Boy*, 37.

98. *Forty-Ninth Star*, July 30, 1916.

99. Ibid., January 28, 1917.

100. *Alaska Labor News*, January 13, 1917.

101. Stephenson, "The Cities of the Far North" in *Land of Tomorrow*, 205–6.

102. See the photographs in Naske and Rowinski, *Anchorage*, 47, 58, 66, 70, 71, 80, 81; Ann Chandonnet, *Anchorage: Early Photographs of the Great Land* (Whitehorse, Yukon: Wolf Creek Books, 2000), 60, 64; John Stromeyer, *Historic Anchorage: An Illustrated History* (San Antonio: Historical Publishing Company, 2001), 12, 21; and Tower, *Anchorage*, 27, 61.

103. *Alaska Labor News*, December 23, 1916.

104. *Forty-Ninth Star*, September 24, 1916.

105. Ibid., February 18, 1917.

106. "Alaska's New Railway," *National Geographic* (December 1915), 567, 574.

107. *Forty-Ninth Star*, November 19, 1916.

108. Ibid., July 9, 1916.

109. U.S.A. v. A.D. Sweet, District Court Records, Alaska, Anchorage Criminal Case Files, record group 21, file 719, NARA-PAR.

110. C. H. Sheets to Andrew Christensen, February 17, 1917, Records of the Alaska Railroad, record group 322, box 66, file "public school," NARA-PAR.

111. H. W. Nagley vs. Johann Bartels and L. D. Ellexson, U.S. District Courts Alaska (Anchorage), Civil Case Files, 1915–1960, box 1, case no. A00001, NARA-PAR.

112. Peter Boudreau vs. Alaska Labor Union, U.S. District Courts Alaska (Anchorage), Civil Case Files, 1915–1960, box 2, case no. 32, NARA-PAR.

113. Mitchell Weisberg vs. H. Seidenverg, U.S. District Courts Alaska (Anchorage), Civil Case Files, 1915–1960, box 4, case no. A00077, NARA-PAR.

114. Margaret Hilda Bell vs. Fred Schiller Bell, U.S. District Courts Alaska (Anchorage), Civil Case Files, 1915–1960, box 1, case no. A00011, NARA-PAR.

115. Anna Gleason vs. George Gleason, U.S. District Courts Alaska (Anchorage), Civil Case Files, 1915–1960, box 1, case no. A00016, NARA-PAR.

116. Estella R. Sherman vs. William A. Sherman, U.S. District Courts Alaska (Anchorage), Civil Case Files, 1915–1960, box 2, no. A00035, NARA-PAR.

117. Hulda Victoria Lathrop vs. Robert Bloomfield Lathrop, U.S. District Courts Alaska (Anchorage), Civil Case Files, 1915–1960, box 1, case no. A00019, NARA-PAR.

118. Olga McCullough vs. Fred D. McCullough, U.S. District Courts Alaska (Anchorage), Civil Case Files, 1915–1960, box 1, case no. A00023, NARA-PAR.

119. Anna E. Ashton vs. Wright Ashton, U.S. District Courts Alaska (Anchorage), Civil Case Files, 1915–1960, box 2, case no. A00027, NARA-PAR.

120. Margaret L. Agnew vs. Benjamin E. Agnew; Clara Viola Foreman vs. Virgil R. Foreman, U.S. District Courts Alaska (Anchorage), Civil Case Files, 1915–1960, box 2, case nos. A00030 and A00031, NARA-PAR.

121. Collin Murray vs. Mercy Roxanne Murray, U.S. District Courts Alaska (Anchorage), Civil Case Files, 1915–1960, box 1, case no. A00006, NARA-PAR.

122. George Bray vs. Rosalie Bray, U.S. District Courts Alaska (Anchorage), Civil Case Files, 1915–1960, box 2, case no. A00042, NARA-PAR.

123. John E. Steen vs. Sade Katherine Steen, U.S. District Courts Alaska (Anchorage), Civil Case Files, 1915–1960, box 2, case no. A00043, NARA-PAR.

INTERLUDE: SOCIALISM

1. Gerig to Edes, May 7, 1919, "Personnel" file, Records of the Alaska Railroad, accession no. 322-69-0966, box 68, NARA-PAR).

2. Ibid., James Wilkinson to William Gerig, May 13, 1919.

3. *Alaska Labor News*, November 11, 1916.

4. Ibid., October 21, 1916.

5. *Forty-Ninth Star*, October 1, 1916.

6. Ibid., November 12, 1916.

7. Ibid., October 8, 1916.

8. *Alaska Labor News*, November 18, 1916.

9. Ibid., September 30, 1916. In its October 7, 1916 edition, the *Labor News* called Marx the "world's greatest political economist."

10. Ibid., October 7, 1916.

11. Ibid., December 9, 1916.

12. Ibid., October 14, 1916.

13. Ibid., October 14, 1916. On November 4, 1916, the *Labor News* declared: "Can we recall the list of republican and democratic presidents and governors of states, who have ordered or sanctioned the use of soldiers to kill our brother workers, and still believe they are out friends?"

14. Lena Morrow Lewis to Christensen, June 9, 1917, "Public School" file, Records of the Alaska Railroad, accession no. 322-69-0966, box 66; and *Alaska Labor News*, November 18, 1916, NARA-PAR.

15. Christensen to Richard Campbell, April 23, 1917, "Public School" file, Records of the Alaska Railroad, accession no. 322-69-0966, box 66, NARA-PAR.

16. *Forty-Ninth Star*, November 12, 1916. In Alaska's third division, the votes for delegate were as follows: Republican (Wickersham) 1965; Democrat (Sulzer) 1680; Socialist (Lewis) 488. See *Alaska Labor News*, January 6, 1917.

17. Sherman Rogers, "The Problems of Alaska's Government," *Outlook* (January 24, 1923), 172. Rogers writes on Alaska generally but his comments hold for Anchorage.

18. For comments on Harding's brief stop in Anchorage and for the general economic equality that existed in Alaska, see Chapple, "Discovering Alaska with President Harding," 22.

19. *Forty-Ninth Star*, October 29, 1916.

20. Mangusso and Haycox, *Interpreting Alaska's History*, 288.

CHAPTER THREE

1. See Alan Bishop and Mark Bostridge, eds., *Letters from a Lost Generation: First World War Letters of Vera Brittain and Four Friends* (Boston: Northeastern University Press, 1998). For example, after a battle Vera Brittain wrote: "The loss of life seems to have been terrible, and the result not worth it, which is worst of all" (106).

2. T. C. Carlson to Helen Van Campen, April 17, 1917, Helen Van Campen Photo Album, University of Alaska Fairbanks archives.

3. *Weekly Alaskan*, May 13, 1916.

4. *Forty-Ninth Star*, January 28, 1917.

5. *AWT*, October 3, 1917.

6. John Barton Payne, "Go North, Young Man!" *Independent* (September 18, 1920), 330.

7. *Knik News*, January 9, 1915; *Alaska Labor News*, February 10, 1917.

8. *Evening News* (San Jose, CA), March 15, 1917; *Grand Forks* (North Dakota) *Herald*, August 10, 1917; and *San Jose* (California) *Mercury Herald*, September 9, 1917.

9. A. W. Greeley, *Handbook of Alaska: Its Resources, Products, and Attractions* (New York: Charles Scribner's Sons, 1925), 105; *Fifteenth Census of the United States: 1930; Outlying Territories and Possessions* (Washington, DC: Government Printing Office, 1932), 8.

10. Thomas Riggs, *Report of the Governor of Alaska* (1918), 7.

11. *Charlotte* (North Carolina) *Daily Observer*, November 15, 1914.

12. *The State* (Columbia, South Carolina), July 31, 1917.

13. *AWT*, April 11, 1918.

14. See, for example, *Philadelphia Inquirer* February 4, 1914. This was a major preoccupation of the U.S. military in the early twentieth century. See Brian McAllister, *Guardians of Empire: The U.S. Army and the Pacific, 1902–1940* (Chapel Hill: University of North Carolina Press, 1997). After the First World War, American strategists opposed independence for the Philippines on the grounds that Japan would soon move in and colonize those islands. See *ADT*, May 17, 1919. For speculation on Japanese designs on Hawaii, see *AWT*, August 18, 1919.

15. Stephenson, *Land of Tomorrow*, 210–15.

16. Lyman A. Cotten, "Our Naval Problem," *North American Review* (March 1917), 370.

17. *AWT*, January 10, 1918; *San Jose Mercury News*, July 20, 1918.

18. Walter R. Borneman, *Alaska: Saga of the Bold Land* (New York: HarperCollins, 2003), 265.

19. *San Jose Mercury News*, July 29, 1918. The article reads that the draft and higher wages had "gradually made impossible the obtaining of experienced men as waiters in the mess hall and lunch room, and after fruitless efforts to maintain the service with elderly men and boys, recourse was finally had to the employment of women."

20. *The State* (Columbia, South Carolina), April 21, 1918; and *Alaska Weekly Times*, November 18, 1917.

21. Riggs, *Report*, 9.

22. *AWT*, January 17, 1918.

23. Ibid., November 22, 1917; October 3, 1918.

24. Ibid., August 15, 1918.

25. *Forty-Ninth Star*, February 11, 1917.

26. *Alaska Labor News*, April 14, 1917.

27. *AWT*, January 24, 1918.

28. *Philadelphia Inquirer*, April 8, 1917.

29. *Grand Forks* (North Dakota) *Herald*, July 31, 1918; Borneman, *Alaska*, 234 and 290; and Stephen Haycox, *Alaska: An American Colony* (Seattle: University of Washington Press, 2002), 241–42.

30. *San Jose Mercury News*, August 30, 1918.

31. *AWT*, September 26, 1918.

32. Riggs, *Report*, 77.

33. *San Jose Mercury News*, October 29, 1918.

34. The *AWT* reported that German-language newspapers in Canada came under pressure to stop their presses (October 31, 1918).

35. Anti-immigrant sentiment in wartime also seemed largely absent in Nome. See Jones, *Empire's Edge*, 79–83. For a typical textbook narrative see, for example, William Bruce Wheeler and Susan D. Becker, *Discovering the American Past: A Look at the Evidence* (New York: Houghton Mifflin Company, 1998), 132–58. There we read, for example, that the German American conductor of the Boston Symphony Orchestra needed a police escort for security when he conducted a concert in New York in 1918 (151).

36. *ADT*, August 13, 1919.

37. Selective Service System, WWI, Records Related to Delinquents and Deserters, 1918–1919, "Final Lists of Delinquents and Deserters—Alaska" file, Record Group 163, box 1, 1–48, NARA-PAR.

38. *ADT*, May 16 and August 13, 1919.

39. *Alaska Weekly Times*, October 3, 1917.

40. Ibid., January 24, 1918.

41. United States vs. Sula Makala, Records of the U.S. District Court, Fourth Division, Iditarod Alaska, Criminal Case Files, 1910–1924, record group 21, box 4, case no. 58, NARA-PAR.

42. Selective Service System, WWI, Records Related to Delinquents and Deserters, 1918–1919, Record Group 163, box 1, "Delinquent Classification List," NARA-PAR.

43. Ibid., "Final Lists of Delinquents and Deserters—Alaska" file, Record Group 163, box 1, 14, NARA-PAR; and *ADT*, January 6, 1919.

44. *ADT*, November 1, 1917.

45. *AWT*, February 28 and July 11, 1918.

46. Ibid., January 31, 1918; June 6 and 13, 1918.

47. Ibid., April 11 and June 13, 1918.

48. Ibid., June 13, 1918.

49. Ibid., April 11 and July 4, 1918. In the January 4, 1918 edition of the *Weekly Times*, Anchorageites read about Anna West, an African American who had been arrested and imprisoned for violating the city's prohibition law. The article focused on her crime, not her color.

50. *ADT*, May 10, 1919.

51. *AWT*, August 22, 1918.

52. Ibid., September 12, 1917.

53. *Alaska Labor News*, March 24 and April 7, 21, and 28, 1917.

54. Ibid., April 7, 1917.

55. *AWT*, November 1, 1917.

56. *ADT*, May 24, 1919.

57. *AWT*, January 31, 1918.

58. Ibid., February 21, 1918.

59. Ibid., May 16, 1918; October 3, 1918.

60. Ibid., October 10, 1918.

61. *San Jose Mercury News*, November 11, 1918.

62. *AWT*, May 30, 1918.

63. Anchorage criminal case files, 1902–1960 (no. 716–743), file no. 726; record group 21 (U.S. district courts), box 38, NARA-PAR.

64. Ibid.

65. *ADT*, November 24, 1916.

66. Ibid., July 11, 1919.

67. *Cook Inlet Pioneer*, June 5, 1915.

68. See the U.S. wartime propaganda reproduced in Wheeler, *Discovering the American Past*, 145–48.

69. *AWT*, June 6, 1918.

70. Ibid., July 4, 1918.

71. Ibid., September 5, 1918.

72. Ibid., May 8, 1919.

73. Ibid., October 17, 1918.

74. Ibid., November 21, 1918.

75. Ibid., April 18, 1918.

76. Ibid., June 27, 1918.

77. Ibid., September 12, 1917.

78. Ibid., November 8, 1917.

79. Ibid., April 4, 1918.

80. Ibid., March 21, 1918. German women were required to register in August. See Ibid., August 8, 1918.

81. Ibid., April 4, 1918.

82. Ibid., November 18, 1917.

83. Ibid., March 28, 1918.

84. Ibid., April 4, 1918.

85. Ibid., February 7, 1918.

86. Ibid., September 5, 1917.

87. Ibid., April 11 and July 25, 1918.

88. Ibid., February 21, 1918.

89. Ibid., November 8, 1917.

90. Ibid., January 31, 1918.

91. "Labor Mass Meeting" (unsigned record of labor meeting at Labor Temple, Anchorage, August 7, 1918), "Wages," file, Records of the Alaska Railroad, accession no. 322-69-0966, box 68, NARA-PAR.

92. Evangeline Atwood, *Anchorage: All-American City* (Portland, OR: Binfords and Mort, 1957), 15, 16.

93. *AWT*, January 24, 1918.

94. Ibid., February 28, 1918.

95. Ibid., December 26, 1918.

96. *Philadelphia Inquirer*, September 22, 1918.

97. *Anchorage Weekly Times*, February 14, 1918.

98. *ADT*, May 19, 1919.

99. *San Jose Mercury Herald*, October 27, 1918.

100. *AWT*, March 21, 1918.

101. Ibid., March 21, 1918.

102. *Grand Forks* (North Dakota) *Herald*, April 4, 1918; *San Jose Mercury Herald*, April 7, 1918; and the *Miami Herald*, April 8, 1918.

103. Selective Service System, WWI, "List of Men Ordered to Report," Record Group 163, box 71, Anchorage file 1 of 3, NARA-PAR; and *San Jose Mercury News*, July 20, 1918.

104. *AWT*, December 19, 1918.

105. Ibid., June 27, 1918.

106. *ADT*, August 8 1918; January 3, 1919.

107. Ibid., August 1, 1919.

108. *AWT*, July 25, 1918.

109. Ibid., November 28, 1918.

110. *ADT*, February 14, 1918; and May 24 and July 30, 1919.

111. *AWT*, June 20, 1918.

112. *ADT*, May 14, 1919.

113. *San Jose Mercury News*, November 30, 1918.

114. *AWT*, August 1, 1918; and *Alaska Daily Times*, July 30, 1919.

115. AWT, January 17 and February 28, 1918.

116. *Anchorage Weekly Alaskan*, June, 8, 1924.

117. Ron Inouye, interviewer and editor, "Alaska's Japanese Pioneers Research Project" (1991), unpublished manuscript, Archives and Special Collections, University of Alaska Anchorage.

INTERLUDE: Z. J. LOUSSAC

1. *Alaskan*, December 11, 1941.

2. Atwood, *Anchorage*, 12, 14, 15.

3. *ADT*, July 7, 1916.

4. Ibid., September 15, 1916.

5. Atwood, *Anchorage*, 93–94.

CHAPTER FOUR

1. Atwood, *Anchorage*, 25.

2. James A. Wood, "Alaska and Its Future," *Christian Science Monitor*, July 5, 1923.

3. C. E. Hagie, "Alaska—the Land Few People Know," *Overland Monthly and Out West Magazine* (June 1929), 175.

4. "Building Conditions on the Pacific Coast," *American Architect* (May 11, 1921), 572.

5. Wilds P. Richardson, "Alaska," *Atlantic Monthly* (January 1928), 111, 113.

6. "The Advance of Alaska," *Outlook* (October 19, 1921), 244; Sherman Rogers, "The Heart of Alaska," *Outlook* (December 20, 1922), 705.

7. Christensen, letter to the editor, *Time* (May 20, 1935); http://www.time.com (accessed November 12, 2009).

8. Atwood, *Anchorage*, 22.

9. Wood, "Alaska and Its Future."

10. *ADT*, July 10, 1930.

11. Atwood, *Anchorage*, 12.

12. *AWT*, March 6, 1936; Atwood, *Anchorage*, 72.

13. W. B. Greeley, "Alaska—The Last of the Frontier," *Outlook* (February 1, 1922), 180; "Why Alaska is Being Rapidly Depopulated," *Current Opinion* (March 1922), 408–9.

14. Atwood, *Anchorage*, 74.

15. Chapple, "Discovering Alaska with President Harding," 16.

16. Atwood, *Anchorage*, 80.

17. Rogers, "Heart of Alaska," 704.

18. See the advertisement in *Forest and Stream* (June 1927), 322.

19. Philip Laing, William Stolt, Eugene C. Smith, Sidonia M. Gill, letters to the editor, *Time* (April 29, 1935); http://www.time.com (accessed November 12, 2009).

20. Atwood, *Anchorage*, 77.

21. *ADT*, April 10, 1931.

22. *AWT*, November 6, 1936.

23. Ibid.

24. Atwood, *Anchorage*, 31, 81–2.

25. Anchorage, Alaska, City Council Minutes, January 19, 1938, vol. 4, 41, Anchorage Municipal Library (hereafter AML); *AWT*, November 27 and December 11, 1936.

26. *AWT*, October 16, 1936.

27. Anchorage, Alaska, City Council Minutes, December 15, 1937, vol. 4, 24, AML.

28. *Alaskan*, July 14, July 21, 1939; January 12, May 10, 1940.

29. *AWT*, May 21, 1936.

30. Ibid., May 14, 1936.

31. *Cook Inlet Pioneer*, July 24, 1915.

32. Ibid.

33. Ibid., June 26, 1915.

34. Ibid., July 17, 1915.

35. Ibid., June 26, 1915.

36. Ibid., June 5, 1915.

37. Ibid., June 19, 1915.

38. Minutes of the First Regular Meeting of the City Council of the City of Anchorage, Alaska, December 1, 1920–February 9, 1921, 1–18, AML.

39. Ibid., June 1, 1921, 48.

40. *Alaska Labor News*, February 10, 1917.

41. *AWT*, November 15, 1917.

42. Stephenson, *Land of Tomorrow*, 205.

43. Atwood, *Anchorage*, 29, 71, 75, 115–17.

44. *AWT*, February 7, 1936.

45. Ibid., March 27, 1936.

46. *ADT*, February 21, 1931.

47. Ibid., April 27, 1931.

48. Ibid., April 29, 1931

49. *AWT*, 25, 1925.

50. Ibid., May 4 and August 4, 1931; *AWT*, March 13, 1936

51. Anchorage, Alaska, City Council Minutes, June 16, 1937, vol. 3, 371; and December 15, 1937, vol. 4, 23, AML.

52. *AWT*, March 13, 1936.

53. *ADT*, October 16, 1930 and April 6 and 7, 1931.

54. Ibid., July 19 and 25, 1930 and April 23, 1931.

55. Franklin Lane to Chairman of the Alaska Engineering Commission, December 28, 1916, "Public School" file, Records of the Alaska Railroad, accession no. 322-69-0966, box 66, NARA-PAR.

56. Frederick Mears to Ula Thompson; and Mears to William Edes, December 17, 1917, "Public School" file, Records of the Alaska Railroad, accession no. 322-69-0966, box 66, NARA-PAR.

57. *ADT*, November 17, 1930.

58. Ibid., November 20, 1930.

59. *AWT*, October 2, 1936.

60. Christensen to Kuney, June 14, 1917, "Public School" file, Records of the Alaska Railroad, accession no. 322-69-0966, box 66, NARA-PAR.

61. Memo to Christensen, October 25, 1917, "Public School" file, Records of the Alaska Railroad, accession no. 322-69-0966, box 66, NARA-PAR.

62. Christensen to Watts, July 25, 1917; and Christensen to B. H. Barndollar, January 31, 1918, "Public School" file, Records of the Alaska Railroad, accession no. 322-69-0966, box 66, NARA-PAR.

63. Manager (Christensen) to Mears, November 24, 1917, "Public School" file, Records of the Alaska Railroad, accession no. 322-69-0966, box 66, NARA-PAR.

64. Undated memo from T. R. McAnally; and unsigned memo to Christensen, September 1, 1917, "Public School" file, Records of the Alaska Railroad, accession no. 322-69-0966, box 66, NARA-PAR.

65. Anchorage school, *The Anchor* (1917), 3.

66. Ibid., (1917), 22; and 1925, 41.

67. Ibid., (1917), 6.

68. Ibid., 9.

69. Ibid, (1925), 12–15.

70. Ibid.

71. Schlereth, *Victorian America*, 249.

72. Department of Education (Territory of Alaska), *Report of the Commissioner of Education: School Biennium Ended June 30, 1932*, 32.

73. Ibid., 21; Schlereth, *Victorian America*, 249.

74. Atwood, *Anchorage*, 6.

75. Rogers, "Problems of Alaska's Government," 172.

76. *ADT*, October 11, 1930.

77. Naske, "Relocation of Alaska's Japanese Residents," 126.

78. Chapple, "Discovering Alaska with President Harding," 16, 22.

79. Petitions for Naturalization, August 16, 1916–September 14, 1920, Records of the District Courts of the United States, District of Alaska, Third Division, volume 1, box 1, NARA-PAR.

80. Ibid.

81. Ibid.

82. *Report of the Commissioner . . . 1934*, 67.

83. "A Petition for Providing High Schools in the Territory of Alaska," Records of the Alaska Railroad, record group 322, box 65, file "schools—general."

84. See notes from Mrs. Osier in "Public School" file, Records of the Alaska Railroad, accession no. 322-69-0966, box 66, NARA-PAR.

85. Louise D. Gill, Anchorage High School Memorabilia Collection, University of Alaska, Anchorage, Archives (hereafter UAA).

86. Johanson-Erickson Family Collection, part 1, box 1, UAA.

87. *Report of the Commissioner . . . 1932*, 31.

88. Ibid., 32.

89. Johanson-Erickson Family Collection, series 4, box 7, UAA.

90. *Report of the Commissioner . . . 1921 . . . 1922*, 5.

91. See, for example, the class history given in *The Anchor*, 1934, 18.

92. *Congressional Record*, vol. 81, pt. 3, 1st session, 75th congress (1937), 2799.

93. W. J. Lewis to Commissioner of the General Land Office, April 21, 1916, Records of the Alaska Railroad, record group 322, box 65, folder "coal land investigations," NARA-PAR. Emphasis in the original.

94. *Report of the Commissioner. . .1921. . .1922*, 5.

95. *Report of the Commissioner. . .1932*, 31.

96. *The Anchor*, 1925, 48.

97. Ibid., 13.

98. *ADT*, May 22, 1931.

99. Ibid., January 4, 1919; February 10, 1923.

100. Alaska Agricultural College and School of Mines, *Farthest-North Collegian* (April 1934). For an overview of Mikami's biography in Alaska, see Preston Jones, "The Woman behind the Man behind the President," *Fairbanks News-Miner*, August 30, 2009.

101. Copy of Senator Murkowski's speech, October 1, 1999, made available to me by Rachel Lease, Administrative Assistant, Department of Anthropology and Council on Archaeological Studies, Yale University.

102. See, for example, *The Anchor*, 1931, 28; 1936, 4; and the John Bagoy Collection, "Pioneer Anchorage Families," file, photograph number B96.32.66, AM.

103. Mikami family photographs in possession of the author.

104. Copy of *The Anchor*, (1935),17. (Only available copy held by AM.)

105. Louise Gill Collection, High School Remembrance Book and draft of "Last Will and Testament of the Class of '30," UAA.

106. Alice Mikami's family name by marriage is Snodgrass. For the sake of clarity I cite here only her maiden name.

107. Harry Mikami to Alice Snodgrass, April 12, 1976; private collection. Copy in possession of the author. Mikami wrote that his father rarely talked about his personal history.

108. Raymond Leslie Buell, "Again the Yellow Peril," *Foreign Affairs* (December 1923), 299. Italics in the original.

109. "Population is the crying need of Alaska," claimed the *Knik News*, May 1, 1915.

110. Department of Commerce, Bureau of the Census, Fifteenth Census of the United States: 1929; population—Alaska, Anchorage, sheet number 51.

111. Atwood, *Anchorage*, 24. The author has deleted a comma between the adjectives in the quote.

112. *The Anchor* (1937).

113. *AWT*, April 23, 1936.

114. *ADT*, June 11, 1936.

115. Atwood, *Anchorage*, 93.

116. *ADT*, August 2 and 23; September 27; October 19, 1930; April 4, 1931.

117. Ibid., June 27, 1930.

118. Ibid., April 4, 1931.

119. Ibid., October 28, 1930.

120. Ibid., September 27 and October 19, 1930.

121. Ibid., May 10 and 14, 1930.

122. Ibid., October 24, 1930.

123. Ibid., August 5, 1930 and September 11, 1931; *AWT,* November 20, 1936; *Alaskan,* November 15, 1940.

124. *ADT,* January 3, 1919.

125. Ibid., April 10, 1931; AWT, November 6, 1936.

126. Ibid., February 11, 1931.

127. Ibid., May 2, 1931.

128. A challenge being that we must rely overwhelmingly on written sources from non-Natives. This section extends the argument made in Preston Jones, "Yankees in Parkas: Native Influence at Nome, 1900–1920" in *Alaska History,* 20:2 (Fall 2005), 43–58.

129. Donald Craig Mitchell's *Sold American: The Story of Alaska Natives and Their Land, 1867–1959* (Hanover, NH: University Press of New England) says nothing, so far as the author has determined, about Natives living in Anchorage before the Second World War. One Native reports that in Anchorage before the war there were "[l]ots of Natives working." See James Kari and James A. Fall, eds., *Shem Pete's Alaska: The Territory of the Upper Cook Inlet Dena'ina* (Anchorage: Alaska Native Language Center; University of Alaska and the CIRI Foundation, 2003), 335.

130. *AWT,* March 13, 1936.

131. "Living in Anchorage—Natives 1934," Alaska Village Census, record group 75, folder 1306-07, NARA-PAR.

132. U.S. Department of Commerce, Bureau of the Census, Fifteenth Census of the United States: 1930; Outlying Territories and Possessions (Washington, DC: Government Printing Office, 1932), 25.

133. See Kari and Fall, *Shem Pete's Alaska,* 330, 332. For an overview of this topic, see Maria Shaa Tláa Williams, ed., *The Alaska Native Reader: History, Culture, Politics* (Durham, NC: Duke University Press, 2009), 163–64.

134. *ADT,* January 2, 1931.

135. Ibid., May 11, 1931.

136. David Gove, "Educating the Alaska Natives," *Overland Monthly and Out West Magazine* (March 1917), 17.

137. *ADT,* September 25, 1931; and November 4, 1931.

138. "The Advance of Alaska," *Outlook* (October 19, 1921), 244.

139. *AWT,* May 30, 1918.

140. Ibid., June 13, 1918. To what use the hair would be put, the article does not say.

141. Sherman Rogers, "Alaska, the Misunderstood," *Outlook* (December 6, 1922), 608.

142. *AWT,* November 13, 1936.

143. Davis, *Uncle Sam's Attic,* 14, 40.

144. *Knik News,* May 1, 1914.

145. *AWT,* May 21, 1936.

146. Ibid., June 4, 1936.
147. Anchorage Police Department Activity report Book from October 15, 1935 to April 11, 1938. Photocopy of original held at AML.
148. Seller family folder, Bureau of Indian Affairs, Alaska Medical Service; record group 75, box 2, village census roles, 1935–1972, file 1306-07, NARA-PAR.
149. *Cook Inlet Pioneer*, July 24, 1915.
150. *ADT*, May 29, 1931; August 8, 1931; Alaskan, May 10, 1940
151. *ADT*, April 4, 1931; September 2, 1931.
152. *Alaskan*, January 12, 1940.
153. *AWT*, March 13, 1936.
154. In *Anchorage*, Evangeline Atwood notes that events at the Fur Rendezvous included Eskimo dances, along with boxing, hockey, basketball and other events (103).
155. Hagie, "Alaska—the Land Few People Know," 176.
156. Cornelius Osgood, "Tanaina Culture," *American Anthropologist* 35:4 (1933), 696, 704.
157. For commentary on this theme, see *ADT*, November 7, 1916.
158. On the topic of language loss, see the short article about efforts against Native language at Kotzebue, *AWT*, July 4, 1918. For an example of a rather hysterical and misleading overview, see Alan Boraas, "Alaska must deal with its racist past," *Anchorage Daily News*, August 21, 2009. Professor Boraas writes that "Alaska in general and Anchorage in particular have a long history of racism." The writer asked him to provide evidence for this claim for the period 1915–1941. He did not do so.
159. *Daily Miner* (Ketchikan), November 4, 1907.
160. Rogers, "Alaska, the Misunderstood," 608.
161. On this, and for other examples of bias, see Cole, "Jim Crow in Alaska," 429–49.
162. North Construction Company to Miss Rose Walsh, May 10, 1948, available at www.alaskcool.org/projects/JimCrow/cov_res.htm (accessed January 20, 2010).
163. On the Fourth of July competitions, see the *Cook Inlet Pioneer*, July 10, 1915; Kari and Fall, *Shem Pete's Alaska*, 335–6.
164. *AWT*, February 21, 1925. For background, see Stephen W. Haycox, "Racism, Indians and Territorial Politics," in Mangusso and Haycox, *Interpreting Alaska's History*.
165. *Alaska Legislature: Roster of Members, 1913–2000* (Juneau: State of Alaska, 2000), 5–17.
166. *ADT*, November 3, 1930.
167. *AWT*, September 10, 1936.
168. Ibid., September 3, 1936.
169. Ibid., January 24, 1936.
170. Ibid., October 9 and 16, 1936.

171. Ibid., November 13, 1936. As if anticipating the wartime friendliness of Russia and the United States, Ray McDonald, manager of Anchorage's radio station, KFQD, recommended a statue of Peter the Great. See the *AWT,* November 27, 1936.
172. Ibid., October 2, 1936.
173. Ibid., January 17, 1936.
174. Ibid., May 21, 1936.
175. Ibid., January 3, 1936.
176. Ibid., November 27, 1936.
177. Ibid., February 21, 1936
178. "Alaskans Want Refugees to Settle in Wheatfields," *Christian Science Monitor,* February 1, 1923.
179. *Anchorage Weekly News*, March 20, 1936.
180. Ibid., March 20, 1936.
181. See the discussion in Jones, *Empire's Edge,* 112–13. Whereas some anti-Semitic language was found in sources related to early Nome, none was found related to early Anchorage, save perhaps the reference in the poem reproduced in the appendix and published originally in the *Alaska Labor News,* December 23, 1916.
182. Atwood, *Anchorage,* 111, 112, 115.
183. Ibid., 107.

CHAPTER 5

1. Minutes of the City Council of Anchorage, November 26, 1930, AML.
2. Correspondence between Alice, Harry, and Mary Mikami. Private collection; copies in possession of the author.
3. *ADT,* August 13; November 8, 1930
4. Ibid., April 4 and May 2, 1931.
5. See, for example, Ibid., May 4, 1931
6. Ibid., August 1, 4 and 8, 1931
7. Ibid., August 6, 1931.
8. Ibid., September 18, 1931.
9. Ibid., August 8 and September 19, 1931.
10. Ibid., July 8, 1930; July 7, November 3 and 14, 1931.
11. Ibid., May 22, 1930.
12. Ibid., September 22, 1931.
13. *AWT,* January 3, 1936.
14. *ADT,* April 27, 1931.
15. Ibid., September 18, 1931.
16. Ibid., August 8 and September 4, 1931.
17. Ibid., September 19, 1931.
18. Ibid., May 6, 1931.

19. Ibid., March 13, 1931.
20. Ibid., September 19, 1930.
21. Ibid., May 19, 1930.
22. Ibid., October 2, 1930.
23. Ibid., October 9, 1930
24. Ibid., November 24, 1930.
25. Ibid., April 10, 1931.
26. Ibid., May 21, 1931.
27. Ibid., May 18, 1931.
28. Ibid., April 23 and September 22, 1931.
29. Ibid., August 7, 1931.
30. Ibid., May 5, 1931.
31. Ibid., September 30; October 14 and 15, 1930.
32. Ibid., September 30 and October 15, 1930.
33. Ibid., November 4, 1931.
34. Ibid., November 5, 1931.
35. Ibid., May 22, 1930 and July 11, 1930.
36. Ibid., December 22, 1931.
37. *AWT,* January 17, 1936.
38. Ibid., January 24, 1936.
39. *Congressional Record,* vol. 79, pt. 2, 1st session, 74th congress (1935), 2343.
40. Ibid.
41. Ibid.
42. Ibid., 2345.
43. Ibid., 2346.
44. Ibid.
45. Ibid., 2347.
46. Ibid.
47. *AWT,* January 24, 1936 April 30, 1936.
48. Ibid., March 27 and May 7, 1936.
49. Ibid., June 4, 1936.
50. Ibid., April 16, 1936.
51. Ibid., April 30, 1936.
52. Ibid., October 9, 1936.
53. Ibid., November 27, 1936.
54. Ibid., October 9, 1936; June 4, 1936.
55. Ibid., July 9, 1936.
56. Ibid., July 2, 1936; July 16, 1936; July 23, 1936.
57. Ibid., July 9, 1936.
58. Ibid., October 16, 1936.
59. Ibid., November 27, 1936.

60. *Congressional Record*, vol. 81, pt. 4, 1st session, 75th congress (1937), 4056.
61. Ibid., 4014.
62. Ibid., 4015
63. Ibid., 4014–5.
64. Ibid., 4016–7.
65. William Henry Chamberlain, "Hands off Japan," *American Mercury* (March 1939), 304–13.
66. Hanson W. Baldwin, "Impregnable America," *American Mercury* (July 1939), 261 257–67.
67. *AWT*, July 30, 1936.
68. *Alaskan*, December 5, 1941.
69. *Congressional Record*, vol. 86, pt. 17, 3rd session, 76th congress (1940), 4936.
70. *AWT*, February 14, 1936.
71. *Congressional Record*, vol. 81, pt. 4, 1st session, 75th congress (1937), 4018.
72. Ibid., vol. 88, pt. 8, 2nd session, 77th congress (1942), 6811.
73. Ibid., vol. 83, pt. 4, 3rd session, 75th congress (1938), 4167.
74. Ibid., 4169.
75. Ibid., 4168.
76. Ibid., 4168.
77. Brian Garfield, *The Thousand Mile War: World War II in Alaska and the Aleutians* (New York: Bantam Books, 1988), 48.
78. *Congressional Record*, vol. 83, pt. 4, 3rd session, 75th congress (1938), 4169.
79. Ibid., vol. 86, pt. 2, 3rd session, 76th congress (1937), 12513–4.
80. Mitchell quoted by Dimond in *Congressional Record*, vol. 81, pt. 4, 1st session, 75th congress (1937), 4055.
81. *Alaska Weekly Times*, January 3, 1936.
82. *Congressional Record*, vol. 83, pt. 3, 3rd session, 75th congress (1938), 2621.
83. Ibid., vol. 81, pt. 10, 3rd session, 75th congress (1938), 1384.
84. Cited in *Congressional Record*, vol. 86, pt. 4, 3rd session, 76th congress (1940), 4131.
85. Atwood, *Anchorage*, 32, 34.
86. "Territories: Gold Rush 1941," *Time* December 8, 1941. http://www.time.com (accessed November 20, 2009).
87. *AWT*, December 27, 1934.
88. *AWT*, January 3, 1936.
89. *Alaskan*, October 18, 1940.
90. *ADT*, July 24, 1941.
91. *Alaskan*, November 15, 1940.
92. Ibid., November 28, 1941.
93. Ibid., November 28, 1941.
94. Ibid., December 6, 1941.

CHAPTER SIX

1. Quotation in Stephen Haycox, "Mining the Federal Government: The War and the All-American City" in Chandonnet, *Alaska at War*, 203.
2. Subscriber information is reported in "Letters," *Time* (April 29, 1935); http://www.time.com (accessed November 12, 2009). And see "Strategy: Fortifying Alaska," *Time* (August 5, 1940); http://www,time.com (accessed November 12, 2009).
3. "Strategic Map: Northwest Frontier," *Time* (September 30, 1940); http://www.time.com (accessed November 12, 2009).
4. *ADT*, November 21–22, 1941.
5. Atwood, *Anchorage*, 86.
6. *Alaskan*, October 18, 1940.
7. "Army & Navy: Northland Boom," *Time* (August 16, 1943); http://www.time.com (accessed on November 20, 2009).
8. Rogers, "Alaska, the Misunderstood," 608.
9. *Alaskan*, July 14, 1939.
10. Ibid., January 12 and May 10, 1940.
11. *Cook Inlet Pioneer*, June 5, 1915.
12. See the advertisement from the Horning family store in the *Cook Inlet Pioneer*, July 17, 1915.
13. Ibid., July 24, 1915.
14. *AWT*, September 3, 1936.
15. Ibid., September 10, 1936.
16. *ADT*, August 19, 1916.
17. Ibid., November 15, 1916.
18. Terrence Cole, "Boom Town: Anchorage and the Second World War" in *The Pacific Northwest in World War II*, ed. Schwantes, Carlos A. (Manhattan, Kansas: Sunflower University Press, 1986), 79.
19. "Anchorage: A City Planned for the Future," *Alaska Life* (April 1940), 14.
20. Haycox, "Mining the Federal Government," 206.
21. On soldiers living in tents see *Alaskan*, November15, 1940.
22. Cole, "Boom Town," 82.
23. *Alaskan*, November 15, 1940.
24. *ADT*, November 4, 1941.
25. Ibid., November 12, 1941.
26. *Cook Inlet Pioneer*, August 28, 1915; September 11, 1915.
27. Haycox, "Mining the Federal Government," 209.
28. On farmers moving from the Matanuska Valley to work in Anchorage, see Orlando W. Miller, *The Frontier in Alaska and the Matanuska Colony* (New Haven: Yale University Press, 1975), 115 and 141.
29. Edward A. Herron, *Alaska: Land of Tomorrow* (New York: McGraw-Hill Book Co., 1947), 120–5.

30. "Army & Navy: Northland Boom." The casualty figures are given in Atwood, *Anchorage*, 39.
31. *ADT*, November 5, 1941.
32. Ibid., December 6 and 8, 1941.
33. Orville George Herning diaries (1917–1918), December 7, 1941. UAA.
34. *ADT*, December 6, 1941.
35. Ibid., December 8, 1941.
36. Ibid., December 8, 1941.
37. Ibid., December 8, 1941.
38. *Alaskan*, December 12, 1941.
39. *ADT*, September 15, 1916.
40. Haycox, "Mining the Federal Government," 204.
41. *ADT*, August 22, 1916 and December 9,1941.
42. Ibid., December 8, 1941.
43. See, for example, Conrad Cherry, *God's New Israel: Religious Interpretations of American Destiny* (Chapel Hill: University of North Carolina Press, 1998); and Michael Norman and Elizabeth M. Norman, *Tears in the Darkness: The Story of the Bataan Death March and its Aftermath* (New York: Farrar, Straus and Giroux, 2009), 22.
44. *ADT*, December 30, 1941.
45. Stanley High, "Japanese Saboteurs in Our Midst," *Reader's Digest* (January 1942), 11–15.
46. On anti-Japanese unrest in California see Kevin Starr, "Shelling Santa Barbara" in *Embattled Dreams: California in War and Peace, 1940–1950* (New York: University of Oxford Press, 2002). For reports on anti-American unrest in Japan see, for example, *Anchorage Weekly Alaskan*, June 8 and 15, 1924.
47. Jean Potter, *Alaska under Arms* (New York: Macmillan Company, 1943), 14–17.
48. "Railroads for Alaska," *Independent* (January 26, 1914), 116.
49. Harry Mikami to Alice Snodgrass, April 12, 1976; private collection; copy in possession of the author.
50. Jack Snodgrass (son of Alice Mikami), conversation with the author, July 16, 2009, Palmer, Alaska.
51. For example, Mary (Mikami) Rouse to Alice (Mikami) Snodgrass, March 17, 1979; and Harry Mikami to Alice Snodgrass, October 1, 1990; private collection; copies in possession of the author.
52. Alice Mikami Snodgrass interview with Ron Inouye, Alaska's Japanese Pioneers Research Project (1991), Archives and Special Collections Department, University of Alaska, Anchorage; and Alice Mikami Snodgrass conversation with the author, Palmer, Alaska, June 2007. Mikami family photographs in possession of the author.

53. Miné Mikami to her children, June 14, 1949; private collection; copies in possession of the author.
54. See, for example, Anchorage High School, *The Anchor* (1931), 28; and *The Anchor* (1936), 4; and the John Bagoy Collection, "Pioneer Anchorage Families," file, photograph number B96.32.66, AM.
55. Louise Gill Collection, High School Remembrance Book and draft of "Last Will and Testament of the Class of '30," UAA.
56. R. W. Ryder, "The Japanese and the Pacific Coast," *North American Review* (January 1921), 13.
57. *Anchorage Daily News*, February 21, 2009.
58. Ronald Inouye, "Commission on the Wartime Relocation and Internment of Civilians," unpublished manuscript held in University of Alaska Fairbanks library (1983), 90.
59. See, for example, *ADT*, June 2, 1930.
60. City Council Minutes, Anchorage, vol. 3 (June 16, 1937), 37; City Council Minutes, Anchorage, vol. 4 (December 15, 1937), 24; City Council Minutes, Anchorage, vol. 4 (December 14, 1938), 163.
61. United States District Court, Anchorage, Alaska, civil case files, record group 21, file 2733, NARA-PAR; Ron Inouye interview with William Y. Kimura, Alaska's Japanese Pioneers Research Project; Jack Snodgrass conversation with the author, July 16, 2009, Palmer, Alaska.
62. "Petition to the National Code Authority of the Laundry Trade," record group 9, box 8-11/07/13, petitions file, NARA-PAR.
63. *ADT*, July 7, 1919.
64. United States District Courts, Alaska (Anchorage), Criminal Case Files, 1902–1960, box 55, case 1101, NARA-PAR.
65. *ADT*, August 5 and October 28, 1930. It is possible, perhaps likely, that K., T., and George Tanaka may have been just two, or perhaps only one person.
66. *ADT*, July 24, 1941. The assumption here is that the George Tanoke referred to in this notice is the same person with the last name spelled slightly differently. Also see the story about Roy Yoshioko, convicted of murder in the Yukon: *AWT*, January 10, 1918.
67. United States District Courts, Alaska—Anchorage civil case files, record group 21, file A2126, NARA-PAR.
68. United States District Courts, Alaska—Anchorage civil case files, record group 21, file A2599, NARA-PAR.
69. *ADT*, September 15 and October 6, 1930; January 3, 1931.
70. Miné Mikami to her children, June 14, 1949. Private collection; copy in possession of the author.
71. Seizo Abe, "Outline of Goro Mikami's Life," unpublished document in the possession of the author.

72. *Alaska Labor News*, October 28, 1916.

73. Paul R. Spickard, *Japanese Americans: The Formation and Transformations of an Ethnic Group* (New York: Twayne Publishers, 1996), 65, 68, 73, 95.

74. "Population is the crying need of Alaska," claimed the *Knik News*, May 1, 1915.

75. *AWT*, August 22, 1918.

76. L. C. Doheny to Harold L. Ickes, January 1939, Doheny Family Collection, series 2, folder 2, part 1, box 1, UAA.

77. United States District Courts, Alaska—Anchorage civil case files, record group 21, file # A2733, NARA-PAR.

78. *ADT*, January 20, 1942, reprinted in Ronald K. Inouye, ed., "The World War II Evacuation of Japanese-Americans from the Territory of Alaska," unpublished manuscript (1973), University of Alaska Fairbanks Rasmuson Library, 41.

79. *ADT*, January 16, 1942, reprinted in Ibid., 36.

80. M. Terama to "Merciful Judges," (August 6, 1915), record group 21, box 30, case #486, NARA-PAR.

81. *ADT*, December 8, 1941.

82. Ibid., December 9, 1941.

83. Earl H. Ohmer to Ernest Gruening, December 27, 1941, reproduced in Inouye, "World War II Evacuation," 22.

84. *ADT*, November 17, 1941.

85. Ibid., November 18, 1941.

86. Ibid., November 15, 26; and December 8, 1941.

87. Ibid., December 11, 1941, reproduced in Inouye, "World War II Evacuation," 24–5.

88. Inouye, "The World War II Evacuation," 126.

89. See the *Fairbanks Daily News-Miner*'s notice of Flora Mikami's wedding in Inouye, "World War II Evacuation," 94.

90. *ADT*, April 22, 1942, reproduced in Inouye, "World War II Evacuation," 102.

91. Ibid., 108.

92. Ibid., 92.

93. *ADT*, January 13, 1942.

94. United States Commission on Wartime Relocation and Internment of Civilians, "Personal justice denied: Report of the Commission on Wartime Relocation and Internment of Civilians: report for the Committee on Interior and Insular Affairs (Washington, DC: Government publishing Office, 1992), 83, 85.

95. Miné Mikami to her children, June 1, 1949; private collection; copy in possession of the author.

96. *ADT*, December 20, 1941.

97. A historian writes: "Some Alaskans did not share the general hysteria" but provides no evidence that hysteria was generalized anywhere in Alaska. There may have been hysteria in parts of the territory, but not in Anchorage. The same writer notes

that Japanese living in Alaska before the Second World War "gained general social acceptance." See Naske, "Relocation of Alaska's Japanese Residents," 124–5, 126.

98. Ron Inouye interviews with William Kimura and Alice Mikami Snodgrass, "Alaska's Japanese Pioneers Research Project," unpublished manuscript (1991), University of Alaska Anchorage Archives.

99. See the photos of the senior classes in University of Alaska Fairbanks, *The Denali* (1942).

100. *Alaskan*, December 26, 1941.

101. *ADT*, December 10, 1941.

102. *Alaskan*, December 19,1941.

103. *ADT*, December 9, 1941.

104. Ibid., December 13, 1941.

105. Ibid., December 12, 1941; and *Alaskan*, December 19, 1941.

106. *Alaska Daily Times*, December 15, 1941.

107. Ibid., January 13, 1942.

108. Ralph Browne, *Anchorage: An Analysis of its Growth and Future Possibilities, 1951–1952* (Juneau: Alaska Development Board, 1953), 4.

109. *Cook Inlet Pioneer*, July 24, 1915.

APPENDIX

1. On the demise of Council, see Jones, *Empire's Edge*, 50–56.

2. *AWT*, November 15, 1917.

BIBLIOGRAPHY

REFERENCE WORKS

"Anchorage," *Collier's Encyclopedia* vol. II. New York: Macmillan Educational Company, 1988:176–7.

Carlson, Phyllis D. "Anchorage," *Encyclopedia Americana* vol. I. Danbury, CT: Grolier Incorporated, 1990:802.

Hornor, Edith R., ed. *Almanac of the 50 States: Basic Data Profiles with Comparative Tables.* Palo Alto, CA: Information Publications, 1992.

Hovey, Kendra A., and Harold A. Hovey. *CQ's State Fact Finder, 2005: Rankings Across America.* Washington, DC: CQ Press, 2005.

Kennedy, David, et al., *The American Pageant: A History of the Republic.* Boston: Houghton Mifflin, 2002.

"Anchorage," *New Encyclopædia Britannica* vol. 1. Chicago: Encyclopædia Britannica, Inc., 2003:378.

Rose, Cynthia, ed. *American Decades: Primary Sources, 1910–1919.* Detroit: Gale Group, 2004.

———, ed. *American Decades: Primary Sources, 1920–1929.* Detroit: Gale Group, 2004.

United States Census Bureau. *Statistical Abstract of the United States: 2007.* Washington, DC, 2006.

Haycox, Stephen. "Anchorage," *World Book Encyclopedia* vol. 1. Chicago: World Book, Inc., 2007:449–50.

ARCHIVAL MATERIALS

Alaska Railways Photograph Album (University of Alaska Fairbanks).

Alaska Village Census Rolls. Record group: 75; box: 2; file: 1306–7, Anchorage 1934–1940. (National Archives and Records Administration, Pacific Alaska Region.)

Anchorage City Directory, 1917 and 1921 (Anchorage Municipal Library).

Anchorage Criminal Case Files, 1902–1960, record group 21, box 38. (National Archives and Records Administration: Pacific Alaska Region).

Anchorage Police Department Activity Report Book, 1935–1938 (Anchorage Municipal Library).

Anchorage Telephone Directories 1924, 1936, 1939, 1940 (Anchorage Municipal Library).

John Bagoy Collection (Anchorage Museum).

William Cashen Collection; photographs (University of Alaska Fairbanks).

Anthony J. Dimond Collection (University of Alaska Fairbanks).

Doheny Family Collection (University of Alaska Anchorage).

Louise D. Gill Collection (University of Alaska Anchorage).

Ernest Gruening Diary, December 1941 (University of Alaska Fairbanks).

Orville George Herning Diaries, 1917–1918 (University of Alaska Fairbanks).

Ronald K. Inouye File (University of Alaska Fairbanks).

Ron Inouye, interviewer and editor, "Alaska's Japanese Pioneers Research Project" (1991). (University of Alaska Anchorage).

Ron Inouye, ed. "The World War II Evacuation of Japanese-Americans from the Territory of Alaska." Unpublished manuscript, 1973 (University of Alaska Fairbanks).

Johanson–Erickson Family Collection (University of Alaska Anchorage).

Lena Morrow Lewis file (University of Alaska Fairbanks).

Mikami Family Correspondence (1949, 1959, 1976, 1979, 1990). Private Collection; copies in the author's possession.

Minutes of the First Regular Meeting of the City Council of the City of Anchorage, Alaska, November 26, 1920–April 21, 1926 (Anchorage Municipal Library)

Northern Construction Company to Rose Walsh, May 10, 1948. www.alaskool.org/projects/JimCrow/cov_res.htm (accessed January 20, 2010).

Petition to the National Code Authority of the Laundry Trade, record group 9, box 8: November 7, 1933 (National Archives and Records Administration: Pacific Alaska Region).

George M. Pilcher diaries, 1913–1933 (University of Alaska Fairbanks).

Records of the Alaska Railroad, Record Group 322, Accession no. 322-69-0966, boxes 63–68 (National Archives and Records Administration: Pacific Alaska Region).

Records of the District Courts of the United States, District of Alaska, Third Division, Anchorage, Alaska. Petitions for Naturalization, May 5, 1916–September 14, 1920. Volume 1, box 1 (National Archives and Records Administration: Pacific Alaska Region).

Selective Service Records, WWI, Records Related to Delinquents and Deserters, record group 163 (National Archives and Records Administration: Pacific Alaska Region).

United States District Courts Alaska (Anchorage), Civil Case Files, 1915–1960, boxes 1–4, 37, 49 (National Archives and Records Administration: Pacific Alaska Region).

University of Alaska photograph files, "sports, team" and "individuals, general" (University of Alaska Fairbanks).

Helen Van Campen Photo Album (University of Alaska Fairbanks).

Published Primary Sources

NEWSPAPERS (OUTSIDE)

Aberdeen Daily News (South Dakota)
Belleville News-Democrat (Illinois)
Bellingham Herald (Washington)
Charlotte Daily Observer (North Carolina)
Dallas Morning News (Texas)
Evening News (San Jose, CA)
Fort Worth Star-Telegram (Texas)
Grand Forks Daily Herald (North Dakota)
Manatee River Journal (Florida)
Miami Herald (Florida)
Philadelphia Inquirer (Pennsylvania)
San Jose Mercury News (California)
State (Columbia, South Carolina)

NEWSPAPERS (ALASKAN)

Alaska Citizen (Fairbanks)
Alaska Labor News (Anchorage)
Alaskan (Anchorage)
Anchorage Daily Times
Anchorage Weekly Alaskan
Anchorage Weekly News
Cook Inlet Pioneer (Anchorage)
Daily Miner (Ketchikan)
Farthest North Collegian (University of Alaska Fairbanks)
Forty-Ninth Star (Anchorage)
Knik News
Morning Mail (Ketchikan)
Socialist Press (Fairbanks)
Weekly Alaskan (Anchorage)

BOOKS, ARTICLES, SPEECHES, GOVERNMENT DOCUMENTS

"A Rational Coal Policy," *Outlook* (June 20, 1914): 428–29.
"A Review of the World," *Current Opinion* (January 1915): 1–4.
"A Reform for Alaska," Outlook (Aug. 1, 1923): 494.
"A United World," *Outlook* (July 27, 1912): 684–85.

"Advance of Alaska," *Outlook* (Oct. 19, 1921): 244.

"A. E. F. University," *Indiana Farmer's Guide* (June 7, 1919): 11.

Ahl, Frances N. "Alaska: Mighty Empire in the Making," *Overland Monthly and Out West Magazine* 88:2 (Feb 1930): 52.

Alaska Legislature: Roster of Members, 1913–2000. Juneau: State of Alaska, 2000.

Alaska Panhandle: Its Proposed Cession to Canada. Washington, DC: Judd and Detweiler, 1915.

"Alaska's New Railway," *National Geographic* (December 1915): 567–89.

"Alaska Railway Problem," *Outlook* (January 20, 1912): 114.

"Alaska's Resources Neglected," *The Independent* (August 21, 1913): 425.

"Alaskans Want Refugees to Settle in Wheatfields," *Christian Science Monitor* (Feb. 1, 1923): 1

"An Alaska Programme," *The Nation* (January 1, 1914): 7–8

"An Army Needs Recreation," *Christian Science Monitor* (September 16, 1940): 6.

Anchorage High School, *The Anchor*, 1917, 1925, 1929, 1932, 1934, 1936.

"Army & Navy: Northland Boom," *Time* (August 16, 1943). http://www.Time.com (accessed November 20, 2009).

Atwood, Evangeline. *Anchorage: All-America City*. Portland, OR: Binfords & Mort, 1957.

Austin, Harry Albert. "The United States Unprepared for War," *Forum* (April 1914): 526–34.

Baldwin, Hanson W. "Impregnable America," *American Mercury* (July 1939): 257–67.

Ballou, Sydney. "Naval Defense of the Pacific," *The Navy* (March 1911): 28–35.

Barber, Joseph Jr. "Hawaii Counts the Cost," *The Atlantic Monthly* (October 1938): 531–39.

Brown, Ralph. *Anchorage: An Analysis of its Growth and Future Possibilities 1951–1952*. Juneau: Alaska Development Board, 1953.

Buell, Raymond Leslie. "Again the Yellow Peril," *Foreign Affairs* (December 1923): 295–309.

"Building Conditions on the Pacific East," *The American Architect* (May 11, 1921): 572.

Brooks, Alfred H. "The Development of Alaska by Government Railroads," *Quarterly Journal of Economics* 28:3 (1914): 586–96.

Brooks, Alfred H. "The Future of Alaska," *Annals of the Association of American Geographers* (December 1925): 163–79.

Bury, J. B. "Progress in the Light of Evolution" in *The Idea of Progress*. New York: Dover Publications, 1932.

Carter, William Harding. "Public Opinion and Defense," *North American Review* (August 1916): 203–10.

Cary, Otis. *Japan and Its Regeneration*. New York: Student Volunteer Movement, 1904.

Chamberlain, Basil Hall. *Things Japanese*. London: John Murray, 1902.

Chamberlain, George E. "The Future of Alaska," *The Independent* (March 16, 1914): 372–3.

Chamberlin, William Henry. "How Strong is Japan?" *The Atlantic Monthly* (December 1937): 788–96.

———. "Hands Off Japan," *American Mercury* (March 1939): 304–13.

Chapple, Joe Mitchell. "Discovering Alaska with President Harding," *McClure's Magazine* 55 (October 1923): 8.

Cherry, Conrad, ed. *God's New Israel: Religious Interpretations of American Destiny.* Chapel Hill: University of North Carolina Press, 1998.

Christensen, Andrew. Letter to the editor, *Time* (May 20, 1935). http://www.Time.com (accessed November 12, 2009).

Chung, Henry. "Japan Amuck" in *The Case of Korea.* London: Fleming H. Revell Company, 1921.

Coolidge, Archibald Cary. *The United States as a World Power.* New York: The Macmillan Company, 1908.

Congressional Record, vols.79–86 (1935–1940).

Conn, Edward L. "Japan and America: An Interview with Viscount Kaneko," *Outlook* (June 8, 1921): 250–53.

Cook, Katherine M. "Education Among Native and Minority Groups in Alaska, Puerto Rico, Virgin Islands, and Hawaii," *The Journal of Negro Education* (January 1934): 20–41.

Cotten, Lyman A. "Our Naval Problem," *North American Review* (March 1917): 367–75.

Davis, Mary Lee. *Uncle Sam's Attic: The Intimate Story of Alaska.* Boston: W.A.Wilde, 1930.

———. *We Are Alaskans.* Boston: W.A. Wilde Company, 1931.

Department of Education (Territory of Alaska), *Report of the Commissioner of Education: School Biennium Ended June 30, 1932.*

Department of Education (Territory of Alaska), *Report of the Commissioner of Education: School Biennium Ended June 30, 1934.*

"Developing the Nation's Treasure House in Alaska," *Current Opinion* (February 1914): 95–96.

Dew, Gwen. "Horrors in Hong Kong," *American Mercury* (November 1942): 559–63.

Eitman, Wilford J. "Economic Basis of Prices in Alaska," *The American Economic Review* 34:2 (June 1944): 351–56.

"Essential League," *Living Age* (January 19, 1918): 177–80.

Fairchild, Johnson E. "Alaska in Relation to National Defense," *Annals of the Association of American Geographers* 31:2 (June 1941): 105–12.

Faris, Ellsworth. "The Mental Capacity of Savages," *American Journal of Sociology* 23:5 (March 1918): 603–619.

Fifteenth Census of the United States, 1930: Outlying Territories and Possessions. Washington, DC: Government Printing Office, 1932.

Fisher, Galen M. *Creative Forces in Japan.* West Medford, MA: Missionary Education Movement of the United States and Canada, 1923.

Untitled advertisement from *Forest and Stream; A Journal of Outdoor Life, Travel, Nature Study, Shooting,...* (September 1929): 693.

Untitled advertisement from *Forest and Stream; A Journal of Outdoor Life, Travel, Nature Study, Shooting…* (June 1927): 322.

Fox, Edward Lyell. "Menaces to American Peace," *McBride's Magazine* (November 1915): 105–13.

Franklin, William M. "Alaska, Outpost of American Defense," *Foreign Affairs* (October 1940): 245–50.

Franck, Harry A. *The Lure of Alaska.* New York: National Travel Club, 1939.

"Friendship and Foreign Trade," *Nation's Business* (June 5, 1924): 32–33.

Gale, James S. "Korea's Present Condition" in *Korean Sketches.* Nashville: Publishing House of the Methodist Episcopal Church South, 1898.

Garner, James Wilford, and Henry Cabot Lodge. *The History of the United States* vol. 4. Philadelphia: John D. Morris and Company, 1906.

Gideon, Kenneth. *Wandering Boy: Alaska—1913–1918.* Fairfax, VA: East Publishing Co., 1967.

Gilman, Isabel Ambler. *Alaskaland: A Curious Contradiction.* New York: Alice Harriman Company, 1914.

Goto, Baron Shimpei. "The Anti-Japanese Question in California," *Annals of the American Academy of Political and Social Science* 93 (January 1921): 104–10.

Gove, David. "Educating the Alaska Natives," *Overland Monthly and Out West Magazine* (March 1917): 9–17.

Greeley, A. W. *Handbook of Alaska: Its Resources, Products, and Attractions.* New York: Charles Scribner's Sons, 1925.

Greeley, W. B. "Alaska—The Last of the Frontier," *Outlook* (Feb. 1, 1922): 180.

Ernest Gruening, "Colonialism in Alaska," *Current History* (December 1955): 349–55.

Gulick, Sidney. "Are Japanese Assimilable?" in *Americanization: Principles of Americanism, Essentials of Americanization, Technic of Race-Assimilation,* ed. Winthrop Talbot. New York: H.W. Wilson Company, 1917.

Hagie, C. E. "Alaska—The Land Few People Know," *Overland Monthly and Out West Magazine* 87:6 (June 1929): 175.

Hagood, General Johnson. "The United States in the Next War," *Journal of United States Artillery* (July 1920): 1–8.

Hall, Russell E. "Americans Look at their Far Eastern Policy," *Pacific Affairs* 10:2 (June 1937): 190–5.

Hamilton, Angus et al. "The Sorrows of a Coveted Kingdom" in *Korea: Its History, Its People, and Its Commerce.* Boston and Tokyo: J. B. Millet Company, 1910.

Hanaford, Phebe A. *Daughters of America; or, Women of the Century.* Augusta, ME: True and Company, 1882.

Hart, Albert Bushnell. "Pacific and Asiatic Doctrines Akin to the Monroe Doctrine," *American Journal of International Law* 9:4 (1915): 802–17.

Hearn, Lafcadio. *Glimpses of Unfamiliar Japan,* vol. 1. Boston: Houghton Mifflin Company, 1894.

Higginson, Ella. *Alaska: The Great Land.* New York: Macmillan Company, 1926.

High, Stanley. "Japanese Saboteurs in Our Midst," *Reader's Digest* (January 1942): 11–15.

Hill, Grace A. "Along the Alaska Coast," *Overland Monthly and Out West Magazine* (September 1917): 6–17.

Hoffman, Frederick L. "The Economic Progress of the United States during the Last Seventy-Five Years," *American Statistical Association* 14: 108 (1914): 294–318.

Howland, Harold. *Theodore Roosevelt and His Times: A Chronicle of the Progressive Movement*. New York: United States Publishers Association, 1921.

Hrdlička, Aleš. *Alaska Diary, 1926–1931*. Lancaster, PA: Jaques Cattell Press, 1943.

Huddleston, Sisley. *What's Right with America*. Philadelphia: J.B. Lippincott Co., 1930.

Hulbert, W. D. "What Is Really Going on in Alaska," *Outlook* (January 20, 1912): 133–8.

Jacobin, Lou. *Tourists and Sportsman's Pictorial Guide to Alaska*. Juneau: Alaska Tourist Guide, 1946.

"Japan's Proposed Entry into Siberia—An Invasion or a Rescue?" *Current Opinion* (April 1918): 233–5.

"Japanese Bogey Reappears," *Current Opinion* 69 (November 1920): 588–90.

Jenness, Diamond. "The Eskimos of Alaska: A Study in the Effect of Civilization," *Geographical Review* 5:2 (February 1918): 89–101.

Joad, C. E. M. *The Babbit Warren*. New York: Harper Brothers, 1927.

Johnson, Albert. "Government Railroad in Alaska—An Inevitable Step." Washington: Government Printing Office, 1914.

Johnston, R. M. "The Imperial Future of the United States," *Infantry Journal* (November–December 1913): 311–17.

Kari, James, and James A. Fall, eds. *Shem Pete's Alaska: The Territory of the Upper Cook Inlet Dena'ina*. Fairbanks: Alaska Native Language Center, University of Alaska, and CIRI Foundation, 1987.

Kawakami, K. K. "America Teaches, Japan Learns," *The Atlantic Monthly* (June 1932): 37, 650–57.

Kawakami, Kiyoshi K. *American-Japanese Relations: An Inside View of Japan's Policies and Purposes*. New York: Fleming H. Revell Company, 1912.

"Keys to Alaska's Wealth," *Outlook* (June 7, 1913): 267–68.

Kiralfy, Alexander. "The Armed Strength of the United States in the Pacific," *Pacific Affairs* 11:2 (June 1938): 208–23.

———. "Japan's Strategic Problem," *Far Eastern Survey* (Feb. 12, 1941): 15–20.

"Labor Prospects Ahead on the Alaskan Road," *Christian Science Monitor* (January 13, 1916): 13.

Laing, Philip, et al. Letter to the editor, *Time* (April 29, 1935). http//www.Time.com (accessed November 12, 2009).

Lane, Franklin K. "Freeing Alaska from Red-Tape," *North American Review* (June 1915): 841–52.

———. "The Oil Age—and Its Needs," *The Independent* (January 17, 1920): 89–90, 120–3.

Latané, Holladay. *America as a World Power, 1897–1907*. New York: Harper Brothers, 1907.

La Violette, Forrest E. "The American-Born Japanese and the World Crisis," *The Canadian Journal of Economics and Political Science* (Nov. 1941): 517–27.

Law, Frederick Houk. *Modern Great Americans*. New York: The Century Company, 1926.

Lossing, Benson. *Eminent Americans*. New York: John B. Alden, 1890.

Lumpkin, H. H. "Uncle Sam's Newest Town," *Outlook* (October 25, 1916): 455–58.

MacDonald, W. L. "U.S–Canada Peace Axis," *The Living Age* (Sept. 1939): 8–13.

"Mastery of the Far East," *North American Review* (July 1919): 134–35.

Mayer, Herbert B. "America Defenseless," *McClure's Magazine* (Aug. 1923): 71

Mckenzie, Fayette Avery. "America and the Indian" in *Americanization: Principles of Americanism, Essentials of Americanization, Technic of Race-Assimilation*, ed. Winthrop Talbot. New York: H.W. Wilson Company, 1917.

Merriam, Willis B. "Some Recent Trends in Alaskan Commerce," *Economic Geography* 14:4 (October 1938): 413–18.

Millis, H. A. "Some of the Economic Aspects of Japanese Immigration," *American Economic Review* 5:4 (1915): 787–804.

"Missionary Messages," *Herald of Gospel Liberty* (Feb. 2, 1928): 124.

Morrill, Alice V. "Alaska—The Coming Country," *Herald of Gospel Liberty* (February 11, 1915): 172.

Morison, Samuel Eliot, and Henry Steele Commager. *The Growth of the American Republic*, vol. 2. London: Oxford University Press, 1942.

Myers, Philip Van Ness. *The Modern Age*. Boston: Ginn and Company, 1903.

Orth, Samuel P. *Our Foreigners: A Chronicle of Americans in the Making*. New Haven: Yale University Press, 1921.

Osgood, Cornelius. "Tanaina Culture," *American Anthropologist*, New Series (October–December 1933): 695–717.

Overstreet, L. M. "Always on Guard," *Outlook* (Oct. 18, 1922): 290.

Payne, John Barton. "Go North, Young Man!" *The Independent* (September 18, 1920): 330.

Popper, David H. "America Prepares—for What?" *The North American Review* (Summer 1939): 199–218.

Potter, Pitman B. "The Nature of American Territorial Expansion," *American Journal of International Law* 15:2 (April 1921): 189–197.

"Railroads for Alaska," *The Independent* (January 26, 1914): 116.

Redding, J. Saunders. "A Negro Looks at This War," *The American Mercury* (November 1942): 585–92.

Redfield, William C. "Rebuilding Our Foreign Trade," *Forum* (January 1919): 35–43.

Report of the Governor of Alaska to the Secretary of the Interior. Washington, DC: Government Printing Office, 1924.

Richardson, Wilds P. "Alaska," *The Atlantic Monthly* (January 1928): 111–20.

Rogers, Sherman. "Alaska, The Misunderstood," *Outlook* (December 6, 1922): 608.

———. "The Heart of Alaska," *Outlook* (December 20, 1922): 704.

———. "The Treasure-House of Southeastern Alaska," *Outlook* (December 13, 1922): 658.

———. "The Problems of Alaska's Government," *Outlook* (January 24, 1923): 172.

Roosevelt, Theodore. "The New Nationalism" in *The Penguin Book of Twentieth-Century Speeches*, ed. Brian MacArthur. New York: Penguin, 1999.

Roth, Lawrence V. "The Growth of American Cities," *Geographical Review* 5:5 (1918): 396–98.

Ryder, R. W. "The Japanese and the Pacific Coast," *The North American Review* (January 1921): 1–15.

Samuels, Ernest, ed. "Vis Nova" in *The Education of Henry Adams*. Boston: Houghton Mifflin Company, 1973; repr.1918.

"San Francisco," *Banker's Magazine* (September 1915): 346–48.

"Says Japs Want the Philippines," *The Daily Miner* (November 4, 1907)

Schlesinger, Arthur Meier. *Political and Social Growth of the American People, 1865–1940*. New York: Macmillan Company, 1941.

"Seattle Commercial Club," *Banker's Magazine* (September 1915): 332–35.

"Seattle's Important Position," *Banker's Magazine* (September 1915): 314–18.

Sedgwick, Ellery. "The Japanese Mystery," *The Atlantic Monthly* (September 1930): 290–99.

———. "Made in Japan," *The Atlantic Monthly* (October 1930): 454–63.

"Self-Government for Alaska," *Outlook* (June 15, 1912): 320–21.

Shaw, Albert. "Assimilating the Indian" in *Americanization: Principles of Americanism, Essentials of Americanization, Technic of Race-Assimilation*, ed. Winthrop Talbot. New York: H.W. Wilson Company, 1917.

Shiratori, Toshio. "The Reawakening of Japan," *The Atlantic Monthly* (June 1934): 547–50.

Skelton, Oscar D. *The Canadian Dominion: A Chronicle of Our Northern Neighbor*. New York: United States Publishers Association, 1919.

Schlesinger, Arthur. *Political and Social Growth of the American People, 1865–1940*. New York: Macmillan, 1941.

Sommerich, Jane. "New Air Service to Alaska Follows Line of Hemisphere Defense," *Far Eastern Survey* 9:15 (July 17, 1940): 179–80.

Sostek, Anya. "Low Budget Trip to Juneau Turns Out to Be Capital Idea," *Arkansas Democrat-Gazette* (January 27, 2008).

Stephenson, Nathaniel Wright. *History of the American People*, vol. 2. New York: Charles Scribner's Sons, 1934.

Stephenson, William B. *The Land of Tomorrow*. New York: George H. Doran Company, 1919.

Stoddard, Lothrop. *Re-Forging America: The Story of Our Nationhood* (New York: Charles Scribner's Sons, 1927.

Stokes, William. "Canada's War Dilemma," *Forum and Century* (November 1939): 222–25.

"Strategic Map: Northwest Frontier," *Time* (September 30, 1940). http://www.time.com (accessed November 12, 2009).

"Strategy: Fortifying Alaska," *Time* (August 5, 1940). http://www.time.com (accessed November 12, 2009).

Sundborg, George. *Opportunity in Alaska*. New York: Macmillan Company, 1946.

Strackbein, O. R. "Our Empire," *The North American Review* (April 1931): 327–34.

Tarr, Ralph S. "The Alaskan Problem," *North American Review* (January 1912): 40–56.

Taylor, Louis. "The Soul of a Samurai," *The Atlantic Monthly* (August 1932): 235–37.

"Territories: Gold Rush, 1941," *Time* (December 8, 1941). http://www.time.com (accessed November 20, 2009).

The Nation (May 28, June 4, 1914; February 5, June 3, 1915; April 5, 1917).

Thomas, David Y. "A Rational Coal Policy," *Outlook* (June 20, 1914): 428–29.

Tower, Walter S. "Western Canada and the Pacific," *Geographical Review* 4:4 (1917): 289.

Troeltsch, Ernst. "Protestantism and Modern Religious Feeling" in *Protestantism and Progress: A Historical Study of the Relation of Protestantism to the Modern World*, trans. W. Montgomery. Boston: Beacon Press, 1958; repr. 1912.

Underwood, John J. *Alaska: An Empire in the Making*. New York: Dodd, Mead and Company, 1925.

United States Commission on Wartime Relocation and Internment of Civilians. "Personal Justice Denied: Report of the Commission on Wartime Relocation and Internment of Civilians: Report for the Committee on Interior and Insular Affairs." Washington, DC: Government Printing Office, 1992.

University of Alaska Fairbanks. *The Denali* (1942).

Walker, Ernest P. *Alaska: America's Continental Frontier Outpost*. Washington, DC: Smithsonian Institution, 1943.

"Week Reviewed," *Barron's*, April 21, 1924.

Weems, Carrington. "Government Railroads in Alaska," *The North American Review* (April 1914): 573–84.

"Why Alaska is Being Rapidly Depopulated," *Current Opinion* (March 1922): 408.

Wilford, C. G. "Letter," *McClure's Magazine* (August 1918): 36.

Wilson, Woodrow. "The Emancipation of Business" and "The Liberation of a People's Vital Energies" in *The New Freedom*. Englewood Cliffs, NJ: Prentice-Hall, 1961; originally published serially in 1913.

Wood, James A. "Alaska and Its Future," *Christian Science Monitor* (July 5, 1923): 24.

Secondary Sources

Benfey, Christopher. *The Great Wave: Gilded Age Misfits, Japanese Eccentrics, and the Opening of Japan*. New York: Random House, 2003.

Borneman, Walter R. *Alaska: Saga of a Bold Land*. HarperCollins, 2003: 258–70.

Chandonnet, Ann. *Anchorage: Early Photographs of the Great Land*. Whitehorse, Yukon: Wolf Creek Books, 2000.

Clinard, Outten Jones. *Japan's Influence on American Naval Power*. Berkeley: University of California Press, 1947.

Cole, Terrence. "Boom Town: Anchorage and the Second World War" in Schwantes, Carlos A. ed. *The Pacific Northwest in World War II*. Manhattan, Kansas: Sunflower University Press, 1986.

———. "Jim Crow in Alaska: The Passage of the Alaska Equal Rights act of 1945," *The Western Historical Quarterly* 23:4 (November 1992): 429–49.

Crittenden, Katharine Carson. *Get Mears! Frederick Mears: Builder of the Alaska Railroad*. Portland, OR: Binford and Mort Publishing, 2002.

Driscoll, Joseph. *War Discovers Alaska*. Philadelphia, New York, London: J.B. Lippincott Company, 1943.

Dunham, Mike. "New Play Celebrates Pioneers' Love For Each Other and Alaska," *Anchorage Daily News*. http://www,adn.com (accessed January 8, 2010).

Fitch, Edwin M. *The Alaska Railroad*. New York: Praeger, 1967.

Garfield, Brian. *The Thousand-Mile War: World War II in Alaska and the Aleutians*: chapter 5. New York: Bantam Books, 1969.

Haycox, Stephen W. "Racism, Indians and Territorial Politics," in Mary Childers Mangusso and Stephen W. Haycox, eds., *Interpreting Alaska's History: An Anthology*. Seattle: University of Washington Press, 1996.

———. *Frigid Embrace: Politics, Economics, and Environment in Alaska*. Corvallis: Oregon State University Press, 2002.

———. *Alaska: An American Colony*. Seattle: University of Washington Press, 2006.

———. "Mining the Federal Government: The War and the All-America City" in Fern Chandonnet, ed., *Alaska at War, 1941–1945: The Forgotten War Remembered*. Fairbanks: University of Alaska Press, 2008.

Heffer, Jean. *The United States and the Pacific: History of a Frontier*, trans. W. Donald Wilson. Notre Dame, IN: University of Notre Dame Press, 2002.

Hendricks, Charles. "Race Relations and the Contributions of Minority Troops in Alaska: A Challenge to the Status Quo?" in Fern Chandonnet, ed., *Alaska at War, 1941–1945: The Forgotten War Remembered*. Fairbanks: University of Alaska Press, 2008.

Inouye, Ronald K. "Harry Sotaro Kawabe: Issei Businessman of Seward and Seattle," *Alaska History* 5:1 (Spring 1990): 35–43.

Jones, Preston. *Empire's Edge: American Society in Nome, Alaska 1898–1934*. Fairbanks: University of Alaska Press, 2007.

———. "Yankees in Parkas: Native Influence at Nome, 1900–1920" in *Alaska History*, 20:2 (Fall 2005): 43–58.

———. "The Woman behind the Man behind the President," *Fairbanks Daily News-Miner* (August 30, 2009), E1.

Langdon, Stephen J., and Aaron Leggett, "Dena'ina Heritage and Representation in Anchorage: A Collaborative Project" in *The Alaska Native Reader: History, Culture, Politics*, ed. Maria Shaa Tlaa Williams. Durham and London: Duke University Press, 2009.

Linn, Brian McAllister. *Guardians of Empire: The U.S. Army and the Pacific, 1902–1940*. Chapel Hill: University of North Carolina Press, 1997.

Mangusso, Mary Childers. "Political Issues of the 1920s," in Mary Childers Mangusso and Stephen W. Haycox, eds., *Interpreting Alaska's History: An Anthology*. Seattle: University of Washington Press, 1996.

McDougall, Walter A. *Let the Sea Make a Noise: Four Hundred Years of Cataclysm, Conquest, War and Folly in the North Pacific*. New York: Avon Books, 1993.

Miller, Orlando W. *The Frontier in Alaska and the Matanuska Colony*. New Haven: Yale University Press, 1975.

Mitchell, Donald Craig. *Sold American: The Story of Alaska Natives and Their Land, 1867–1959*. Dartmouth: University Press of New England, 1997.

Naske, Claus-M. "The Relocation of Alaska's Japanese Residents," *Pacific Northwest Quarterly* (July 1983): 124–32.

Naske, Claus-M., and Herman E. Slotnik. *Alaska: A History of the 49th State, Second Edition*. Norman and London: University of Oklahoma Press, 1987: 94–123.

Naske, Claus-M., and L. J. Rowinski, *Anchorage: A Pictorial History*. Norfolk: The Donning Company, 1981.

Nielson, Jonathan M. *Armed Forces on a Northern Frontier: The Military in Alaska's History, 1867–1987*. New York: Greenwood Press, 1988.

Norman, Michael and Elizabeth M. Norman. *Tears in the Darkness: The Story of the Bataan Death March and Its Aftermath*. New York: Farrar, Straus and Giroux, 2009.

Ponko, Vincent W. "The Alaskan Coal Commission, 1920 to 1922," *Alaska Journal* (spring 1978): 118–29.

Pratt, Julius W. *America's Colonial Experiment: How the United States Gained, Governed, and In Part Gave Away a Colonial Empire*. New York: Prentice-Hall Inc. 1950.

Schlereth, Thomas J. *Victorian America: Transformations in Everyday Life*. New York: HarperCollins, 1991.

Spickard, Paul R. *Japanese Americans: The Formation and Transformations of an Ethnic Group*. New York: Twayne Publishers, 1996.

Starr, Kevin. "1941: Shelling Santa Barbara," in *Embattled Dreams: California in War and Peace, 1940–1950*. New York: Oxford University Press, 2002.

Strohmeyer, John. *Historic Anchorage: An Illustrated History*. San Antonio: Historical Publishing Company, 2001.

Tower, Elizabeth. *Anchorage: From Its Humble Origins as a Railroad Construction Camp*. Fairbanks: Epicenter Press, 1999.

Wheeler, William Bruce, and Susan D. Becker, eds. "Justifying American Imperialism: The Louisiana Purchase Exposition, 1904" in *Discovering the American Past: A Look at the Evidence*, vol. 2. Boston: Houghton Mifflin, 1998.

Wilson, William H. *Railroad in the Clouds: The Alaska Railroad in the Age of Steam, 1914–1945*. Boulder: Pruett Publishing Company, 1977.

———. "The Alaska Railroad and Coal: Development of a Federal Policy, 1914–1939," *Pacific Northwest Quarterly* (April 1982): 66–77.

———. "The Urban Frontier in the North" in *Interpreting Alaska's Past: An Anthology*, eds. Mary Childers Mangusso and Stephen W. Haycox. Anchorage: Alaska Pacific University Press, 1989.

Wilson, Woodrow. *The New Freedom*. Englewood Cliffs, NJ: Prentice-Hall, 1961.

"The World Over," *The Living Age* (July 1940): 401–6.

INDEX

amusement hall, 31
Anchorage and, 124
colonies created by, 94
dependence on, 29–30, 42, 69, 148
drinking water shortage and, 30
fisheries and, 42
internment policy, 136
investment into Alaska and, 50
jurisdiction of, 32
medical care and, 30
natural resources and, 68
New Deal and, 69–70
public transportation and, 42
railroad and, 2–3, 30, 143–144
religion and, 31
Graham, Isabella, 10
Great Depression, 7, 69, 92, 105
Grigsby, George, 92
Gruening, Ernest, 20, 70, 94, 135
Guveles, Demos, 85

H
Haddad, Hamma, 36
Harding, Warren G., 20, 44, 68, 77
Hawaii
  immigrants in, 14, 15, 18
  national defense and, 110–111
  Pearl Harbor, 118, 125, 133, 134–135, 137
  vulnerability of, 25, 27, 113
Hayes, E.L., 13
Henry, Jack, 61–62
Herald of Gospel Liberty, 28
Herning, Orville, 125
Herron, Charles, 123
Hettel, Bernard, 56
Hill, Grace, 20–21
Hirano, Kay, 131
History of the American People (1934), xiv
Hitler, Adolph, 108, 111, 112, 128
Hoffman, Frederick, 4
Home Guard, 60, 118, 126
homelessness, 123

Hooker, William, 62
housing shortages, 123
Hubbard, Bernard (Father), 114
Hughes, George, 83
Humphrey, William E., 27

I
ice cream, 22, 34
Ickes, Harold, 133
identity, 146–147
illiteracy rates, 6
immigrants
  "Alaskanizing" of, 38
  "Americanization" of, 47, 85–86
  citizenship petitions and, 35–36
  English language and, 44
  illegal, 14
  military service and, 55
  policy on, 152–153
  views of, 7, 53
  waves of, 5–7
imperialism, xiv–xv
Industrial Workers of the World
  ("Wobblies"), 58
interpersonal relations, 145–146
Italian Relief Committee, 60

J
Japan
  economic power, 12–13
  embargo on, 118
  invasions from, 18
  Manchuria and, 14, 106–107, 109
  military power, 12–13, 14, 28, 106, 108
  proximity to Alaska and, 105
  United States and, 13–14, 18, 26–27, 63, 105–106, 118, 128–129
  war with, 114, 125, 145
Japanese. *See also* Mikami family
  Americans, 128, 136
  Christians, 10, 14
  citizenship, 36